Praise for Jim Gilreath's *Skin in the Game* Searches

"Metapoint Partners has had a relationship with Jim Gilreath for more than 17 years. We have never experienced anyone who does a more thorough and complete evaluation of candidates. Gilreath Consultancy has handled 24 searches for Metapoint Partners. We are happy to recommend his services without reservation."

~Keith C. Shaughnessy, President & CEO of Metapoint Partners

"In all my years of corporate consulting, I have yet to meet an executive search professional with greater integrity, diligence, or expertise than Jim Gilreath. Jim understands that every new hire ultimately contributes either to moving a business forward or holding it back. We've collaborated successfully in a number of critical hiring situations for companies whose prior selection errors had been costly. Combining Jim's careful, exhaustive search discipline with expert psychological assessment technology, we were able to hire by design rather than by chemistry."

~David Pellegrini, Ph.D., Principal of The Global Consulting Partnership

"Gilreath Consultancy has many years experience in matching up high performance individuals with high performance opportunities. Jim's process is extremely thorough for both the client and the prospective candidates. It ensures that the clients understand the candidates, the candidates understand the opportunity and both understand what is required for success. I know because I am a satisfied hired candidate."

~Gregory J. Biederman, former President and CEO of Nylon Corporation of America

"Jim Gilreath's tenacity in pursuing candidates, the thoroughness of his reference and work experience checks and his patience in seeking out only the most qualified candidates separates him from the other retained search firms with whom I have worked."

~Peter Bransfield, former President of Altair Avionics Corp

"The strength of a Gilreath Consultancy search is in the defined process they use to assure a good match between the private equity company's desires, the portfolio company's needs and the candidate. As a placed CEO, Jim did a great job in making sure that my experiences and professional strengths were the right matches for Roscoe Medical. He did this through a variety of steps that included traditional, but thorough, search steps (e.g. references) as well as ones that seem to be unique to Gilreath Consultancy. While unique, they were valuable in completing the match between Roscoe and myself."

~Paul J. Guth, President & CEO of Roscoe Medical, Inc.

"Jim Gilreath sets a very high benchmark for retained recruiters hiring C-level executives. I learned this as a candidate when I was hired as CEO by one of his private equity clients. Jim works to really know the human being behind the titles and marketing. In his process of revealing my life, from youth through my formative years and education, to reasons behind career choices and decisions, we both learned a lot about me. He is a consummate professional and a pleasure to work with."

~Bob McKinley, former CEO & President of Sidump'r Trailer Company

"I have been through the Gilreath due diligence process twice. The thoroughness of the process impressed me as a candidate. Doing the biography that Jim calls the "Indiana Jones" provided me with an opportunity to summarize my career in the most advantageous light; answering the detailed questionnaire Jim put together about the position I was being considered for was a great help in preparing for the in-person interview. Several of my references commented about how in-depth the reference checking process was (the most in-depth that any of them had ever encountered). From the candidate's perspective, this meant that there would be no surprises, allowing you to concentrate on preparing for the interview process."

~Wayne D. Pedlar, former General Manager of Tower Industries, Inc.

"As a CEO hire and beneficiary of Gilreath Consultancy services, I have never participated in a more comprehensive or thorough vetting process. At the end of the day, both the candidate and company will have all the information necessary to make an informed decision."

~Timothy L. Friedel, former President & CEO of Stone Panels, Inc.

To Christy Dencause

A real professional. Enjoyed our dealings as Bronze Sponsors twice at ACG annual conferences. Also during my years as an ACG member. Best wishes

Regards,

Jim [illegible]

04-19-16

SKIN IN THE GAME

Skin in the Game

No Longer Just a C-Level Employee

by Jim Gilreath

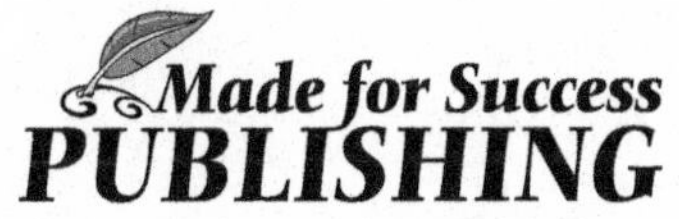

Made For Success Publishing
P.O. Box 1775 Issaquah, WA 98027
www.MadeForSuccessPublishing.com

Distributed by Made For Success Publishing

Library of Congress Cataloging-in-Publication data

Gilreath, Jim
Skin in the Game: No Longer Just C-Level Employee
p. cm.
ISBN: 9781613398098 (Paperback)
ISBN: 9781613398340 (Hardback)
LCCN: 2015915800

Printed in the United States of America

For further information contact Made For Success Publishing
+14255266480 or email service@madeforsuccess.net

Skin in the Game

No Longer Just a C-Level Employee

CONTENTS

Praise for Jim Gilreath's Skin in the Game Searches............1

CHAPTER 1

The Concept of Skin in the Game....................................17
What's Involved?..18
Pros and Cons 19

CHAPTER 2

Preparing For Your Skin in the Game Job Search 23
The Difference Between PEGs and VCs 24
Here's Your Master Job Search To Do List: 30

CHAPTER 3

What Do Lower Middle Market PEGs Seek
In SITG C-Level Executive Talent?...................................35

CHAPTER 4

Writing Your Indiana Jones Bio..55

CHAPTER 5

Resume and Cover Letter Tips..63
Skin in the Game Job Search Resumes 65

CHAPTER 6

Four Exhibits of C-Level Hires from Skin in
the Game Searches..75

CEO Hire....76
Resume....94
Cover Letter....103
Correspondence....105
CFO Hire....108
Resume....145
Cover Letter....151
VP Operations Hire....153
Resume....168
Cover Letter....174
VP Sales and Marketing Hire....176
Cover Letter....189

CHAPTER 7
Organizing Your References Before Launching a Skin in the Game C-Level Job Search....191
Dealing with Problem References and an Inconsistent Job History....203

CHAPTER 8
Fine Tuning Your Presentation....209
Perfecting Your Three Minute Personal Elevator Pitch....213
Become a Member of LinkedIn....224

CHAPTER 9
Networking....229
Jim's Master List of M&A Professionals....237

CHAPTER 10
Skin in the Game PEG 1st & 2nd C-Suite Job Interviews....287
Preparing for a PEG C-Level Job 1st Interview from Networking Referral:....288

SITG CEO Candidate: Harvey Goldstein........................297
SITG CFO Candidate: Bruce Clayborn...........................308
SITG COO Candidate: David Ritter..............................320
SITG VP Sales and Marketing: Randall Swanson............335
Exhibit Items to Bring to your PEG
Interviews in your Multi-packet Portfolio........................349
Face-to-Face Generic SITG C-Level Job
1st Interview with a PEG Partner....................................350
The SITG C-Level Job Candidate's Suggested
1st Interview Questions for the PEG Partner....................353

CHAPTER 11
From the Job Offer to Being Hired.................................387
Negotiating Your SITG C-Level Job Offer......................389
Let's Review an Actual SITG CEO Job Offer................392

CHAPTER 12
Conclusion...421

INTRODUCTION

BY JIM GILREATH

During more than 40 years of national C-Level retained search consulting, I developed a unique and successful hiring model that was well received by my lower middle market and middle market Private Equity Group (PEG) clientele. I only presented qualified and interested skin in the game C-Level candidates for my PEG retained searches. They all had to satisfactorily pass through my meticulous screening and coaching process. Each finalist C-Level candidate would be required to provide me with certain documents for the PEG client's information package. Each finalist SITG (skin in the game) search candidate and I collaborated together to produce an impressive three ring binder on the candidate. It was titled "Highly Confidential Information File on John Wxyz" for the client's eyes only. Specifics are in my book, *Skin in the Game.*

One of my long-term PEG SITG search clients explained that once they reviewed a typical candidate binder from me, typically the search candidate was 80% hired. There was some pushback from finalist C-Level SITG search candidates, especially CEOs, about submitting 9-12 of their key references for me to check, even before they met my PEG clients. I would explain the reasoning behind my completing this part of my hiring system, how it has made the difference between many past successful hires.

Unfortunately, these highly confidential reference checks also can uncover good reasons that this SITG search candidate isn't a good enough match and they are eliminated. Of course now with LinkedIn, it's open house on calling anyone connected to a C-Level search candidate with or without the candidate's approval. I always write in my SITG retained search agreement with our PEG client that no unauthorized reference checking is allowed by myself or the client.

"Skin in the game" was a term attributed to Warren Buffett, the famous multi-billionaire investor. He was known to publicly advise executive insiders to buy stock in a company they were running or helping grow profitably. Their skin in the game was the amount of their own money used to buy some of that stock

The majority of my SITG C-level hires haven't had any previous experience working for a company owned by a PEG. These C-level hires had never bought stock in their company until I placed them. Typically these SITG hires had to have C-Level experience in the same industries as my retained search clients' portfolio companies. Also each of my finalist candidates had to fit the PEG's business culture.

My due diligence oriented, retained search hiring process for each of my C-Level search assignments is based, in principle, on the typical due diligence approach employed by my client PEGs in their meticulous evaluation of all aspects of a targeted acquisition.

Though our SITG C-Level searches typically take 3-4 months to complete, PEGs evaluating a company acquisition often take several months or longer to complete or decline. That's because of the potential financial risks involved once the deal is consummated.

So, who will benefit from this book?

Skin in the Game is an essential read for:

- M&A industry professionals
- Proven C-level executive job seekers
- Middle market PEG partners
- Retained Search Consultants
- Human Resource Executives
- Corporate Hiring Authorities
- Fresh MBA graduates

Even if you aren't seeking a STIG C-Level job, there are many aspects of my system that can help your candidacy succeed in your being hired. I am giving you what I call proven "evidential candidacy" search support techniques.

Skin in the Game was intended to be priced as a $50 manual on SITG C-Level hiring. I decided instead to price it at $19.99 so it would help a wider audience because my hiring model works for many, big time!

-Jim Gilreath

Chapter 1

The Concept of Skin in the Game

"Skin in the game" (SITG) is a term coined by famous investor Warren Buffett, referring to a situation in which high-ranking insiders use their own money to buy stock in the company they are running or helping grow. Theoretically, putting skin in the game makes certain that the people who run a company have a direct interest in running the company well. In the majority of my completed skin in the game senior management searches, the majority have consistently performed well and have reaped their monetary rewards at the liquidity event (company exit). When management owns stock in a company, they want their company to perform at a high level to generate returns and will put forth a consistent effort to accomplish or exceed company Earnings Before Interest, Taxes, Depreciation & Amortization (EBITDA) goals. Having skin in the game is different from having performance-based bonuses and other types of compensation because there will be direct consequences to management if the value of the company's equity drops. Skin in the game management will definitely lose money if their company loses money.

On the Private Equity Capital Growth Council's website, watch *Private Equity Minute*, a six-part video series featuring Dartmouth College's Tuck School of Business Professor Colin Blaydon. The series is a primer on the private equity model and how value is created for private equity-backed companies. Check out: http://www.privateequityatwork.com/what-is-private-equity/.

What's Involved?

Chief Executive Officer (CEO) hires would typically invest $100K of their own funds in exchange for, typically, a double digit percentage of company equity depending on the market capitalization amount. Vice Presidents (VPs) would invest $60K-$100K for a single digit percentage of the company. Generally all hires made soon after the portfolio company has been acquired by the private equity firm are given the "strike price" per share, which is the same price per share as the original private equity ownership. Some hired candidates have asked for and been allowed to purchase more shares. Vesting is typically 20% per annum; full vesting takes five years or at the sale of the company. Stock option plans often require the company attaining annual goals and objectives to be earned individually for each year. Normally companies are held by the ownership for four to five years, but can be up to seven years (or more) until they are sold to either a financial buyer or strategic buyer. If you end up joining a portfolio company as a skin in the game hire a few years after it has been acquired, you may incur tax obligations due before the company is sold to another ownership. Often our Private Equity Group (PEG) client will loan our hired candidate the money to pay such taxes and deduct it from the hired candidate's future bonus earnings or at the liquidity event.

I always advise my skin in the game candidates to discuss their job offer letters with appropriate legal and tax advisors before making their decision.

Below are the results of several of my random skin in the game C-Level hires:

Manager	Company	Original Investment	Shares Purchased	Options Earned	Total Shares	Value at Sale
Bob H	ATI	$364,224	1,200	180	1,380	$3,582,811
Bob H	Pengo			7	7	$99,094
Marty S	ATI	$53,556	50	75	125	$324,530
Charlie H	Lab Tops	$100,000	1000	1440	2440	$2,344,694
Kent T	Lab Tops	$75,000	750	720	1470	$1,412,582
Randy S	NPC	$96,100	961	1,200	2,161	$1,699,907
Al S	Vutek	$500,000	5,000	1,840	6,840	$11,552,760
Al S	Marathon	$300,000	1,500.00	1,105	2,605	$3,124,177
TOTALS		**$1,488,880**				**$24,140,554**

Pros and Cons

Do you enjoy being in a risk reward situation? What does it mean for you to be a peer equity owner in a company you are helping grow versus being just an employee? Do have any money to invest in a skin in the game job opportunity at the title you are seeking with a middle market portfolio company? I have been involved in senior manager hires involving as little as $20K hired candidate investment. Sometimes a client will offer earned stock options with no out of pocket expense to the hiree. If you are presenting yourself as a CEO, Chief Financial Officer (CFO), or VP seeking a signing bonus, maximum starting salary, automatic raises and bonuses, perks, and four weeks' vacation, odds are the private equity owners of the portfolio company you are considering won't be interested if you can't put skin in the game. Forewarned is forearmed.

Investing your own money in portfolio company equity depends on your own interpretation of your due diligence research. Consider the Confidential Descriptive Memorandum of the PE firm's acquisition of the company and their financials as well as the PE firm's strategy going forward to grow the company's EBITDA towards a successful exit plan.

How much challenge do you want in your employment situation? You have to conduct your own research regarding the company, industry, markets, reputation, and track record. How many prior hires in your function has the PE firm recruited since they bought this company? How do the financial statements and balance sheet look? How leveraged is this deal for the PE firm? Does it need major Capex? Can it meet its covenant obligations with reasonable assurance? Are you joining a company whose current mission is getting it ready for sale or to grow?

The more you know about the PE firm investors, this business, industry, and markets in relation to your own experience and expertise, the more likely your success. Check out the private equity owners and ask to speak with someone in your corresponding management function from another of their portfolio companies. What feedback have you gotten? Even if you meet or exceed the company job specs, are the owners a good match for your integrity, temperament, ethics, and management style?

The other career advantage for you is that once you are successful in a skin in the game job function for a private equity firm, the more likelihood of you being sought after by other PE firms once your deal is over and you're looking for your next opportunity. Reputation means a lot in the PE sector.

Welcome to the middle and lower middle market Mergers & Acquisitions (M&A) sector. Joining the right private equity group (PEG) offers a risk and results-oriented, fast-paced, non-political, transparent, hands-on, exciting environment. These employment circumstances apply to you, your boss, the PEG Managing Partner and your direct and indirect subordinates. If management all has skin in the game there is a general camaraderie, a "you watch my back, I'll watch yours" environment. Plus your equity could multiply by five or seven, and your payoff for helping the company grow could be sensational.

Chapter 2

Preparing For Your Skin in the Game Job Search

This book has good advice for any job seeker or PEG hiring authority. However it was written for skin in the game Chief Officer (C-Level) executives to help them become hired by PEGs for one of their middle market portfolio companies. That's my expertise. I have no retained search experience handling skin in the game C-Level assignments for any Venture Capitalists (VCs).

If you are entrepreneurial, a risk taker, and have a C-Level background in technology, visit NVCA.org and click on "About NVCA" then on "Members" and open up their list of over 400 mostly VC and some Leveraged Buyout (LBO) firms. Click on a VC's website and click on "Portfolio". See if any of their invested companies are a match with your credentials, experience, and industry background. If so, click on "Team" and then locate the person to email, such as the Partner in Charge or Managing Partner, General Partner, or Partner. Let them know you are a C-Level executive (give specific title sought) and attach your resume. Would they be interested in discussing you putting some skin in the game in the right VC company in exchange for some equity? What would the next step be? Take it from there and do plenty of sound due diligence. Consult an attorney and tax accountant about any eventual agreements involving money, stock acquisition terms, and written job offers.

The Difference Between PEGs and VCs

PEGs raise funds from Limited Partners, accredited investors, endowments, insurance companies and the firm's Partners. Such funds are not open to the public. Lower middle market PEGs often use LBOs to acquire existing companies in the $10M-$50M sales range. Middle market PEGs acquire private companies typically in the $50M-$250M sales range. Companies come from all industries. They will provide growth capital, as required, to increase the return on funds. PEGs typically hold their equity investments in companies for four to five years. Then they successfully sell their holdings to either a strategic buyer or financial buyer and share the equity profits according to each investor's stock holdings. This is called the "exit" or liquidity event. Most of my C-Level hires have multiplied their initial skin in the game investments in my client PEG's portfolio companies for lucrative payouts.

VCs pursue riskier startup ventures and will loan capital at 20%-30% interest rates. Companies who default on their exit loan payments are obligated to exchange VC loans for company equity. VCs also invest capital in equity, focusing on technology companies promising big potential returns. They usually invest their risk capital taking minority equity positions below 50%. VCs may each invest small amounts in a dozen pre-revenue and early stage companies. VCs experience much higher failure rates than

PEGs. VCs' successes can often make up for their more frequent failures.

Ask yourself, "Can I work and thrive in a private equity owned portfolio company after putting some of my own skin in the game?" Do you have the temperament to risk some of your own money in the equity of your next employer?

In one scenario, I was asked to fill a SITG CEO position that had two previous CEOs in sixteen months. It can be a "take no prisoners, all or nothing" environment, depending on what your due diligence turns up in certain PEG investor C-Level job opportunities. However, working for the right PEG can have growth challenges, growth opportunities, and spectacular financial results. In the mid-1990s, I filled a search for a SITG CEO with a New Hampshire manufacturer owned by a prestigious, profit-oriented, successful PEG. My candidate, Al S., invested $100K in equity, performed well, received additional equity bonus shares, and earned more than $11M at the company's liquidity event five years later. I have been involved with dozens of successful SITG C-Level hires. They have put up to $100K in skin in the game for company equity, amassed additional stock options, and earned millions for helping increase PEG companies' targeted EBITDA growth levels at the time of their liquidity event.

That is why I have written this book. During your networking efforts to meet PEGs through mutual contacts, try to be in contact with SITG C-Level executives about their own PEG employment experiences. Ask for PEG referrals.

In tight lower middle job market cycles, like the 2008-2014 era, highly qualified competition for C-Level job opportunities have been the norm in a number of industries. If you have an undergraduate degree and an MBA from one of the branded schools, and have been in the top 10% of your classes, your resume will attract immediate attention with certain PEGs and their headhunters.

If your employment record demonstrates you have moved up the promotional ladder with branded companies, again, you will generate instant interest from a number of PEGs and their headhunters, especially if you are still employed. You may have influential branded contacts. If so, they will positively impact your chances of being interviewed by a PEG. Congratulations, you are off and running. Hopefully you can duplicate this winning formula until you make a match with the right PEG to secure a SITG C-Level job. In my experience, such top branded job candidates do not typically undergo deeply probing interviews or comprehensive reference checks by the PEGs. PEGs will typically leave most or all of a branded candidate's references to be checked by their search firm.

The following is a good example of the tough competition in the current job market if you are a non-branded (though highly qualified) C-Level job applicant/candidate vying for similar jobs. A job competitor might submit a more impressive resume than yours, claiming many accomplishments, or have their MBA or MS degree from a prestigious university. Your competition may be well positioned in that they are fully employed with sterling resumes without breaks in their employment dates nor frequent job changes. You may also be a lot older than most SITG job competitors.

Such challenges for job openings face non-branded but qualified candidates. This also applies to typical retained search firms flush with resumes of qualified, interested, and branded job candidates. These candidates are often surfaced by the big branded search firms' research departments.

Ask yourself: do you think your well-prepared resume alone is likely to secure you an imminent phone or face-to-face interview if it's screened by a headhunter for a PEG's C-Level job, or by the PEG itself?

If you follow my advice and prepare yourself properly for the skin in the game job search campaign, you will become a formidable contender for the right job opportunity. I suggest you follow the chapters sequentially so you understand my overall strategy, and then execute my instructions. My advice requires effort on your part with no short cuts and will help you overcome your lack of top school branded education or and having worked for unbranded companies. Furthermore, these chapters help overcome any unfortunate short tenured employment periods and will alleviate your "old age" concerns. Expect keen competition for any potential job for which you may be considered. You'll be ready to deal with the competition after you have finished this book.

I will prepare you for the PEG interview, if it's a job you really want and for which you are qualified. I will help you gain confidence with referral sources, even those you do not know well, who will in turn recommend you to PEGs.

After forty years of retained searches predominantly for Fortune 500 clients, privately held companies, and lower middle market PEGs, an alarming number of interviewers do a poor job of screening candidates. Too many interviewers are ill-prepared, relying only on the candidate's resume, their gut feeling, mutual chemistry, and whether the candidate is a dynamic interviewer saying all the right things. A significant number of C-Level executive job interviewers include those that are unqualified, surly, or simply incompetent. In certain cases I have asked to sit in on the candidate's interview with the hiring authority to try to keep the interview process on track and productive. Fortunately none of my referred candidates were allowed to interview with our client PEGs before undergoing significant reference checks and credentials screening.

To counter this major hiring problem, I offer our PEGs a complete turnkey hiring process. I do the dirty work myself. I handle everything from getting the Non-Disclosure Agreement (NDA) signed to producing a life bio on each candidate (later named the Indiana Jones Bio). I verify the candidates' academic degrees and certifications. Almost every search turns up at least one phony MBA or a candidate omitting a past job or two from their resume. I have each search candidate rate themselves from one to ten on their degree of qualifications for the key aspects of the C-Level job for which I am screening them. I complete a written interview of twenty-five questions for each candidate to answer, and I do all the major reference checks in writing before any candidate's information binder is sent to our client. The end result has been an average of four search candidate binders referred per completed search assignment. My successful hire completion rate has been in the ninetieth percentile over the past twenty-eight years.

Why am I describing my search process to you? Because I am applying my proven due diligence C-Level job search approach to your successful pursuit of a skin in the game job.

Occasionally, PEGs will complain that they didn't know what to ask my candidates in a face-to-face interview after reviewing an SITG candidate's 3 ring binder from me. My philosophy is the more details a client is presented about my candidates, the better their hiring decisions.

This book will help you better manage your skin in the game job search process. Remain motivated, focused, humble, and courteous to all, especially anyone in a position to be of help to your ultimate job search goal. There are untold numbers of competitor job seekers after the same jobs you are seeking. Become a well-prepared, organized, and confident "evidential" skin in the game candidate loaded with your due diligence backup. Too often, many potentially good C-Level executive hires are inadvertently sabotaged by someone on the hiring authority's interview team. These saboteurs have no real stake in the hiring outcome and often go with their gut reaction to a candidate. Many times the latter interviewer is a board member, trusted friend, or someone in charge of another business owned by this PEG. Often such a person doesn't even have a copy of the C-Level job specs. You will be ready if that happens if you follow my preparation advice before interviewing. If you do the work, you'll see positive results.

Let's say you are a senior executive seeking the right skin in the game job opportunity. You're impatient, you want action. You want a steady flow of networking meetings, job interviews, and SITG C-Level executive type job offers. You are ready to write your equity check, start working, and lead your team, producing results towards your upcoming liquidity event. Okay, I hear you loud and clear. Let's get started now!

Here's Your Master Job Search To Do List:

- If you lack a home office then rent an inexpensive, established, private temp office set up with a receptionist, desk, file drawers, computer, email, fax, and long distance phone with voicemail.
- Write your Indiana J. (optional), especially if you haven't looked for a job in many years. Your IJ Bio should help strengthen your interviewing skills and your resume whether you have it done professionally or do it yourself.
- Write your powerful, influential resume reflective of your credentials, results, contributions to company growth, sales, profits, and functional title(s). Instead of listing just responsibilities, mention obtained results. Avoid adjectives. Provide data, key performance indicators (KPIs), performance measures you tracked, critical key metrics achieved such as EBITDA, and sales growth. Keep the PEG hiring authority target for your resume in mind (see chapter 5).
- Write a focused, influential, persuasive cover letter (see chapter 5).
- If you want expert help writing your resume, check out the three qualified and proven professionals I recommend in chapter 5 and select one to best assist you with your resume and cover letter (mention that I referred you).

- Select references that you have worked with and for, and mail them your resume to obtain reference letters from them. Ask for at least a paragraph on their letterhead confirming any of your accomplishments stated in your resume that they can verify (see chapter 7). Most PEG clients I have represented view typical reference checks with a grain of salt. Exceptions would be other PEGs that employed my clients and people known to my clients. My approach to references has been successful through trial and error for over twenty-five years. It's based on you producing a people profile who know you professionally and are authoritative within their company. Even list those individuals you might prefer the PEG not to contact for reasons discussed later. For many skin in the game job seekers, chapter 7 may be the most difficult chapter to emulate.
- Set up your LinkedIn profile (see chapter 8).
- Are you consulting part time while seeking skin in the game job opportunities? PEGs often engage specialist consultants on projects that can lead to full-time opportunities. Make up and order 100 inexpensive tasteful consulting brochures and business cards (see chapter 10).
- Prepare your presentation portfolio for PEG meetings. Order a dozen Esselte Oxford Poly 8-Pocket Folder-Letter Size (see chapter 10).
- Rehearse your three minute personal elevator pitch (see chapter 8).
- Organize your networking plan (see chapter 6).
- Order 500 business cards with your name, address, city, state, zip, your email, cell phone, and home phone (with 24/7 voicemail capability) on the front. On the reverse

side print your skin in the game function and whatever industry or industries you are focusing on.

- Do your research for targeted middle market PEGs to contact and targeted PEG portfolio companies in industries your background matches (see chapter 9).
- Once you're ready for a job offer, check out chapter 11.
- Conclude your to skin in the game job search (see chapter 12).

Maybe you are one of the lucky ones who is a graduate of a branded school with high class rankings and have your MBA. You are employed with no job history gaps and you have the right connections, a dynamite resume, and you interview famously. If there is a PEG with a SITG C-Level job match for you, congratulations; you will be hired. For the rest of you, this book will help you get there if you are interested, qualified, and can actually do the SITG C-Level job well. The advice I offer in this book will definitely help you if you're willing to do the work. Good luck!

Chapter 3

What Do Lower Middle Market PEGs Seek In SITG C-Level Executive Talent?

Working for a lower middle market private equity firm as a skin in the game portfolio company CEO is not for everyone. It involves surviving due diligence prior job screening by the PEGs. In these weak economic conditions that are dampening the current job market in many industries, there is keen competition for every skin in the game CEO opportunity. There is a significant increase in PEGs hiring through their M&A network and social media sites because of the glut of good talent available to them. Overall, in the lower middle market, CEOs are competing harder for fewer skin in the game job opportunities. On the other hand, when M&A industry headhunters are retained for a CEO search, they can almost cherry pick from their A player database generally available at the time.

Don't be discouraged by what you've read so far. Later in this publication I offer strategies and options on how to make a powerful, effective, due diligence-oriented presentation of your CEO candidacy. If you are willing to put in the necessary effort, you greatly improve your odds of landing interviews for skin in the game job search opportunities.

Based on my twenty-eight years of skin in the game senior executive hiring for mostly lower middle market portfolio companies, the PEG clients generally seek to improve operations, overhaul strategy, thereby increasing their enterprise value for the sale of the company. Lower middle market PE firms I've worked with typically have their sights set on acquiring several fragmented competitors and want a CEO who can integrate the acquisitions into the main company. In manufacturing scenarios, PEG ownership seeks to eliminate duplicity of excess equipment and labor as well as reduce any inherited real estate.

PEGs want their CEOs to keep after sales, cash flow and EBITDA, guard against high Capex, and spend three quarters of their time with customers, operations, and strategy. In manufacturing or process companies there are KPIs using a dashboard accessible through the CEO's smartphone to monitor daily or weekly. Can they insightfully understand a financial statement and balance sheet? Have they worked closely with their past CFOs to understand these critical financial documents?

A CEO candidate's resume should include:

- Metrics
- EBITDA percentage growth
- Sales increase percentages
- Operating income growth
- Inventory reduction percentages
- Increased market share percentages
- New product revenues
- Increased top line revenue percentages

Getting hired in a skin in the game senior executive position with a PE-owned portfolio company doesn't always ensure remaining there until the company exit, especially since there was an above average CEO turnover in the hiring process in 2013. Candidates have to conduct as much due diligence on the PE firm and the potential portfolio company employer as the PEG conducts on the candidate. You have to determine whether the culture of the portfolio company and the PE Managing Partner's management style represents an ideal fit for your environment over the anticipated job duration.

Boston Consulting Group's press release of November 13, 2013 stated their research into 198 companies currently under PEG ownership found that 57% have already changed CEOs since being acquired. Some of those changes were planned prior to the acquisitions, but many occurred because the PE owners came to the conclusion that the incumbent CEOs, including recent hires, were not suited to the task at hand. Not all new hires were skin in the game. It's not automatic that every PEG CEO job interview states that putting skin in the game is a must. At times it's an option. For the most part, most of my PEG clients are impressed that a qualified and interested CEO candidate wants to put some skin in the game; typically $100K. I've had certain CEO candidates for PEG job opportunities earning larger total compensation who have agreed to take less total compensation for the opportunity to buy more equity.

In the lower middle market where portfolio companies are typically in $10M-$100M plus in sales, our PEG clients look mostly for what I call "dirty fingernail" manufacturing, or chemical processing CEOs. Generally, the smaller the company, the larger the equity amount offered, typically up to 10% plus a merit stock option plan. The larger the company, the smaller the equity percentage offered. PEGs seek hands-on leaders with direct or related industry knowledge and experience, including similar markets and major or target customer awareness. Qualified former Division or Subsidiary Leaders, or Business Unit General Managers (GMs) with proven full Profit & Loss (P&L) responsibility and multi-functional direct reports with large corporations are preferable to former full P&L executives from smaller or equal-sized companies as the portfolio company in need of a new CEO.

I have found that senior executive candidates have been judged on merit versus their age. Employed candidates have the inside track over unemployed candidates. However, proven qualifications and solid references matter most overall. Forewarned is forearmed. Is the CEO big picture focused or strictly tactical and short-term focused? A lot depends on what the PE firms seek in a CEO.

A new CEO must:

- Have a transparent operating style.
- Be able to accept staff accountability and responsibility.
- Have no hidden agendas.
- Demonstrate focus on mutually agreed upon priorities and routinely track KPIs.
- Be detail-oriented.
- Delegate and follow up.
- Know his future boss' management style and why the CEO position is open, have a clear understanding of what their value creation will consist of going into the job, and whether he is calling the plays as far as the company board's strategy, priorities, Capex financing requirements, and timetables.

- Know if the former CEO or owner is on the board and whether their CFO has a dual reporting relationship to the PE firm and to the CEO.
- Know whether any incumbent executive was an active candidate to become the new CEO and the company's reason for them not being promoted to the position.
- Identify potential mutual points of friction with the PE ownership and determine if he can tolerate them. It's beneficial here to evaluate this CEO opportunity on a big picture basis. Examples might be learning that there are one or more sacred cows to be inherited among their direct reports and why.
- Ask to speak to one or two of the PE firm's other portfolio company CEOs to get up to speed on the PE firm's typical management style and whether there are areas of mutual friction.
- Do your own due diligence.

Ideally, the CEO prospect should be particularly strong in more than one function. In a lower middle market manufacturing business, the CEO would be strong in operations and quality. If the portfolio company is mainly in distribution, their CEO specs may require he be strong in supply chain management and sales management, which focus mainly on customers' objectives. The CEO should know how to read and understand a balance sheet and the company financial statement. You may be handed financial statements during an interview with the PE firm. If you fail to react appropriately, your candidacy might disintegrate.

The CEO who lacks certain required functional experience sought after by the PE firm must be prepared to show evidence of being able to hire and retain an A player in that necessary function.

This capability is most evident in manufacturing companies where the new CEO may be strong operationally, but lacks sufficient financial and accounting experience such as in budgeting, cost reduction, and planning.

The middle market PE ownership may consist of one or more Operating Partners depending on the number of portfolio companies actively owned. Alternatively, the portfolio company CEO may deal directly with either the PE firm's Managing Director, a Partner, or Principal.

Most PE firms I have represented usually want the CEO to land on their feet running and have them prioritize operational matters. The new CEO must get thoroughly up to speed on the direct reports and learn if they also have any skin in the game. Inheriting a strong staff is very fortunate, but keeping them in the company is a CEO's imperative. I have found staff equity ownership helps them remain on board. I have been a witness to many lucrative liquidity events at the company's exit by our hired senior executives.

One interview question that frequently arises is: what would the new CEO do in his first month on the job? A new CEO's early priority is visiting the company's most important customers with the VP Sales and Marketing. The new CEO should also schedule visits to all the company's plants or facilities as soon as possible with the VP Ops or Chief Operating Officer (COO).

Skin in the game CEO prospects should realistically evaluate themselves in terms of whether they can do the job well and what perceived shortcomings they might have versus the PE firm's specifications. Most hiring authorities (in my over forty years of headhunting experience) are unduly influenced by grading the CEO candidate compared to the job specs. Proven CEO prospects lacking an MBA often are thrown out with the bath water. Be prepared to contend with this issue and overcome it effectively by discussing your advance educational credits, specialized training certificates, and your expertise. If you firmly believe it, state that you feel you can land on your feet running in the CEO job and bullet point why you feel that way.

Stress your proven track record and value with specific facts and be prepared to furnish a supportive reference name or two. Some qualification deficiencies are almost sure knockouts, such as the company having plants in Asia and the CEO prospect having no Asian operation management track record. Not every CEO candidate has global management experience, however.

Similarly, it is desirable if a CEO has multi-location facilities management experience, especially if there are integration possibilities. The SITG CEO and all skin in the game senior executive candidates who encounter job openings at PE firm portfolio companies should email their resume to the firm if they feel qualified to pursue any verbally described open CEO position. Next, request a copy of the CEO requirements or other senior functional titled job specs as soon as possible. Then break the job requirements into "must haves" versus "preferred items". List the must have requirements and rate your own qualifications between one and ten.

If you survive your initial job interview and mutually remain a candidate, sign a non-disclosure agreement (NDA) and request a copy of the company's offering memorandum, usually written by the investment banker of the company's former owner. It details the company's financial track record, describes the business, and identifies their customers/clients. This memorandum is vital to your overall due diligence effort and is what the PE firm used as part of their due diligence effort before acquiring the company.

The above criteria for CEOs of PEG's portfolio companies in the aggregate are overwhelming, but it is unlikely that any SITG CEO candidate has mastered them all. I am providing a pattern of similar traits and requirements to help candidates with hiring aspects particular to SITG CEOs.

What do PEGs seek in their portfolio company CFOs?

What attracts CFOs to PE owned middle market portfolio companies? Why are they willing to invest $60K to $100K and sometimes more of their own money in the equity of their next employer? Simple answer: risk and reward. What is the typical CFO position like? Exhilarating and exhausting.

The newly hired skin in the game PE backed portfolio company CFO must get up to speed with the private equity agenda and quickly get a good handle on the complexities of the company's debt agreements. From day one, it's about the CFO building trust with the PE owners, the CEO, the banks, and any Limited Partners who typically are also board members. Building trust with the management team is almost as critical.

The competent and proven CFO is required to have the unquestionable traits of integrity, expertise, skills, and convictions to challenge the portfolio company's CEO and management team on key strategic and tactical decisions. The private equity environment revolves around the PE Partners craving a unique dashboard highlighting cash flow, margins, and leverage ratios. PE ownership believes that numbers speak louder than words. A CFO should fit the PE firm's strategic plan profile. Those CFOs heavily experienced in organic growth are better at performance management and containing costs. If the strategic plan is heavily M&A focused, the preference would be for a CFO with significant transactional experience and industry insight. A CFO with heavy turnaround experience or consolidation expertise, who is helping businesses get ready for sale, would not typically be ideal for a company facing a dynamic growth situation.

A CFO needs a balance of technical and leadership skills. Their responsibilities can span strategic planning, analysis, preparation, and presentation of monthly financial reporting including:

- Generally Accepted Accounting Principles (GAAP) financial statements
- Bridges
- Key performance indicators
- Weekly rolling forecasts
- Budgeting
- Credit, collections, and cash management
- Financial and tax audits
- Policy, procedure, and internal controls
- Compliance processes
- Cost accounting (standard and average costing)
- Product costing
- Capital expenditures/depreciation
- Contract review

PE partners are hungry for details and fussy about presentation. The typical CFO mantra is, "No shocks, no surprises."

The CFO is responsible for compiling the numbers; they better be accurate! Expectations are usually high, demands from constituencies countless, and tight deadlines numerous. The typical CFO must be a "stand up" executive, impartial and passionate, even ruthless when necessary. The CFO reports directly to the PE firm Managing Partner with a dotted line to the company CEO. CFOs are the main conduit of information flow to the PE ownership and the company CEO. He often has to balance completing the priorities of the PE ownership and the company's management team. This balancing act can be especially difficult if the business is performing in a downward trend.

The PE ownership often puts the CFO on the spot and asks the CFO's opinion about the portfolio company's tactical plans to increase the top line and the company's chance of success. In a middle market portfolio company, it is rare that a controller is promoted to CFO because it would be on the job training. However, M&A expertise is not always required of the CFO since the PE firm typically has that expertise. However, past experience with integrating acquisitions in partnership with operations is valuable. Familiarity is beneficial with IT systems, processes, and controls, particularly Enterprise Resource Planning (ERP) software implementation.

CFOs typically know how the entire day-to-day company works and how the various departments fit together. The CFO is continually involved in operations and is seen as the non-stop furnisher of their financial data requests. He projects a sense of urgency and surrounds himself with passionate "all hands on deck" subordinates. The CFO typically needs a strong experienced team including a solid financial controller to help maintain control over the financial function and enable him to deal with wider issues and requests. Hiring, managing, and retaining solid subordinates is typically a major challenge as the CFO will surely fail without adequate direct reports. The CFO's leadership approach creates an open, collaborative environment that sparks ideas and results in cross-functional, consensus-driven solutions.

From day one, the hands-on CFO must know the company's P&L and work on improving cash management, credit/collection, working capital, EBITDA, and profit margins. The CFO drives value creation, guards against unnecessary company spending, and meets debt covenants and all deadlines. He alerts the PE ownership and the CEO to potential problems and will challenge sales forecasts and undocumented assumptions from the various departments and satellites.

The CFO must keep a number of different constituents satisfied which requires timeliness, execution, results, good communication skills, and adequate analytical and consensus building attributes. The CFO must share the company's financials accurately, transparently, on time, and be willing to clarify what insights his numbers should signify to the PE ownership as well as the company's management team.

The CFO is the strategic Partner spearheading the portfolio company towards the most attractive exit or liquidity event culminating in the greatest value creation for all the equity stakeholders. If he has any time for reading, the CFO should bone up on *How to Win Friends and Influence People* by Dale Carnegie. When change management collaboration is important to a company's transformation and growth, people skills become almost as important as the numbers. Peers must be treated as people rather than just functions. Healthy debate and conflict are part of wrestling with company issues and their solutions. This consideration calls for teamwork, versus the Lone Ranger approach, to reach an action plan consensus going forward, and keeping goals and objectives on track.

Many otherwise highly qualified, interested, and desirable CFOs do not survive their peer and subordinate reference checks, giving feedback such as, "He's caused too many personality clashes, even in routine dealings."

The CFO has a major involvement in planning and executing an exit from the PEGs. Typically the exit was four to five years, but nowadays, given the market conditions, the exit is more like six to seven years and counting. I have read that turnover of the PE backed CFO has significantly increased from 2009 to 2013. In my twenty-eight years' experience, if the CFO is an A player and a good fit with the portfolio company's PE owners, and after exhaustive due diligence, job screening, and some of his skin in the game, there won't be any CFO turnover during the typical four to five year employment lifecycle.

The CFO is usually a master in due diligence, but must keep his eyes wide open in entering into his own CFO employment situation. There are issues to flush out before accepting a job offer, even with some skin in the game.

- Can you meet the board? What type of company culture are you feeling and is it giving you culture shock?
- Are there too many CPAs and/or former CFOs in the PE firm overlooking your shoulder with what seems like daily requests?
- Ask to speak with a few CFOs of other PE firm owned portfolio companies to learn their management style

- Is the portfolio company you might be joining highly leveraged?
- Can the portfolio company's management systems deliver the data needed by all concerned?
- How long does the PE ownership typically maintain its holdings?
- Meet the CEO. Is he the former owner or is he new blood outside the industry? How much skin in the game do the CEO and the rest of management team have?

The above criteria for CFOs of PEG's portfolio companies in the aggregate is overwhelming, but it is unlikely that any SITG CFO candidate has mastered them all. I am providing a hiring pattern of similar traits and requirements to help SITG CFO candidates with aspects particular to hiring skin in the game CFOs.

What do PEGs seek in their VPs of sales and marketing?

PEGs for their middle market portfolio company typically want a VP Sales and Marketing (S&M) who has been a significant part of one or more successful related portfolio companies owned by private equity and can land on his feet running. He must be a high energy hands-on leader by example who manages subordinates with a focused sense of urgency. The VP S&M champions the fact that in this age of social media, the Sales Department (and the company itself) must beware of the consequences of unsatisfied customers.

The VP S&M must:

- Be marketing savvy and have an acute sales management focus embracing consultative system selling and solution selling.
- Be familiar with the company's products, industry, and markets.
- Deliver business growth market validation and market entry strategy, as well as valuable analytics on sales force effectiveness and customer response.
- Drive revenue, sales efficiency, Return On Investment (ROI), and close deals.
- Be able to formulate a comprehensive business plan to establish strategic sales direction and if required, define product features needed to satisfy target market requirements.
- Be responsible for competitive analysis, product positioning, pricing strategy, promotional materials, customer service, training, and publications.
- Interface well with operations and finance in a collaborative style.
- Select various appropriate channels of distribution either through independent Sales Reps, Distributor Salespeople, or Employee Salespeople as required.
- Knowledge of various effective sales compensation plans is a must.
- Be budget conscious, setting and achieving aggressive sales forecasts as well as goals and objectives oriented, KPI and metrics driven, and delegate well with strong consistent follow up.
- Be a "no surprises" professional, a motivator, and able to hire, manage and retain a productive loyal superior sales force and a capable marketing assistant.

In certain portfolio companies, new product introduction experience would be vital. Again, PE firms tend to match VP S&M hires industry to industry, markets to markets, products to related products. Desirable background would be fluency in both social media environments and the monitoring and measuring tools for more industry visibility.

In a global PE owned portfolio company, international market development in Europe and Asia will be required, including strategic alliances and periodic overseas travel.

A VP S&M's expected technical knowledge includes Customer Relationship Management (CRM), such as Salesforce, Goldmine, and Sugar. Also he should have general knowledge of online marketing Search Engine Optimization/ Search Engine Marketing (SEO/SEM), and web analytical tools experience such as the offerings of Adobe Analytics. Travel 30%-40% of the time is often necessary.

It can be very challenging in the confidential interview process for the VP S&M because of his normal work and travel commitments. I have a few suggestions to deal with this interview challenge (see chapter 10, SITG PEG Interviews).

The above criteria for VPs of Sales and Marketing of PEG's portfolio companies in the aggregate is overwhelming, but it is unlikely that any SITG VP S&M candidate has mastered them all. I am providing a pattern of similar traits and requirements to help SITG VPs of S&M candidates with hiring traits particular to skin in the game VPs of S&M.

What do PEGs seek in their SITG VPs of Operations?

My twenty-eight year skin in the game VP Operations (VP Ops) hiring experience is heavily tilted towards lower middle market diverse manufacturing portfolio companies. There are a number of good points worth noting from this focus. PEGs typically focus on hiring hands-on VP Ops candidates responsible for the production of goods or provider of services. They consistently track KPIs to drive internal and external customer satisfaction and to encourage constructive behavior from the entire workforce. The VP Ops additionally hold subordinates accountable to goals and objectives. These characteristics are key ingredients for all VP Ops.

The VP Ops is the "go to" position to deliver the promised goods and/or expected company services to always satisfy the customers. The VP Ops is typically a take charge leader by example with a sense of urgency and accountability, taking initiative in identifying, analyzing, and solving problems. He needs strong oral and written communications skills to deal with all levels of the business, and must especially express numerics including metrics, percentages, margins, and profit and loss numbers.

The VP Ops oversees the production of company products and/or provision of services. Their role is ensuring that the organization is running comfortably and efficiently according to plan, and that the products and/or services meet client or customer needs.

The VP Ops reports to the CEO and typically manages all company functions except IT, finance, sales and marketing, and is responsible for the Operations Department P&L. Responsibilities are:

- Hands-on management of functional areas of supply chain, manufacturing engineering, quality assurance, production, shipping and receiving, inventory, and facilities
- Reducing the labor content across all products by targeted percentage objective as percentage of sales
- Exceeding operating plan goals in measurements of safety, productivity, quality, and on-time delivery within an ISO9000 2008 workplace
- Integrating product acquisitions, new product/ technology introductions (NPI), lean strategy implementation, production transfers, and facilities/ equipment investment
- Turning around underperforming operations by transforming company operations and culture into a highly effective manufacturing entity
- Incorporating lean manufacturing techniques and continuous improvement to create a sustained favorable cash flow position while increasing production capacity on a global basis
- Showing specific metrics and percentages for having improved EBITDA , improved productivity, improved Direct Labor (DL) costs, improved on-time delivery, improved quality metrics, reduced OSHA recordable incident rate plus submitting a company record of consecutive days without a lost time accident
- A major driver in successful new ERP system implementation and in establishing a land not previously developed (Greenfield) facility for a new product launch
- Overhauling manufacturing flow of materials from receipt to shipment

- Conducting training for knowledge and practical application of lean manufacturing methodologies and world class principles to continually drive improvements in EBITDA, cost, delivery, quality, safety, and employee involvement while placing the customer at the center of everything
- Rearranging a facilities plan to create flow and eliminate waste
- Being grounded in shop floor fundamentals with ability to connect with shop floor personnel in both union and non-union environments
- Having extensive experience in buy and sell side M&A, product line consolidation and rationalization, functional consolidation, and re-engineering of business processes post acquisition
- Possessing personal characteristics which include being a high integrity, trustworthy, hands-on executive leader with credibility amongst customers, employees, board members, suppliers, and other stakeholders that is underscored by an intuitive business focus
- Retaining a reputation for driving positive change that enhances the bottom-line, translates strategy into reality, and implementing best practices across organizations, unifying a winning company culture
- Having expertise in operating budget management, acquisitions and integration, product development and introduction, supply chain, operational excellence, lean Six Sigma, quality, customer service, customer satisfaction, facilities, human resources and environmental, and health and safety
- Providing multi-operational site responsibility for products, including annual operating budgets, three year

strategic planning, and being sponsor/champion of process improvement programs utilizing operational excellence and lean Six Sigma disciplines

- Taking responsibility for manufacturing, materials, procurement, manufacturing engineering, quality engineering, customer service, order entry, facilities and environmental, and health and safety

Achieving all the above responsibilities is utopic; it would be considered unusual for anyone to achieve every single responsibility.

The above criteria for VPs of Operations of PEG's portfolio companies in the aggregate is overwhelming, but it is unlikely that any SITG for VPs of Operations candidate has mastered them all. I am providing a pattern of similar traits and requirements to help SITG for VP of Operations candidates with hiring traits particular to skin in the game for VPs of Operations.

Regardless of the SITG C-Level job you apply for, after you ask for and receive a copy of the PEG's job specifications, you should complete a self-rating quiz, rating yourself from one to ten against the job requirements. Then write down the name of one or two references who can verify your high ratings. Also include their contact info for the PEG (see the self-rating quiz example in chapter 10).

Chapter 4

Writing Your Indiana Jones Bio

Definition of an IJ Bio and its Purpose

Before you produce a final resume, consider first writing your IJ Bio, especially if you haven't looked for a job in a while. Making the effort to complete your IJ Bio can help you conduct more effective networking and PEG job interviews. Our PEG clients liked the due diligence aspect of the IJ Bio. Our C-Level candidates grew to appreciate it after completion. I discovered years ago that a significant number of our A player skin in the game C-Level search candidates from the Midwest, Southwest, and from manufacturing industries had unimaginative, job responsibility-dominated resumes. Top level candidates, particularly at the full P&L and operations level, found it difficult to legitimately give themselves credit for their major career employment achievements.

The majority of my PEG clientele for the past twenty-eight years has been the lower middle market, not the billion dollar companies serviced by the big name headhunters. The skin in the game search assignments I fill demand hands-on C-Level candidates able to do more than the job for which they were hired. Their resumes need to demonstrate an ability to wear many hats in small portfolio companies. If you are trying for a job in this market, your resume must show these skills and characteristics.

Bringing out such legitimate abilities in your Indiana Jones Bio will provide you with ammunition for a more effective resume that addresses your target audience's hiring priorities.

I began calling my candidate bio request the Indiana Jones Bio based on the adventurous Indiana Jones movies, and the bio moniker stuck. Afterwards, our senior level candidates began focusing on their value added achievements and began putting numbers, metrics, EBIT/EBITDA figures, results, percentages etc. into their IJs and subsequently into their resumes instead of just bland generalities.

Presently there is a tight market with many A player senior executives actively looking for a job for over eighteen months or longer. Other highly qualified senior executives have actually stopped seeking their ideal job and lowered their career expectations.

When investigating their own possible company acquisitions, private equity firms, including our PEG clients, employ a due diligence screening process before they spend millions in assessing and verifying as much critical, relevant, and confidential information as possible. Some PEGs spend years evaluating a key acquisition. I have always employed that same due diligence approach and investigative detail regarding our executive search candidates. The more the clients know about our finalist referred candidates, the better their hiring decisions. Clients appreciate this opportunity to really know their C-Level candidates and eventual hires. Gilreath Consultancy's Indiana Jones Bio tool has been well received by our PEG clients right from the beginning.

My pet peeve with the middle market PEGs in general is their insufficient concern with a C-Level candidate's "soft skills". These are personal attributes that enable someone to interact effectively and harmoniously with other people, encompassing leadership, empathy, communication, and sociability. Too many middle market PEGs focus almost solely on hard skills, defined as a person's technical skills, and ability to perform certain standalone functional tasks.

If you have not looked for a management or executive job in many years, the Indiana Jones exercise will be helpful to you in communicating your life and career accomplishments and setbacks. This presentation should be in a "cut to the chase" manner, especially in face-to-face networking sessions and PEG job interviews. You might consider completing an Indiana Jones Bio to be overkill. Don't. I have found that it strengthens the SITG C-Level candidate's resume, networking, and job interviews.

The IJ Bio, done right, is a cathartic, comprehensive review of your career to date. It demonstrates your soft skills and hard skills. The best approach, on a rough draft basis, is to list each employer, company, sales, number of employees, job location(s), parent company, products or services, job title, and key job criteria. Be sure to mention the job challenges you faced. Start getting in the habit of rating your individual job performance (and why) versus the job specs, from one to ten. Concisely explain circumstances, if any, beyond your control for poor performances. Naturally, using the IJ Bio as a helpful tool for a more impactful resume, you should focus on your accomplishments.

The IJ Bio is to be treated confidentially regarding its distribution. If your first interview has gone well with a PEG and resulted in a follow-up interview, use your IJ Bio as a leave behind with the interviewer once the second interview session has ended positively. Remember, you will be competing for that skin in the game job. Odds are, your competition will only have a resume to leave with the hiring authority. You will have an effective resume, a due diligence-focused IJ Bio, and more. Be sure to mark the top "PRIVATE AND CONFIDENTIAL" before printing a copy.

The IJ Bio can help you psychologically when fine tuning your resume and for improved interviewing. Most hiring interviewers are not skilled enough to recognize if their interviewee can do the job they seek to fill. They are better at determining whether the interviewee meets all the job specs or not. The IJ Bio can reinforce your SITG C-Level candidacy looking at the entire person, not just what the resume covers. If you have an interview concerning a skin in the game job, give a copy of your Indiana Jones Bio to the PE Partner upon leaving, if he expresses further interest. Use it judiciously, as it's not for just anybody who gets your resume. The IJ Bio will help you as much as the PEG hiring authorities you interview with.

Indiana Jones Bio Basic Outline Exhibit:

- Avoid duplicating your resume contents.
- Don't be overly modest.
- Don't exaggerate.
- Don't constantly make generalizations.
- Back up your claims with numbers, facts, data, and specifics.
- Avoid using too many adjectives.
- Be factual, clear, concise and enlightening .
- Be careful not to breach any non-disclosure agreements using too much specific detail.

Your Indiana Jones Bio can also help with your LinkedIn bio. Here's how your Indiana Jones Bio should flow according to the many highlighted checklists:

Early Background

Include a few words about your upbringing location, your parents (professionally speaking), siblings, noteworthy high school era accomplishments or Eagle Scout achievements, and any significant part time jobs. Also include any college scholarships.

College/University Years

This should include your top grades, whether you attended a self-financed college, any noteworthy varsity sports, part time jobs, Co-Op jobs, Reserve Officers' Training Corps (ROTC), etc.

Early Employment Years

- Mention your initial job / career objectives and why.
- Describe any early mentor(s) and each one's significance as well as the circumstances of their impact on you.
- If married, mention circumstances of your meeting, any commonalities and what brought you and your spouse to commit your lives together.
- Describe your reasons for doing so, if you left your home area.
- What were the specific motivations, whether for employment opportunities including functional learnings in line with your goals and preferred function exposure to engineering, finance, or sales and marketing?
- Briefly touch on your military background.

- As you explain your employer(s) and various job titles you've held, mention significant accomplishments, your collective positive job performances, and results that led to promotions.
- Did you ever pursue a specific career enhancing job opportunity?
- Describe any special training you mastered such as Lean Manufacturing and how you used it to produce targeted company objectives.

Later Employment Years

This should include titles, accomplishments, setbacks, lessons, promotions, awards, special training, challenges, problems solved, examples of leadership traits, and teamwork examples. Connect your career progressions to employer profits, functional developments, and reasons for changing each job. Add a short paragraph about your wife and kids (avoid using their names).

Certifications and Awards

Hobbies

Volunteer Activity

Don't worry about the length of the first draft. Have a trusted colleague or former mentor look it over and be frank about their critique. Give it an overnight review to settle and make necessary word reductions. Re-read it for action items and insert numbers whenever possible such as sales, growth, EBITDA, cost reductions figures, percentage increases, labor rate reduction, profit margin improvements, and value added. That's why it's called the Indiana Jones Bio!

Gilreath Consultancy typically presents PEG clients the fully vetted backgrounds, including exhibits and reference checks on three to four search candidates in separate three ring binders. Many client interviewers take a quick look at the contents of each candidate binder before they interview our candidates, and then close it. In comes the job candidate to the interview with the client representative. This includes Fortune 500 corporate search assignments I used to handle as well as skin in the game searches for PEGs. They say, "Tell me about yourself." Each candidate's resume portrays their public profile with lots of adjectives, not too many metrics, dollar signs, EBITDA, and dashboard KPIs.

I wanted my skin in the game candidates to offer the clients more than just their elevator pitch in response to "tell me about yourself". In manufacturing and chemical processing industries, managers/executives tend to be conservative and do not automatically start bragging about their exploits, skills and achievements. Writing out your life results, warts and all, gives most managers and executives more confidence in themselves. I have each C-Level SITG candidate complete their IJ Bio and become accustomed to communicating their bio highlights naturally, confidentially and succinctly. More than once, if need be. Prepare to be asked, "Tell me about yourself" unless you're Tom Brady or Jack Welch.

Chapter 5

Resume and Cover Letter Tips

Your cover letter to a PEG firm Partner should state that you are highly qualified for and interested in a skin in the game position with an appropriate portfolio company owned by this PEG. Based on your research, you note that this PEG owns a number of portfolio companies in industries and markets where you have proven expertise in growing certain competitor companies to achieve profitable sales, EBITDA, acquisition integrations, and successful liquidity events.

This cover letter presumes you have researched your PEG targets, including their portfolio companies. You should inform your targeted PEG audience if you have proven experience in growing a company or companies that compete with one or more of the PEG's portfolio companies.

Targeted PEGs you are pursuing for skin in the game senior jobs will typically be interested in proven senior executives from related or competitor middle market portfolio companies, especially those seeking to invest some of their own money in a business whose equity they can own, then they can help it grow profitably towards a typical successful exit in five years or less. PEG target firms also react well to you mentioning upfront that you have worked successfully for XYZ PEG firm in one of their prosperous LBO deals, putting your own skin in the game.

Your cover letters to targeted PEG firms must communicate any of your past company achievements depending on your line management function.

Show if you have:

- Helped add value
- Increased cash flow or improved sales
- Introduced new products
- Opened new markets
- Profitably outsourced production
- Reduced debt
- Kept Capex manageable
- Met all covenants
- Improved EBITDA

Other typical PEG interests include integrating acquisitions, reducing inventory, eliminating duplicate facilities and unprofitable products, and measuring key performance indicators weekly. Be sure to mention any past successful portfolio company employment under a PEG. Your experience will get the quick attention of your targeted PEG.

Your cover letter should state your functional expertise when you are seeking to partner with a like-minded PEG. If you know other like-minded functions in which you are also qualified and in which you are interested, state that as well. Indicate metrics, product line profitability dollars saved, percentages of EBITDA increased where applicable to zero in on your level of profit improvement, cost reduction or sales increase, and function as leader or team member.

If you say you have P&L experience, make sure it's full P&L line management experience as a CEO/President/GM over Sales, Marketing, Operations, and CFO. Do your homework before you write your cover letter. Know your PEG audience, portfolio companies, their business model, and backgrounds of Partners you are emailing. In chapter 6 I cover how to approach PEG targets.

If you have a profile on LinkedIn, you might include the link as you are ending your cover letter. Personally, I prefer quality ivory bond paper snail mail to emails. The end result is a greater likelihood of your cover letter and resume being read by your target PEG audience. The better the fit between your background and experience to the targeted PEG, the more you should use the US Postal service and an ivory bond paper letter and envelope for your message and resume. It's also critically important to have an accurate targeted recipients list. Such a list should have correct titles, spelling of names, and accurate addresses. Just because your peers predominantly use emails in their job approaches doesn't mean you should as well. Check out chapter 9 and Bob Bronstein, "blast mailer" friend of mine.

Skin in the Game Job Search Resumes

Finding a good senior executive job is more difficult than it used to be in the current economy. Furthermore, it is important that you are comfortable with current communication technology, including social media. Most PEG hiring authorities will ask you to email your resume before they will talk with you, much less interview you.

You need to have a very impactful resume considering the potential value of a SITG executive position that will be charged with growing a PEG's portfolio company. Hopefully your resume will cause targeted PEG Partners to contact you, or meet you about a confidential portfolio company need (hidden job market). Some PEGs are seeking to partner with skin in the game CEOs to acquire a company in select industries and niche markets (more about this subject in chapter 6).

You can always update your old resume, or buy a book on writing an executive resume for senior SITG executives. However, later in this chapter we have examples of resumes for this purpose, and recommendations to three top proven resume writing professionals.

If you are a "branded" SITG C-Level job seeker, graduated from a big name school (ideally with an MBA), and have worked for top branded companies, count your blessings. If your disposition is pleasant and you are not arrogant, you have quite a combination of positives going for you in seeking an SITG job with a middle market PEG. Additionally, if you have represented branded products, not job hopped or made a questionable job change or two, your resume will automatically attract the attention and interest of a certain number of PEG hiring authorities.

However, especially in a tight job market, a less stellar resume is typically viewed differently if your degree is from a "minor" branded school. If your functional employment history has been with non-branded companies or those ranked below the leaders in their respective industries, your resume must focus on your roles in goals achieved, metrics results, and contributions to employer growth. PEGs will notice your resume numbers rather than adjectives. Focus on numbers such as: KPIs, cutting dollars wasted, improvement metrics, percentage sales increase, and profitability. Lean, no-nonsense, action-oriented resumes.

You can't expect your resume alone to get you hired for a skin in the game job opportunity, but done well, it's a critical first step. Your goal is to get a face-to-face interview with a middle market PEG hiring authority whose company is a match with your skills, experience, and interests. If you managed a brassiere manufacturing company, you will probably not be a fit with a missile systems designer and manufacturer. When I was a Vice President with Weidemann Consultants in New York City years ago, there was a saying, "Macy's wants Gimbels." Like attracts like. Remember, key references from your most recent employment periods will be asked to verify your resume claims.

Produce a resume stating facts and details of your results that you are prepared to back up in an interview with knowledgeable references and related documentation such as a self-rating quiz. Provide metrics, percentages, monetary values, and numbers related to your stated results.

Be sure to sufficiently identify each of your past employers in the line following the company's name. List sales volume, manufactured or distributed products, or types of services, markets, various locations, and parent company's name. A pet peeve of mine is that numerous resumes I receive do not explain what the applicant's company does.

Avoid using jargon. Use language understandable by most business people. Be concise, curb using too many adjectives. Instead use data, numbers, and metrics. "Cut to the chase". I wouldn't worry about length since your PEG target employer is in the due diligence business. Their approach is typically the more info they have, the better hiring decision they will make. Aim for brevity, facts, data, numbers, results, and sufficient detail.

Based on your past affiliations, the more branded names in your resume of products, employers, vendors and markets, the more interest to the reader. Brand names typically connected with any of the PEG's current portfolio companies or targeted acquisition prospects are preferred.

Be careful of putting specific sensitive or confidential financial information in your resume about your current or most recent employer if you are under a confidentiality agreement.

I like to see "reason for leaving" after each employer change and state the employment period. Many promising SITG senior executive job offers are lost if this information is misinterpreted. Your job change explanations (covering the last twenty years or so) should be credible and optimally verifiable.

Regardless of your motive, never omit former jobs from your employment history. You have to behave as if fifteen of your former employer references will be checked by the PE firm before they make you an offer. Social media sites like LinkedIn will probably contain most or all of your former bosses' bios free for the PEG's perusing. So again, be prepared for PEG cold reference calls about you.

Does your current resume and cover letter adequately show your real overall financial values, results, and potential contributions in metrics? Depending on your C-Level function, you should touch on productivity measurement versus industry norms in Sales, Operations, Marketing and Support productivity. Also indicate when you have been employed in any PEG owned portfolio companies in similar industries and related markets to your own career achievements. Mention if you have previously put your money into a portion of the company's equity.

Remember to write a frank and honest resume, especially regarding your job titles, experiences, and accomplishments. I advise most executives to ask their most important references in their most recent jobs to provide them with a written one paragraph reference. I always recommend they send each reference a copy of their resume and a reference request confirming the resume statements covering the time they worked with the job seeker. If the resume is not truthful and contains gross exaggerations, most references will not agree to confirm their mutual experiences with the resume's statements. Numerous times I have emailed a job candidate's resume to the reference I am checking and the first thing I am asked is, "Who wrote this bull crap, anyway? It's mostly baloney!"

Do you need a proven first class executive resume writer to help produce an effective resume? Below are proven experts I recommend if you want top notch help producing a high quality resume and cover letter.

Mark S. Freedman, Director, The
Resource Planning Group, Inc.
http://www.resourceplanning.com/#!bios/c20r9
Ph. 1-413-458-9462
Email: mfreedman@resourceplanning.com

Mark is skilled in creating a cutting-edge personal branding presentation as well as the traditional resume format. He applies that expertise in both consulting assignments and resume production.

In 1994 Mark founded the Career Strategies Division that provides resume and cover letter development and production, direct targeted mailing, and search strategy coaching and counseling to senior level executives worldwide. His clients represent all line and staff functions within a broad range of industries. They include food service, biotech and pharma, consumer products, manufacturing, hospitality, telecommunications, IT and high tech, and sports management. He has established alliances with national job banks and outplacement organizations to provide resume consultation and development to their clients and members.

Previously, Mark served as Executive Director of large and medium-sized human service agencies in California and New York. He has developed leading-edge programs and procured the grant funding for persons with a broad range of disabilities to maximize their potential and integrate them into an independent life in their communities.

Mark has been a featured speaker at many New York City metropolitan area organizations on the topic of executive job search strategy. He has been published in *Resumes! Resumes! Resumes!*, Career Press, 1997, *and Resume Winners from the Pros*, Wendy S. Enelow, Impact Publications, 1998.

He received his B.A. from California State University, Hayward, pursued his M.A. at Dalhousie University in Halifax, Nova Scotia, and earned credits toward a Ph.D. while teaching Political Science at the University of California, Santa Barbara.

Jan Melnik M.A., MRW, CCM, CPRW, Specialties: Professional Career Management, Interview Coaching, Job Search Coaching, and Resume Writing Services... create branded resumes, cover letters, LinkedIn profiles, critical leadership initiatives addenda, bios, and other targeted career-search tools for the highly motivated and accomplished professional... Executive Coach | Career Strategist | Keynote Speaker | LinkedIn Coach |

www.janmelnik.com
Ph. 860-349-0256
Email: compspjan@aol.com

As a regular career expert on NBC, Jan speaks frequently at libraries, universities, and conferences nationwide, and is quoted in the media regularly (from the *New York Times* and *Entrepreneur* to *USA Today*).

Since 1992, Jan has written seven books, five in the entrepreneurial field for Globe Pequot Press and two for JIST Publishing. In 2006, JIST published *Executive's Pocket Guide to ROI Resumes and Job Search* (co-authored with Louise Kursmark). In 2007, *One-Hour College Application Essay* was published by JIST.

John Marcus, award-winning author whose books include *The Resume Doctor: How to Transform a Troublesome Work History Into a Winning Resume* (Harper Collins), *The Resume Makeover* (McGraw-Hill) and *The Complete Job Interview Handbook* (Harper Perennial).

Ph. 941-363-0340
Email: Jobauthor@aol.com

Your local library will likely have a copy of these gems for you to peruse. *The Wall Street Journal's* career website hailed *The Resume Makeover* as, "The authoritative guide to resume writing."

C-Level executives always ask me what type of resume format I prefer: the chronological format or the resume featuring skills and accomplishments. I prefer the chronological resume. Should you worry about whether your resume is one page, two pages, or three pages? Again PEGs are due diligence-oriented deal makers. If you need three pages to incorporate your credentials, skills, accomplishments, and experiences, then three pages it is. I favor a black and blue and white resume with blue highlighting featured metrics, sales, numbers, and data.

If you feel confident that you can produce a legitimate attention-getting resume as opposed to a Barnum & Bailey version, go ahead and create one. I suggest you consult a professional resume and cover letter veteran expert writer. I recommend, in this highly competitive job market where there are many C-Level job contenders and fewer C-Level jobs, that you make a modest investment in your next SITG career move. Bob Bronstein has more to say in support of that at the end of chapter 9.

A final suggestion regarding your missing yet desirable credentials. If you lack an MBA, I suggest you look into local MBA programs online where you can study according to your schedule and time availability. While you are seeking an SITG job with a PEG, your time will be otherwise occupied for the most part. Securing an MBA takes longer that way, but I have seen instances where my SITG C-Level candidate enters an online MBA program, say in Operations Management, and lists it in his resume as currently enrolled in an MBA Operations Management degree curriculum. That will look better than your "lonely" undergraduate degree on your resume. The PEG client who hired this manager was impressed that this VP Operations, twenty years out of college, was continuing his education part-time and staying current in his career focus. It's not a make or break issue but could be beneficial to you in more ways than just educationally.

Chapter 6

Four Exhibits of C-Level Hires from Skin in the Game Searches

Below are the Indiana Jones Bio, resume, and cover letter exhibits of four skin in the game senior executive functions: hired CEO, CFO, VP Operations and VP Sales and Marketing.

**Read only the Indiana Jones Bio, resume, and cover letter exhibits pertaining to your own particular functional job title.*

N.B. stands for Nota Bene or Note Well. All names of candidates, companies and locations have been changed for confidentiality purposes. Any similarity of fictional names used to actual names of persons, employers, and locales is purely coincidental.)

CEO Hire

Below are the Indiana Jones Bio (IJ), resume, and cover letter exhibits of Tom Frederick, a skin in the game CEO hired as Architectural Building Products Manufacturer CEO.

Indiana Jones
Early Background

Tom Frederick was born at Altus Air Force Base, Altus, Oklahoma. When Tom's father completed his military service, the family settled in a suburb of Philadelphia, Pennsylvania until the family moved to Denver, Colorado when Tom was thirteen. Tom's father worked as a mining engineer consultant in the domestic oil and gas mining sector. His mother was a stay-at-home mother for most of his early childhood. After moving to Denver, CO, his mother went to work in the library of the local school. Both parents are currently retired.

Tom is the second of three siblings. He has an older brother who now resides in Houston, Texas, where he directs marine operations for an international engineering and construction company. His younger sister graduated from The University of Oklahoma. She resides in Tulsa, OK, where she teaches high school algebra and trigonometry.

During high school, Tom was very active and achieved a high degree of academic and athletic success. He was the valedictorian of his class and received several merit-based scholarships. Tom also lettered in football, wrestling, and track. Tom was the East High School football team captain and earned All-District honors.

Secondary Education

Tom attended The University of Texas, Austin. During the school year, he worked twenty hours a week at various jobs including tutoring in calculus and substitute teaching at a local high school. He was also a leader in the Residence Hall Association and active in intramural sports. Tom was recognized as a Distinguished Student and graduated cum laude in August 1980 with a Bachelor of Science degree in Civil Engineering (Structural Engineering concentration). He was awarded membership in the Tau Beta Pi, Chi Epsilon, and Phi Eta Sigma national honor societies.

After a few years of work experience, Tom returned to school to broaden his understanding of business operations. He attended The University of Chicago. Under a graduate assistantship program, he worked thirty hours a week as a career counselor in the Business Placement Office at The University of Chicago. Tom graduated in May 1984 with a Masters of Business Administration in Finance.

Throughout Tom's career, his professional education has been continually enhanced through attendance in numerous seminars and short courses in topics including leadership development, strategic planning, corporate development, sales and marketing, communication, lean manufacturing, recruiting, safety, and software applications.

For several years, Tom served as the Diamond APG industry representative to the Remodeling Futures Program of the Joint Center for Housing Studies. This program was based at the Kennedy School of Harvard University.

Entry Level Work and Early Work History
Transocean, Inc., Houston, TX – summers (two years)

While attending The University of Texas, Austin, Tom worked during the summers on offshore drilling rigs. He started as a roustabout and was promoted to roughneck and derrickman. Work hours were long, sometimes requiring thirty-six-hour shifts. The compensation was good, but the job was hard, dirty, and dangerous. This experience gave Tom a great appreciation for the value of a good education.

McGregor International, Inc. ($6.6 billion - revenue)
Houston, TX and New Orleans, LA - 1980 to 1982
Title(s): Structural Design Engineer - 1980 to 1981
Field Engineer - 1981 to 1982

McGregor International is a market leader and worldwide provider of engineering, construction, and project management services to offshore oil and gas developments. Tom was hired as a Structural Design Engineer in McGregor's Houston office. Initial projects included the design of a compressor station, flair boom tower, deck extensions, and jackets for offshore platforms. He was a lead engineer on a unique jacket replacement for a storm-damaged structure.

In 1981, Tom was selected from a pool of over twenty candidates for a one year reassignment to McGregor's New Orleans office. In his new capacity as a Field Engineer, Tom supervised offshore construction and subsea pipeline installations. He was second in command of construction barges with crews ranging from 200 to 350 men.

When he returned to the Houston design group, Tom realized that his passion was in operations vs. office-based design work. At the same time, he recognized that he would benefit from a greater understanding of business fundamentals. To accomplish these goals, Tom applied for admission to graduate business schools.

Reason for Leaving

Tom left McGregor International to pursue a full-time MBA curriculum at The University of Chicago, IL.

D.W. Alexander LLC Management Consulting
($9.9 billion - revenue)
Dallas, TX - 1984 to 1995
Title(s): Associate Consultant - 1984 to 1986
Senior Consultant - 1986 to 1987
Manager - 1987 to 1990
Senior Manager - 1990 to 1995

D.W. Alexander LLC is a leading management consulting and financial advisory firm to top organizational leadership on issues of strategy, organization, and operation.

The consulting challenge was to diagnose complex business problems and implement corrective solutions in a time sensitive environment. Tom enjoyed the dynamic, high pressure environment where he was constantly exposed to new ideas and practices, and fresh challenges. He thrived as a consultant and was promoted three times in eleven years.

Tom was a member of D.W. Alexander's Reorganization Advisory Services Group. He led business reorganization teams to improve marketing and sales, product mix, cost controls, customer service, cash management, financing, compensation systems, and asset deployment. Project teams consisted of managers and senior staff from D.W. Alexander's consulting, audit, tax, actuarial and benefits, and business valuation groups. Representative engagements included Hale Corporation, Wethersfield Communities, Universal Homes, John Deere, Dallas Fort Worth Bank, Silicon Valley Bank, and Third Republic Bank.

Many of Tom's engagements required complex financial and operational analysis. He directed teams that identified billions of dollars in annual cost savings and productivity enhancements in supply, distribution, marketing, customer service, finance, work force management, and support services. In other projects, he assessed the economic viability of three multi-billion dollar projects.

Tom was an active participant in the sales and marketing of professional services including client research, preparation and delivery of proposals, cold calling, and conducting seminars and training sessions. He collaborated with Beaumont Partners to develop and roll-out the firm's Shareholder Value Maximization product.

When the firm was looking for new avenues to capture talented recruits, Tom joined a group of senior professionals to found D. W. Alexander's Business Analyst Program. After establishing objectives, procedures, and action plans, the program was rolled-out nationally. Tom developed, recruited, trained, counseled, and administered the Dallas Business Analyst Program.

Exposure to many successful Partners and the rigors of the consulting environment allowed Tom to hone his skills and talent for leadership, team-building, strategic analysis and planning, quantitative analysis, process improvement, collaboration, and communication.

Reason for Leaving

The management consulting lifestyle that required near 100% travel made it difficult to maintain family relationships and support the development of children. In addition, Tom desired to return to a construction-related field. When an attractive corporate opportunity was presented to join the Diamond Industries, Inc. Architectural Products Group, Tom accepted the offer.

Chronological Job Titles during Later Career:

Diamond Industries, Inc., Architectural Products Group (APG) ($3 billion - revenue)
Atlanta, GA and Dallas, TX - 1995 to 2003
Title(s): Vice President, Corporate Development - 1995 to 1996
President, Pontiac Aggregates - 1996 to 1998
President, APG South Region - 1998 to 2001
President, APG West Region - 2001 to 2003

Diamond Industries, Inc. is the U.S. holding company for Glasgow, Scotland based HCR plc. and the largest manufacturer of building materials and architectural products in North America. It employs a lean, flat organizational structure with limited overhead. Diamond Industries made a practice of hiring engineers with consulting backgrounds to staff corporate development positions.

This filled a needed role and provided bench strength for future management needs.

As Vice President of Corporate Development, Tom was responsible for the Architectural Products Group's internal and external growth initiatives including acquisitions, new plant development, strategic planning, and special projects. He also served as a consultant to Diamond Industries APG Company and regional presidents, recommending business alternatives and assisting with any quantitative analysis.

During his tenure, external growth was fueled by the acquisition of three manufacturing companies. Tom identified companies, followed up on leads, analyzed the opportunities, designed acceptable offers, prepared the board proposals, and coordinated the integration of the acquired companies.

Internal growth was supplemented by the development and execution of plans to construct four Greenfield plants. Previously when Diamond Industries APG built Greenfield plants, there were often cost and schedule overruns. Tom used MS Project to establish critical paths and budgets for all Greenfield projects. Employing these tools and closely monitoring progress, each project came in on time and under budget.

The development position allowed Tom to meet many successful entrepreneurs. He benefited from the stories of their triumphs and accomplishments.

In 1996, Diamond Industries APG experienced trouble with one of its operating companies, Pontiac Aggregates, in Atlanta, GA. The CEO and CFO were fired after they were implicated in a corporate fraud leading to a $4MM loss. The group CEO asked Tom to take over the troubled operation.

As the new President of Pontiac Aggregates Industries, Tom assumed leadership of a distressed $32MM, 140 employee, lightweight aggregate manufacturing company. He was challenged to turn around a company that cumulatively had not made a profit in the last ten years. Morale was low; employees were afraid they would be fired and fearful the company would be sold. Problems under the previous administration made Pontiac Aggregates an HCR board level issue. In the first few months of the turnaround, the level of administrative scrutiny was oppressive.

Tom orchestrated a dramatic three-year turnaround. EBIT improved from -$3.9MM to +$6.4MM and Return on Net Assets (RONA) increased from -12.9% to +22.3%. The product line was expanded, and new channels were developed thus expanding distribution. The result was a $16MM, or 62% increase in sales. Output was increased by 25% and unit costs were lowered from $17.01 to $13.16. A record was established for four years without a lost time accident. Many of the tactics that were employed to achieve these results were subsequently implemented in comparable situations throughout Tom's career.

When Tom joined Pontiac Aggregates, he brought the remaining management group together as a team by increasing accountability, sharing information, putting together plans, prioritizing key issues, and making sure that everyone was on the same page.

Much of the initial focus centered on improving the production quality, capacity, and efficiency of the plants. The production process employed natural gas and powdered coal-fired kilns. Fuel made up the largest component of the cost structure. By improving the flame characteristics and heat dispersion, product quality and output was dramatically enhanced. Costs were lowered yielding large positive production variances.

To further improve production, steps were taken to implement a comprehensive preventive and predictive maintenance program. Thermography (infrared photography) was used to identify electrical issues and address potential failures. Vibration analysis was used on all motors to eliminate bearing failures. Oil was scrutinized at a micron level to improve filtration and prevent hydraulic failures. These efforts combined to significantly reduce equipment failures and avoid thousands of dollars in downtime.

Sales procedures were also transformed to be more effective. Pontiac Aggregates' traditional selling practice was linear and time consuming. Tom saw opportunities to consolidate the selling process by addressing activities concurrently instead of consecutively, thereby shortening the sales cycle. Tom brought key management on all large sales calls. This procedure allowed Pontiac Aggregates to address any objections and close sales immediately.

Lightweight concrete using Pontiac Aggregates offers design flexibility and substantial cost savings by providing lower dead loads, improved seismic structural response, longer spans, better fire ratings, thinner sections, less reinforcing steel, and lower foundation costs. Tom worked with the deans of the schools of architecture at Georgia Tech, North Carolina State, and Clemson to convey these important concepts to their graduating students. Tom was appointed to the Development Board at the Duke School of Architecture. This provided an immediate connection to many of the leading architects in the South. The heightened exposure greatly improved Pontiac Aggregates' product specification.

With expanding product specification, sales reached the production capacity of the plant. To further enhance profitability, prices were selectively increased. Certain product segments that were not profitable were pushed to competitors.

Plant safety was also a critical area of focus and priority. A full-time Director of Environmental, Health and Safety (EHS) was hired. Employee-directed safety committees were formed and industry experts were consulted. This emphasis reduced lost time accidents from four or five per year to no life-threatening accidents in a four year stretch.

To improve distribution, Pontiac Aggregates began shipping product at off-peak times to strategically located strategically located inventory terminals. These stores were drawn down when demand exceeded plant shipping capacity. Efforts were made to ship with the most economical carrier. Barge-shipped product could lower transportation costs by as much as 80%.

Formal strategic and capital planning processes were implemented. These processes were year-round and incorporated a great deal of feedback from the field. Key goals and objectives were communicated to all employees in the form of charts and graphs. Progress was tracked against budget and prior year performance. These initiatives stimulated many conversations about what could be done to further improve performance.

Tom groomed the Vice President of Production to be his successor and arranged for him to study for an MBA degree on a part-time basis. As the VP assumed more responsibility, Tom had more time to help with other struggling operations in the Diamond Industries APG organization.

In 1998, Tom was promoted to Regional President, Diamond Industries APG South. This group was newly-formed and initially consisted of six manufacturing and distribution companies with sales of $132MM. Group building products included masonry, architectural stone, bricks, patio products, retaining walls, bagged stone and concrete, fly ash, and lightweight aggregate. Tom was challenged to expand the region and convey the important strategic lessons learned at Pontiac Aggregates.

Many of the programs started at Pontiac Aggregates were rolled out to all APG South companies. These initiatives included detailed preventive and predictive maintenance, strategic planning, capital effectiveness programs, financial and operational reporting of key metrics, transportation effectiveness, and working capital management.

New safety initiatives were also adopted. Machine lock-out procedures were standardized and communicated. Yards were paved to prevent stacking failures. Plant interior walls were painted white to improve visibility. All accidents required immediate investigations; plants were shut down to share the investigation results. In quick order, APG South established the best safety record in Diamond Industries APG.

While leading APG South, Tom directed the acquisition of three manufacturing companies. He identified the prospective companies, analyzed the opportunities, designed suitable offers, reviewed the contracts, wrote the board proposals, and coordinated the integration of the acquired companies. Combined annual revenue of these acquisitions exceeded $67MM.

Team selling processes were streamlined and two new sales channels were introduced to the region. When these initiatives were combined with the new acquisitions, regional sales increased from $202MM to $209MM.

Tom was the first regional president to conduct formal sales and management training at a group level. In addition, he spent an inordinate amount of time individually coaching, mentoring, and training promising young managers. Seven of these employees went on to become presidents of Diamond Industries affiliated companies.

Diamond Industries APG management wanted to construct a new prototype manufacturing plant. Tom was integrally involved in the site selection, design, construction management, and start-up of the facility. He employed new methods to reduce costs and save time on the critical path schedule. The state of Tennessee was successfully solicited to fund staff training costs. This plant was generally regarded as the most successful start-up in APG history.

After three years, the APG South region grew to nine companies, $240MM in revenue and 1,000 employees in twenty-seven locations. Group EBIT was at $19.2MM with a RONA of 20.2%.

In 2001, Tom was promoted to Regional President, Diamond Industries APG West. He directed all aspects of the largest APG region with ten diverse manufacturing and distribution companies, \$280MM in revenue and 1,400 employees in thirty-five facilities. Regional building products included masonry, architectural stone, bricks, ornamental precast, roof tile, ready-mix concrete, patio and landscaping products, retaining walls, bagged stone, and concrete mixes. In a post 9/11 environment, Tom's emphasis shifted to controlling cost to maintaining profitability in a declining market.

Administrative operations were consolidated to eliminate \$2.0MM of redundant overhead.

Lean manufacturing techniques were utilized to increase production and lower unit costs. Manufacturing operations were filmed, broken down, and analyzed. Root causes of machine downtime were rigorously scrutinized. Machine set-up procedures, yard layout, and product staging were also examined. Innovative process improvements were adopted that lowered operating cost by \$5.0MM and increased throughput by 8%.

Tom spent a considerable amount of time directing the turnaround of three APG West operating companies: Kevtile, Celsus Pre-Mix, and KCI Manufacturing.

Kevtile - Refocused product strategy and consolidated dealer operations, upgraded sales team, improved plant efficiencies, and eliminated production variance. Took operations from breakeven to \$1.9MM profit in one year, \$3.4MM in two years.

Celsus Pre-Mix - Improved production efficiency, lowered unit cost, added new product, and expanded distribution. Improved EBIT from \$490k to \$1.8MM in one year.

KCI Manufacturing - Outsourced truck fabrication, reduced inventory, consolidated operations, and improved preventive maintenance. Boosted EBIT from $370k to $2.0MM in one year.

Like APG South, many of the programs started at Pontiac Aggregates were rolled out to all APG West companies. New safety initiatives rolled out in the West cut historical accident rates in half.

As a result of leadership training successes in APG South, the Diamond Industries APG corporate group developed its own in-house training program. Tom helped to put together many of the training modules. He also taught courses on leadership, recruiting, staff development, and training.

Regional EBIT improved by $5.0MM despite a 2% post 9/11 decline in sales. RONA for the group increased from 10.1% to 16.2%, the largest incremental increase in the six-region architectural products group.

Reason for Leaving

At Diamond Industries, Inc., Tom enjoyed unprecedented success and was promoted three times in eight years. He was responsible for turning around several companies. Eventually, he managed the group's largest region comprised of twelve companies operating out of forty facilities.

In 2000, new management was installed and the culture of the Architectural Products Group changed significantly. Most of the prior administration ended up moving on. By 2003, Tom was the fifth of six regional presidents to leave. After his departure, he was retained as a consultant to assist Diamond Industries APG with acquisitions and several special projects.

Lynx Building Group ($216MM - revenue)
Dallas, TX - 2003 to 2006
Title(s): Vice President, Corporate Development - 2003
President, Southwest Division - 2003 to 2006

Lynx Building Group is a privately-owned real estate developer and national homebuilder based in Chicago. The company operates in Illinois, Wisconsin, Ohio, Florida, Texas, and Arizona. Tom was hired to lead corporate development and was subsequently promoted to Southwest Division President.

The challenge was to rebuild the management team and turn around operations in a very competitive market. Tom restructured the sales team, launched new product, and added joint ventures, thereby improving sales by 78%. He closed under-performing locations, sold excess assets, and reduced inventory by 8.3%. Purchasing and production were streamlined, thus lowering Cost of Goods Sold (COGS) by 3.7%. At the same time, Selling, General, and Administrative Expenses, (SG&A) was reduced by 12.6%. The combination of these efforts improved EBIT by $3.0MM in two years.

Reason for Leaving

With the start of an industry-wide downturn, Lynx Building Group consolidated its operations under family members. The Texas operations were combined with operations in Florida under the leadership of the CEO's younger brother. The Division President position in Texas was eliminated in the consolidation.

Excalibur Homes ($116MM - revenue)
Dallas, TX - 2006 to 2008
Title: President, Texas Division - 2006 to 2008

Excalibur Homes is a privately owned real estate developer and national homebuilder based in Memphis, TN. The company operated in Georgia, Tennessee, and Texas. Tom was recruited by the Board of Directors to create a new Texas-based, high-end homebuilding division. The competitive market in Dallas and the industry downturn combined to present a huge challenge.

This was Tom's first true start-up company and he relished the freedom to create a new, ideal organization. He formed a legal operating entity, acquired attractive land positions, established an effective management team, developed a new attention-grabbing product line, value-engineered a cost effective product, created compelling marketing materials, and built trial product under-budget and ahead of schedule.

In preparing the division's strategic plan, Tom developed an interactive financial model to project a five year income statement, balance sheet, and cash flow forecast. This model was subsequently adopted by the corporate parent organization.

Tom was very involved with the sales and marketing of the new product line. He hired and directed the sales staff, prepared competitive analysis, developed marketing materials, coordinated realtor functions, and assisted with the overhaul of the corporate website.

A cash crisis at the corporate parent made it difficult to fund local payables. Consequently, mechanics' liens prevented sales from closing.

Reason for Leaving

The parent company was caught with too much inventory in Tennessee and Georgia. Working capital requirements and the debt burden generated a cash crisis. Management in Georgia was unable to negotiate an acceptable settlement with its creditors and national operations were suspended.

Longhorn Banking Corporation ($2.0 billion - assets)
Dallas, TX - 2008 to Present
Title: Team Leader, Loan Acquisition
Group - 2008 to Present

Longhorn Banking Corporation is a Texas-based bank founded by billionaire Arthur Ewing and headquartered in Dallas, Texas. Through its Loan Acquisition Corporation (a Longhorn Banking affiliate) the bank buys individual loans and loan portfolios from different sellers including the Federal Deposit Insurance Company (FDIC), the Small Business Administration (SBA), and numerous private sellers. In the last few months, Longhorn Banking Corporation has purchased over $750MM of loans from failed banks.

Tom was contacted to consult on issues concerning residential construction. This quickly transitioned into a position as an acquisition Team Leader. Tom currently directs a team of securities and loan analysts who devote 100% of their time to analyzing potential transactions. All transactions are reviewed in detail including validating loan documents and other agreements, considering market factors and business viability, determining lien position, evaluating collateral, and assessing guarantees. Tom and his team present all prospective deals directly to Arthur Ewing.

This experience is challenging and a tremendous growth opportunity. It allows Tom to evaluate many different business models from a variety of industries. In addition, it provides an in-depth exposure to the financing side of the business. He now has a better appreciation of the banker's perspective.

Family

Tom met his wife, Mary, at The University of Texas graduate school of business. After completing their degrees, they married in June 1984.

Mary graduated from Notre Dame University with a Bachelor of Science in Speech. Before attending graduate school, she worked as a Marketing Representative for CXL (computer software), and Sheraton Corporation. At The University of Texas, Mary earned an MBA in Finance. Mary enjoyed a long and successful banking career in the Wells Fargo organization. She retired as a Trust Officer in 1999.

Tom and his wife have been married for twenty-three years and have two sons and a daughter. Their daughter, Alexandra, is a senior finance major in The University of Texas. Their older son, Howard, will graduate from Fort Worth Senior High School in June of 2009. He will attend Texas A&M University and plans to major in management information systems. Their younger son, Erik, is ten years old and will be a fifth grade student in the fall.

Associations, Personal, and Leisure Time Activities

Tom is a member of the national, state, and local Homebuilder's Association. He served for several years on the Development Board for the Duke School of Architecture. He is also a past Vice President of ESCSI (national industry association for lightweight aggregate producers).

His leisure time is spent attending athletic events (including helping with his son's baseball team), taking part in a men's basketball league, chess, and participating in family activities.

RESUME

CONFIDENTIAL RESUME (Still Employed)
TOM FREDERICK
1341Langham Place
Fort Worth, TX 76110
(682) 444-3030
tfrederick@yahoo.com

Chief Executive Officer
Accomplished in driving revenues, growth, and profit improvement

Career Highlights

- Doubled sales from $102MM to $209MM in three years through development of new channels, strategic growth initiatives and successful merger integration.
- Reduced operating costs by $5.0MM via consolidation and innovative process improvements.

- Identified, evaluated, and acquired six companies with $155MM in combined revenue.
- Successfully turned around an under-performing home-builder and four distressed manufacturing companies.
- Recruited, coached, and mentored seven employees who became Presidents of affiliated companies.

Professional Experience

Longhorn Banking Corporation, Dallas, TX

$2.0 billion (assets) privately owned bank. Longhorn Bank acquires individual loans and loan portfolios from different sellers including the FDIC, the Small Business Administration (SBA), and numerous private sellers.

Team Leader, Loan Acquisition Corporation, Dallas, TX

Recruited to consult on issues concerning residential construction; promoted to acquisition Team Leader. Directs a team of securities and loan analysts who devote 100% of their time to analyzing potential acquisitions. Transaction analysis includes validating loan documents and other agreements, assessing market factors and business viability, determining lien position, and evaluating collateral and guarantees. All prospective deals are presented directly to Andy Beal, owner and President of Longhorn Bank. In six months, Longhorn Bank has purchased over $750MM of loans from failed banks.

Excalibur Homes, Memphis, TN - 2006 to 2008

$116MM privately owned real estate developer and national homebuilder.

President, EH Group Texas LLC, Dallas, TX

Recruited by directors to start up a new Texas-based high-end homebuilding division. Directed all aspects of operations including corporate formation, land acquisition, staff retention, product development, and management of purchasing, construction, sales, and marketing.

Reason for Leaving

The parent company was subject to too much inventory and not enough cash, and creditors forced operations to be suspended.

Lynx Building Group, Dallas, TX - 2003 to 2006

$216MM privately owned real estate developer and national homebuilder based in Chicago, IL. The company operates in Illinois, Wisconsin, Ohio, Florida, Texas, and Arizona. Tom was hired to lead corporate development and was subsequently promoted to Southwest Division President.

Vice President, Corporate Development - 2003

President, Southwest Division - 2003 to 2006

- Responsible for rebuilding the management team and turning around the operations of a newly acquired division. Improved EBIT by $3.0MM over two years.

- Restructured sales team, launched new products and added joint ventures improving sales by 78% to $47MM.
- Closed under-performing locations, sold excess assets, and reduced inventory by 8.3%.
- Streamlined purchasing and production lowering COGS by 3.7%, reduced SG&A by 12.6%.

Reason for Leaving

With the start of an industry-wide downturn, Lynx Building Group consolidated its operations under family members. The Division President position in Texas was eliminated in the consolidation.

Heavy Construction Categories (public limited company) (HCC plc.) / Diamond Industries, Inc., Architectural Products Group (APG) - 1995 to 2003

HCR plc. is a publicly traded Glasgow, Scotland based international leader in the construction materials industry with $10B in annual revenues. Diamond Industries is a U.S. holding company with $3B in revenues, the largest manufacturer of building materials and architectural products in North America. Domestic operations are based in Atlanta, GA.

President, Diamond Industries APG West Region
Dallas, TX - 2001 to 2003

- Directed the largest APG region with ten diverse manufacturing and distribution companies, $280MM revenue and 1,350 employees in thirty-five facilities.
- Improved EBIT by $6.0MM (27%) despite a 2% post 9/11 decline in sales.

- Boosted RONA from 14.1% to 18.2%; best performance of six-region architectural products group.
- Consolidated operations to eliminate $2.0MM of redundant overhead.
- Lowered operating costs by an additional $6.4MM and increased production by 10% through innovative process improvement initiatives.
- Cut accident rates in half; best performance in the architectural products group.
- Executed a restructuring and revitalization program for a $40MM roof tile manufacturer with 240 employees.
- Improved from breakeven to a $1.9MM profit in one year; $3.4MM profit in two years.
- Formulated and taught leadership courses on recruiting, skills development and coaching.

President, APG South Region
Atlanta, GA - 1998 to 2001

- Created and led a new APG region with six manufacturing and distribution companies, $102MM revenue and 1,000 employees in twenty-four locations.
- Established and upheld the best safety record in Diamond Industries APG.
- Almost doubled regional sales from $132MM to $250MM while maintaining a RONA over 20%.
- Led the acquisition and integration of three manufacturing companies.
- Directed the design, construction management, and start-up of a new plant; considered the most successful start-up in APG history.

- Combined annual revenue of acquisitions exceeded $67 million.
- Designed and implemented capital effectiveness programs.
- Recruited and developed seven employees who became Presidents with affiliated companies.

President, Pontiac Aggregates
Atlanta, GA - 1996 to 1998

- Assumed leadership of a distressed $32MM, 140 employee lightweight aggregate manufacturing company.
- Orchestrated a dramatic three-year turnaround.
- Improved EBIT from $3.9MM to +$6.4MM; RONA from -12.9% to +22.3%.
- Expanded product line, added new channels and improved distribution resulting in $16MM in sales, or 62% increase resulting in national product leadership.
- Increased output by 25% and lowered unit cost from $17.01 to $13.16.
- Established record production of four years without a lost time accident .
- Rated first in safety among forty-six other Heavy Construction Categories (HCC plc.) companies, groups, and divisions.

Vice President, Development, Diamond Industries, APG
Atlanta, GA - 1995 to 1996

- Coordinated corporate development for a $220MM product group including acquisitions, strategic planning, and special projects.

- Identified, evaluated, and acquired three manufacturing companies; actual results substantially exceeded board criterion.
- Developed and executed plans to construct four Greenfield plants; each came in on time and under budget.

D.W. Alexander
Dallas, TX - 1984 to 1995

Leading management consulting and financial advisory firm based in New York, NY with U.S. revenues of $9.9 billion. Management consultants to top organizational leadership on issues of strategy, organization, and operation.

Senior Manager, D.W. Alexander Consulting
Dallas, TX - 1990 to 1995
Title(s): Manager - 1987 to 1990
Senior Consultant - 1986 to 1987
Associate Consultant - 1984 to 1986

- Directed client teams of up to forty-five professionals.
- Analyzed complex business issues, applied quantitative methods to diagnose problems, and identified and implemented specific solutions.
- Led business reorganization teams to improve marketing and sales, product mix, cost controls, cash management, financing, compensation systems, and asset deployment; representative engagements included Hale Corporation, Wethersfield Communities, Universal Homes, John

Deere, Dallas Fort Worth Bank, Silicon Valley Bank, and Third Republic Bank.

- Identified cost savings and productivity enhancements in supply, distribution, marketing, customer service, finance, work force management and support services; documented $13 million annual cost savings for a $900 million utility in a typical engagement.
- Assessed economic viability of three multi-billion dollar projects.
- Developed, recruited, trained, counseled, and administered the Dallas Business Analyst Program; coordinated the firm's national recruiting efforts at three major universities.

McGregor International, Inc. Houston, TX
1980 to 1982

McGregor International is a $6.6 billion in revenue market leader and worldwide provider of engineering, construction, and project management services to offshore oil and gas developments.

Structural Design Engineer, Houston, TX
1980 to 1981

Tom was hired as a Structural Design Engineer in McGregor's Houston office. Initial projects included the design of a compressor station, flair boom tower, deck extensions, and jackets for offshore platforms. He was a lead engineer on a unique jacket replacement for a storm-damaged structure.

Field Engineer, New Orleans, LA - 1981 to 1982

In 1981, Tom was selected from a pool of over twenty candidates for a one year reassignment to McGregor's New Orleans office. In his new capacity as a Field Engineer, Tom supervised offshore construction and subsea pipeline installations. He was second in command of construction barges with crews ranging from 200 to 350 men. Tom loved to make things happen in day-to-day field operations.

Education

MBA, Finance
University of Chicago, 1984

BS, cum laude, Civil Engineering
University of Texas, 1980

Elected to Tau Beta Pi, Chi Epsilon, and Phi Eta Sigma honoraries.

COVER LETTER

From: Tom Frederick, tfrederick@yahoo.com
Sent: Sunday, May 03, 2009 9:49 PM
To: S982@gilreathsearch.com
Subject: - Title: Investor President & CEO, Dallas, Texas

Dear Mr. Gilreath:

As a company and regional President with Diamond Industries APG Architectural Products, I led the growth and profit improvement initiatives for many mid-sized architectural product companies. I am a Civil (Structural) Engineer with an MBA, and I am based in Dallas.

Implementing innovative process improvements, expanding sales, turning around under-performing companies, and acquiring and successfully integrating complementary businesses are ways I add value. Successes include:

- Doubled building product sales from $132MM to $250MM in three years through new channel development, strategic growth initiatives, and successful merger integration.
- Reduced operating cost by $8.4MM via consolidation, Lean Manufacturing principles and process modifications.
- Identified, evaluated, and acquired six building product manufacturing companies with $155MM in combined revenue.
- Successfully turned around a troubled homebuilder and four distressed building product manufacturing companies.

- Recruited, coached, and mentored seven employees who became Presidents of affiliated companies.

Please give me a call to discuss how my team-focused approach and commitment to excellence can add value to your private equity client's architectural product manufacturing and distribution operation.

Sincerely,

Tom Frederick

CORRESPONDENCE

Example of a Skin in the Game Job Search Update Email

I have another cover letter example from a skin in the game CEO prospect who is updating me on what he is qualified for and would consider. This type of cover letter update and cut to the chase resume could be used to keep in touch with PEGs you have met or have encouraged you to stay in touch. To me, it's short, sweet, and effective:

Hello Jim,

How are you? It has been a while since we last spoke and I am reaching out with two short updates.

I am now considering a short term CEO role with an online media company. I am most interested in a full time C-Suite role and wish to stay on your radar. Below the signature block is my short updated profile. My goal is to have an ongoing leadership role for a media company in the content, licensing, or technology sectors. I would be delighted to learn about your current activity and where my network might be useful to you.

Please let me know what the news is in your world. What is a good time for a short catch-up call?

Warm regards,
Arthur

941- 339-0878
http://www.linkedin.com/Arthur

Company Goals Where I Can Lead

Scaling a company onto a growth trajectory
Raising investment capital
Business development and strategic relationships

Roles Desired

CEO, Executive, or Board role at media, licensing, content, or technology company
Executive role at a consumer or B2B media services company

Core Skills

Creative deal maker for all levels corporate growth and expansion
Leadership at operating and governance levels, public and private
Capital sourcing from extensive network of private equity and VC investors
Growing revenue and business development
Turnaround success at Century Comics and Dorrance Greeting Cards
Executive roles in finance, sales, and operations at emerging growth

Leadership and Experience

Chairman, Malito - software game producer and distributor
Operating Partner, Magnum Capital - VC fund investing in media and software

President and CEO, AG Media Ventures - VC growth and investment advisor
President, DC Comics - raised capital for growth
President and CEO, Millenium Resources - B2B services software provider
EVP and CFO, Hallendorf Enterprises - $51MM cash flow improvement
VP and MD, Tolland Entertainment - worldwide deal maker and business development
VP and GM, Discovery Cable - broadband cable franchising and business scaling

Education

MBA, Beta Gamma Sigma Honors in Finance, Harvard University
Masters, International Fellow, Columbia University
Bachelor of Arts, Phi Beta Kappa, Russian Language & Literature, Stanford University

CFO Hire

Below are the confidential Indiana Jones Bio (IJ), resume, and cover letter exhibits of Ed Garvin, CFO, hired as SITG CFO of MA based Service Industry Machinery Designer and Manufacturer.

N.B. All names of candidates, companies and locations have been changed for confidentiality purposes. Any similarity of fictional names used to actual names of persons, employers and locales is purely coincidental.

Early Background

Ed was born and raised in Waterford, CT. His father (Ernie Garvin) was a nuclear submariner in the Navy until he retired as a Chief Electrician when Ed was in the ninth grade. His father went to work for the Electric Boat Division of General Dynamics after his retirement from the Navy. He commuted to western Pennsylvania and returned home every other weekend throughout Ed's high school years. Ed's mother stayed at home and raised her four children.

Ed was the oldest of the four. His brother, Maurice, earned his BA degree from Harvard University and his JD from UCONN, and is an attorney for the State of Rhode Island. His sister Millie graduated from The University of Bridgeport with a degree in Computer Science. She is the mother of four children and handles the accounting for her husband's IT consulting company, Cloud Systems LLC, based in New Haven, CT. Ed's youngest sister, Carrie, graduated from Yale University with a Bachelor's degree in Communications and received her Master's degree in Education from Bucknell University. She is the head women's basketball coach at Lehigh University.

Ed has always enjoyed sports and competition and earned a Varsity letter three times each in football and baseball during high school. He was elected captain and was All Conference for each sport during his senior year. His other activities during high school included Yearbook Editor, Boy's State Delegate, National Honor Society, Senior Class Officer, and Altar Server.

He purchased a paper route in the fifth grade and has held some position of employment every year since. Ed graduated in the top 10% of his high school class of 450 students and was awarded the Citizenship Award, among other awards. Ed grew his paper route from fifty papers to 250 papers by the time he sold it in the eighth grade. His high school jobs included self-employment (painting, landscaping, snow removal, and delivery for a florist). He also had a maintenance job for an apartment complex, he umpired, and he interned at IBM in Endicott, NY during his college summers.

Ed went back to Waterford after his college graduation in May 1983 until his General Electric Corporation (GE) position began in December 1983. During that time, he worked for the highway department, taught as a substitute teacher for the junior high and senior high school, and coached football at Waterford High School. At an early age, Ed assumed a lot of responsibility at home with his dad being out to sea and then later commuting to Pennsylvania. As a result, Ed matured quite early and was well prepared for life after high school.

Secondary Education and Other Training

Ed was recruited to play football and baseball by several schools including the Naval Academy, Coast Guard Academy, Union College, Trinity College, and Worcester Polytechnic Institute (WPI). He chose Harvard University, recognizing the advantages it had to offer. His research indicated that the combination of an undergraduate engineering degree with an MBA to follow might be most desirable and a practical use of his quantitative aptitude.

Ed graduated with honors and a B.S. in Business Management and Marketing. His GPA was 3.6 for the four years. Ed financed 90–95% of his education through scholarships, on-campus work-study, and summer employment. In addition to maintaining work-study positions all eight semesters, he participated in the Big Brother program, played baseball freshman year, and football the two years thereafter. He would have played football during his senior year but he had sudden surgery for a hernia during August and elected to not play football and concentrate on his job search.

Ed earned his MBA in 1996 from Columbia University. Other company training he has received includes: GE Financial Management Program (FMP), Effective Presentation, Developing Managerial Effectiveness, New Manager Development Course, Advanced Financial Management Course, Volvo Trucks Total Quality Transformation, Looking Glass Experience, American Flooring Industries, Six Sigma Greenbelt, and Six Sigma Champions Training.

Professional Work History

Ed was recruited by GE for the Financial Management Program (FMP) through the Harvard Career Center and was offered a position to start in December 1983. He targeted GE's training program because he felt the combination of the rotational work assignments and after-hours course instruction would be a great broad and rigorous introduction to the world of business. He also liked the fact that financial managers were trained to become general managers.

FMP Trainee in GE Turbine Division - 1983 to 1986

For the first two years, Ed was in Lynn, MA with the Medium Steam Business and the third year at the Turbine Division in Schenectady, NY. This was followed by six-month rotational assignments through General Accounting (Accounts Payable), Manufacturing Finance, Business Unit Financial Planning and Analysis, and Cost Accounting.

Division Level Financial Planning and Analysis, Project Analysis

The on the job and classroom training developed a solid financial/general management foundation for Ed. Principals such as understanding the details of the business, driving accountability throughout organizations, integrating business/ financial processes, integrity of data, engagement of all employees, continuous improvement, teamwork, planning and execution, and clear leadership have served Ed well throughout his career.

Since the rotations were only six months long, Ed learned how to quickly assimilate into new roles, teams, understand the business, and identify opportunities for improvement. Some of the contributions that he was able to make during these training assignments included reducing open credits from suppliers from $330,000 to $75,000, developing an indirect manufacturing expense budget of $70 million, reconciling unfilled orders backlog of $600 million and a contribution margin of $225 million, developing material input budget of $120 million, and developing a mechanized income statement for six consolidated businesses to streamline monthly closing routines.

His performance in the program earned Ed an invitation to join the Corporate Audit Staff. Even though he had targeted the Corporate Audit Staff since his initial research of GE, he had to make the very tough decision to turn it down and pass on the fastest career track. He had just been married and he did not want to be away from home primarily 100% for the next four to five years. Instead, he elected to broaden his experience by going to different businesses within the company.

Senior Auditor, GE Aircraft Engines
Evandale, OH - 1987 to 1988

This assignment would not have been Ed's first choice because it was not a traditional finance role. However, the experience and skills he acquired proved to be invaluable and he appreciated the opportunity. At the time GE was establishing its self-policing/ reporting rigor in its government-related businesses as a reaction to the allegations of improprieties at its Aerospace business.

The businesses were having a difficult time attracting internal talent, and the Manager of the Corporate Audit Staff recommended Ed to the Aircraft Engines Auditing team. Ed elected to take the position since the company was very accommodating and offered his wife a position in the business too.

The nature of the work involved accessing employee's allegations of improprieties and determining impact and corrective actions, including employee punitive measures, if the allegations proved true. Besides broadening his knowledge in financial, manufacturing, and quality functions, Ed developed skills in project management, dispute resolution, investigation, presentation to senior management, and leadership. His operational and financial reviews included areas such as government contract cost charging, employee incentive plans, quality, disbursements, and inventory systems.

Some of Ed's key findings were a $3 million contract overcharge due to improperly documented overhead rates, a petty cash fraud of $250K involving plant and vendor personnel, and a flawed employee incentive plan resulting in hundreds of thousands of improper payments, including those to the Plant Manager and Finance Manager. Ironically, the Finance Manager was the individual that had recommended Ed for the Corporate Audit Staff (CAS) based on his review of Ed's performance during a CAS pilot assignment. That particular experience of Ed having to expose his former manager reinforced his ethics to always do what is right and not compromise his values.

Financial Analyst, Commercial Operations, GE Plastics Pittsfield, MA - 1988 to 1990

Based on Ed's auditing performance, he was able to pursue promotional opportunities after only sixteen months and elected to gain experience with Sales and Marketing. In this role his primary responsibilities were to prepare and analyze budgets, forecasts, and actual results for sales and standard margins ($1.9 billion sales), base costs ($45 million), and distribution costs ($80 million). He provided leadership for two employees. Ed's key contributions included the development of mechanized monthly sales reports, providing more efficient and accurate reporting of results, performing financial analysis in support of $1.5 billion Borg Warner Chemicals acquisition, and the integration of the Borg Warner data and processes into GE. In addition, he was acting Manager of Finance, Commercial Operations, and provided leadership for six employees for six months until the position was filled.

The acquisition and integration of a new business was a great learning experience for Ed. One critical lesson he learned was to make sure one understands the importance of the go to market function for any acquired business. Most of the Borg Warner sales force was let go and GE tried to just add the Borg Warner products to the group of products sold by its own existing sales force. However, relationship selling was a critical basis for selling the Borg Warner (commodity type) products, and GE struggled to retain customers as a result of its decision to let most of these relationships evaporate.

Sr. Financial Analyst, Manufacturing Div., GE Appliances Louisville, KY - 1990 to 1991

Having acquired commercial experience, Ed went to GE Appliances to gain manufacturing experience. GE Appliances, at that time, had been typically staffed with home grown talent, but the company was looking to infuse some new perspectives and ideas into the business. Ed welcomed the opportunity to go and work in Dick Bowman's (VP Manufacturing) organization. Dick was recognized as a very good leader and had been asked personally by Jack Welch to go to Louisville and optimize the manufacturing costs.

Ed prepared and analyzed operating budgets, estimates, and actual results for a Manufacturing Division with $2.7 billion of costs, 15,500 employees, and eleven plants (nine US, one Canada, one Mexico). Products manufactured included washers, dryers, ranges, refrigerators, freezers, and dishwashers, while microwaves and room air conditioners were sourced from foreign suppliers. Ed provided leadership for three very senior employees (two men and one woman). Through his strong leadership he was able to raise the performance of this team resulting in a promotion for Donald Stapleton to the Dishwasher Plant.

Key contributions made by Ed and his team were automating and streamlining estimating/budgeting processes resulting in elimination of one man year of effort and identifying $1.8 million of reimbursement from the state of Kentucky for costs related to the development and implementation of employee skills training. This position enabled Ed to gain significant experience cultivating relationships and building credibility with multiple plant managers, controllers, and senior leaders of the division.

Plant Controller, Dishwasher Plant, GE Appliances Louisville, KY - 1991 to 1992

Ed was promoted to Plant Controller and provided financial leadership and controllership for a plant with $325 million costs and 1,450 employees. He had direct leadership for four finance employees including two long tenured Appliance gentlemen, and a Financial Management Program (FMP) trainee. He performed analysis resulting in closure of a $22 million production facility generating $8 million annual savings.

Ed developed financial reporting packages with emphasis on root cause analysis, productivity drivers, and process improvements resulting in $1 million annual reduction in overtime and doubling productivity. Controllership was tightened through improved communications and increased discipline.

Ed focused on developing his leadership skills to elevate the performance of his finance team and help turn around the plant's declining performance. He identified gaps in the team's skills and developed individual improvement plans for each member. He communicated clear requirements for his vision for a value added business integrated finance team. These actions helped moved the team to a higher level of performance. Ed also simplified presentation of analyses to plant staff to increase their understanding of plant costs.

Ed was able to establish credibility with the plant staff early in this assignment despite being the bearer of bad news. Members of the manufacturing team had completed a "Work Out" session, just prior to his arrival, and identified a project to save $2.4 million annually by bringing production of wire racks back into the plant. Shortly after assuming the role, Ed realized that this level of savings was not going to materialize. Working with his finance team he discovered an error in the analysis of the "Work Out" team and the real savings would only be $1.6 million. He quickly communicated the savings shortfall to the Plant Manager by laying out the flawed original analysis and the correct analysis side by side. However, Ed also had his team identify opportunities to try and make up the shortfall. The finance and manufacturing teams worked together to identify initiatives to make up $0.5 million of the gap.

Manager, Programs and Productivity, GE Appliances Louisville, KY - 1992 to 1993

The GE Appliances management team wanted to implement site productivity/profitability capabilities. Ed was asked to lead this effort and to oversee the capital budgeting process ($210 million) as well. Per the words of his manager, "Ed took on a new unstructured position with inadequate staffing (one FMP) and no systems support. Through extremely long hours, a diligent focus on details, and facilitating compromises from the four product line Finance Managers, Manufacturing, and Customer Service, Ed has implemented site productivity/profitability capabilities." During this assignment Ed analyzed the sales and costs for all the product lines. Two recent college graduates (one female/one male) rotated through the FMP assignment, and Ed enjoyed helping them establish a strong, broad foundation of analytical skills.

During this assignment, Ed continued to be courted by a former GE Plastics manager, Bob Gross, to join him at Volvo Trucks. Volvo had lost money nine out of ten years and at the time was owned by Porsche. Bob was the head of finance for the Sales,

Marketing, and Parts and Service organization. He wanted Ed to join him as his understudy and contribute to the turnaround. Bob had been pursuing Ed soon after his arrival at Volvo, but Ed had not really given Bob's offer much consideration until the last few months in his current position.

Ed decided to leave GE and join Volvo because he was excited by the prospects of a broader leadership role and the challenge of trying to turn around the performance of a widely recognized branded product. Bob also agreed to get Volvo to sponsor Ed for an Executive MBA program and pay all the costs if he was accepted into such a program in the future. Ed's intent was to apply to Columbia University because it was within driving distance of Bethlehem, PA.

Assistant Commercial Controller, Volvo Trucks Bethlehem, PA - 1993 to 1995

Ed's major responsibilities included truck pricing, margin analysis, budgets and forecasts, expense analysis and control, and customer billing for the Sales and Marketing Division (included Parts and Service). This division employed over 800 people with $70 million annual expenses and generated sales of $1.1 billion for the full year 1992 through direct sales to 300 distributors worldwide. The operating loss for the full year 1992 was $141 million. The Executive Vice President for Sales and Marketing, Mike Gregory, gave day-to-day control of pricing to the Finance department. Bob Gross gave Ed the responsibility for the pricing and approval of deals that went through the distributor channels. In addition, Ed worked with the marketing group and Regional Sales VPs to strategize the price points that they would target.

The commercial elements to the turnaround plan were the following:

- Implement product and channel profitability analysis by customer to understand where pricing and margin was by dealer
- Develop targeted market segments by customer where Volvo products commanded a premium or were more competitive
- Implement pricing strategies for the various products, channels, customers, etc.
- Implement discipline to define customer requirements and pro-actively price the total package
- Establish timely reporting and analysis to drive accountability and execution

Ed really enjoyed this general management type role and working with the internal teams of people in marketing, sales, and customer fulfillment, and the external teams of dealers to drive the volume, price, and mix improvements needed to get Volvo back in the black. Ed led efforts to develop partnership type relationships with the dealers to collaboratively identify mutual winning opportunities.

Another interesting component to this role for Ed was trying to develop a self-directed work team for the custom billing organization. The individual that had been leading this group was very autocratic and resistant to change. He had created a lot of animosity between his long tenured team of six women and two men. Bob eliminated the leader's position and asked Ed to assume leadership for this group and see if he could create a self-directed work team. One of the joys of Ed's career was seeing this team shine once the individuals were asked to contribute their ideas and were given responsibility to make decisions.

Ed feels the keys to unleashing their potential were establishing his credibility as a leader by trying to understand the processes and issues first, taking an interest in each one as an individual and demonstrating that he wanted to help them succeed, attempting to eliminate barriers, and letting them develop a plan of corrective action and process improvement. Each of them was reenergized with Total Quality training they were provided. Ed gave them some formal training and informal coaching to assist them along the way. The end result was that Ed was able to decrease the operation from eight to six at the time volumes were increasing 40%. The two displaced individuals were reassigned within the company. The change in attitude of the team was so noticeable that they were recognized and asked to present their results to the top 100 leaders of the company.

Executive Director Commercial Operations, Volvo Trucks, Bethlehem, PA - 1995 to 1998

Ed was promoted to Bob Gross' position when Bob moved into a product GM role. In addition to his previous responsibilities, Ed assumed all of truck pricing (retail as well as wholesale and all of international sales), parts pricing, capital planning, and controllership for seven company-owned retail dealerships (five US and two Canada).

In addition to his increased leadership responsibilities (twenty employees in total organization), Ed's strategic role was expanded. He worked much more closely with Mike Gregory, the members of Mike's staff, and the CEO's staff. More of Ed's time was spent structuring and closing national account deals, large domestic regional fleet deals with the distributors, and more complicated international deals, providing the commercial implications for capital budgeting projects, and developing sales and marketing programs with Volvo staff and members of The Associates, (Volvo's financing vendor partner). Ed's direct reports included Manager of Truck Pricing (Joe Kern), Manager of Parts Pricing (Bruce Scott), Finance Manager company-owned dealerships, Co-Work Leaders of Customer Billing (Don Smith), Financial Planning & Analysis (FP&A) Leader (Jack Cook), and Special Projects. The experience of leading such a diverse team of individuals contributed to the development of Ed's leadership skills.

Ed continued to drive process improvements. He led the development of an automated means to produce an order backlog profitability analysis by region, specification, and customer.

The above information was important because Volvo had backlogs which ranged at times from six months to eleven months. By knowing the margin on the books, Ed and the team could more aggressively and strategically price their new business. Ed led a cross functional "Work Out" team to reduce lead times. His team produced pricing books to enable Volvo to increase its speed to market with new pricing or specification features.

VOLVO SUMMARY

- Sales grew from $1.2 billion in 1992 to $3.0 billion (annualized) estimated for 1998
- Volume contributed $1.4 billion of the increase, and price/mix contributed $300 million and an average of

$50 million/year with price and mix each accounting for approximately 50%

- The operating loss of $151 million in 1992 was reversed and grew to an estimated operating profit of $160 million in 1998
- At least $150 million of the $300 million improvement can be directly attributable to increased prices that the team was able to achieve through the improved processes, communications, accountability, and execution that were implemented

Being part of the Volvo team was very rewarding for Ed. The team worked hard and well together and Ed enjoyed being part of an organization that had a real esprit de corps amongst the team members. However, Ed needed to leave Volvo to pursue other career growth opportunities. The CFO role was the only financial position that was of interest to him at Volvo, but Porsche was not going to put an American in that role.

Ed might have entertained trying to move cross functionally in a Product Line GM role, but the majority of the commercial team that he most respected, as potential mentors, had followed Marc Gustafson (he became President and CEO of North America in 1996) to Volvo Trucks in Raleigh, NC. Ed had offers to go to Volvo Trucks but decided to pursue other opportunities outside of the trucking industry.

Director, Operations Analysis, American Flooring Industries Pittsburg, PA - 1998 to 2000

Ed was recruited to American Flooring by the executive recruiting firm of Korn Ferry out of Chicago. Other recruiters had put him in front of Reynolds Aluminum and 3M Company at the same time. He pursued American because he believed the company gave him the best long-term opportunities to match his interests. American had just purchased Tandem Polymer (hardwood flooring company in Detroit) and DKM (linoleum and sports flooring company in France and Norway) in the summer of 1998.

The intent was for Ed to take this position in the Controller's department and establish a more rigorous and consistent operating rhythm between corporate and the various business units, assist in the financial integration of the two acquisitions, and support Investor Relations and the Controller's group in producing the MD&A for the company.

After this initial assignment, which would be a great way to learn about the company and establish relationships, it was intended for Ed to advance into M&A or Treasury. The plan excited him as M&A and Treasury were areas of interest. However, plans changed. During late 1999, asbestos claims related to a pipe insulation business the company sold in the 1960's started increasing at an alarming rate and all M&A activity was ceased. Having accomplished the three objectives of this role, Ed's manager, Neil Carter, suggested that Ed move into the Flooring Division since M&A and Treasury were not going to be options in light of impending chapter 11.

Ed had concerns about the position he was being asked to take.

1. It was not a growth position in terms of responsibilities.
2. The operational and financial teams appeared to be dysfunctional.
3. Business performance had deteriorated.
4. Business results were significantly worse than estimated.

Items two and four would not have concerned him as much if he were being placed in the CFO role and could more directly drive the changes needed. He did take the role with his rationale being that he would be in a better position to get the CFO role for the Flooring Division once he had experience in the business.

GM Finance, Residential Products American Flooring Industries Pittsburg, PA - 2000 to 2001

Ed provided financial leadership for Sales and Marketing for a $550 million flooring business. He implemented reporting for product, channel, and customer profitability to drive strategic planning and improve forecasting capabilities. Through these efforts Ed and his team increased the integrity of the financial data, integrated financial functions, and educated financial and commercial personnel on business metrics. Ed's direct impact in this role was to generate $3 million savings through tightening pricing controls and identifying $4 million distribution cost savings by providing line of sight to "real" actual costs.

GM Finance, Americas, American Flooring Industries Pittsburg, PA - 2001 to 2005

The Flooring Division was comprised of the hardwood business ($1.0 billion sales) acquired in 1998, and the original American vinyl and laminate business ($1.0 billion sales). Ed was given full financial responsibility (P&L, balance sheet, and cash flow) for both the residential ($600 million sales) and commercial ($400 million sales) businesses that made up the vinyl and laminate businesses.

Direct responsibilities now oversaw finance managers, credit and collections, personnel and plant controllers, plus dotted line responsibilities for general accounting. During these four years, Ed's team was comprised of approximately thirty people and was roughly 50% men and 50 % women. Ed was indirectly the leader of several general accounting personnel too. These individuals were critical to some of the specific accounting, closing, and reporting activities for Ed's team, but they reported directly to John Fischer, Worldwide Controller for Flooring, as their responsibilities included other businesses.

Ed and John developed a good working relationship to identify the appropriate accounting actions for the business despite the awkwardness of the matrix organization at times.

During late 2000, the President and the CFO of Flooring were both removed from their positions. Thus, Ed's intuition that the CFO position would be available relatively soon after his move to the Flooring Division was correct. He had not anticipated that the President would be replaced too. The new President had previously been the President of American's Building Products

Division and he brought his CFO (Don Lenahan) with him. Don and Ed had developed a great relationship from their experience working together when Ed held the Director of Operations analysis role. Shortly after Don joined the Flooring Division, he gave Ed full responsibility for the vinyl and laminate businesses. In addition to these responsibilities, Ed helped Don integrate the hardwood and vinyl/laminate businesses and assisted him with the European businesses ($260 million in sales).

After six months the new President left for a position with American Standard; former GE employee Chad Gerber replaced him. The "political" dynamics became quite interesting. Chad was a former financial officer and much younger than Don. Initially Don resisted Chad's style that was more aggressive, direct, quick to judge, and less personal than Don was accustomed to. However, with Ed's assistance, Don quickly became a fan of Chad's business savvy and sense of urgency.

Ed was able to quickly help Don understand Chad's perspective and implement the business metrics and operating rhythm rigor that Chad desired. Although Ed did not work for Don, he did know Chad from the days they both worked at GE Aircraft Engines. Since Ed preceded Don and Chad into the Flooring Division, he was able to objectively identify for them areas that were broken and needed to be fixed in the business.

The impact of a significant number of new hires from outside the company and the rate of turnover of these individuals increased the importance of understanding the "political" dynamics that impacted the flooring organization. The Flooring Division's efforts to assimilate many new external hires coming from very different corporate cultures was consistent with the company's direction as a whole. The cultural change was accentuated because the vinyl and laminate markets were shrinking, and tough strategic decisions needed to be made to maximize results for these product lines.

Chad Gerber and Don Lenahan, just like Ed, were able to objectively see the sense of urgency of the issues facing this business.

The market for the vinyl and laminate products declined 12% and there was significant erosion in the product mix over Ed's four years in this position. The factors driving the declines were consumer preferences shifting to wood and ceramic products, and the improved performance and appearance of the lower priced vinyl products. Other significant pressures facing the business were high raw material inflation and the unfavorable exchange rate for the euro (currency for source laminate products).

During the four years, with the help of Ed's innovation and persistence, the team:

- Realized manufacturing cost productivity increased 3% to 4% annually
- Reduced SG&A costs
- Rationalized the manufacturing footprint to reduce manufacturing costs-$50million annually
- Identified alternative suppliers for laminate
- Implemented price increases of $25 to $30 million
- Developed a plan to reduce investment to increase ROC from 12% to 20%

Some of Ed's innovation and leadership skills included developing the financial reporting rigor to identify the profitability and ROC by product, channel, and customer. He also engaged the business leaders to identify the corrective actions required to offset the volume and mix declines and higher costs of materials and labor needed to produce these results.

Chad Gerber left American in the summer of 2003 and was replaced by a long term American Flooring employee. Don Lenahan remained as CFO until early 2005 and since he had earned the support of the CEO, was able to continue to drive the actions needed with the new President of Flooring. Although Ed is proud of the results the team was able to achieve in the vinyl and laminate segment, he admits he stayed in the position probably about two years longer than he would have preferred. Why did he stay? He had the chance to control provisions and retention payments given to him which enticed him to remain in the business despite the uncertainty of the company's future as a result of chapter 11.

The company had a reorganization plan to emerge from chapter 11 within three to four years. However, as the company moved into the sixth year, Ed felt the opportunity to do something new far outweighed the continued wait for the change of control provisions to maybe materialize into something of value. Also, with the departure of Chad and Don, the cultural challenges were not worth the battle anymore to him.

The new CFO of American brought in Ben Elliott to replace Don Lenahan. Ed recommended to Ben that the finance team should be restructured so that one individual had the responsibility for all the product lines. Vinyl, laminate, and hardwood would all be integrated under one finance leader. Ed recommended that this organizational structure would better align Finance with the rest of the business team's structure and improve the efficiency of the financial support to the President and his team.

Ed's peer for hardwood (Tim West) had only been in his position for one year, so Ed recommended that Tim be retained. Brian was very supportive, and actually implemented all of Ed's organizational recommendations, even offering Ed a severance package. Ed knew that he would get a year of severance per the chapter 11 terms, and he was anxious to pursue another personal growth opportunity.

Shortly after starting his transition, Ed discovered he needed hernia surgery. As a result, he decided to take care of some personal business, have his surgery, recuperate, spend some time with his family and enjoy the holidays for the balance of 2006. He also took that time to explore some entrepreneurial opportunities presented to him. Ed passed on these opportunities because they would not have offered the scale of business or the peer stimulation that he desired. He also passed on the opportunity to be CFO of a private equity owned truck parts manufacturer after his due diligence left him with doubts about the company's potential.

GE Working Capital Solutions Manager Business Planning and Analysis, Equipment Services, Trailer Fleet Services (TFS) and Mobile Office Trailers Philadelphia, PA - 2005 to 2006

During the holidays of 2006 a friend of Ed's at GE Money in Atlanta referred him to the CFO (Mike Harris) of GE Equipment Services, Trailer Fleet Services (TFS) and Mobile Office Trailers. In early 2007 Mike set up some exploratory interviews for Ed. The business was comprised of two segments, Trailer Fleet Services ($500 million in sales) and Mobile Office Trailers ($500 million in sales). Mobile Office Trailers was in the midst of a turnaround and was openly being shopped to potential buyers. Trailer Fleet Services had been a very cyclical business and a relatively newly formed team was trying to implement a strategy to invest and grow. Although this would not have been the GE business Ed would have elected to re-enter the company, he decided to take the position for the following opportunities:

- The offer of senior level management structure and the applicable benefits that could accrue with his continuity of service could prove to be quite lucrative.
- To be able to add value quickly to both businesses and re-establish himself within the company.
- To get GE financial services experience.
- The potential to quickly land the CFO position at this location or be promoted to another business within a couple of years.
- The potential to gain divestiture experience.
- To experience GE again and assess his long term interest in the company before relocating his family.
- Leverage GE business unit CFO experience if Ed decided to leave GE.

At the time, Ed and his wife, Louise, desired to stay in Levitton, PA, through the high school graduations of their two children. Those two children are now juniors in college. With limited opportunities in Levitton, this commutable GE position in Philadelphia was a nice professional and personal balance at the time to satisfy Ed and Louise's short-term goals.

In this position, Ed implemented consistent, comprehensive, efficient business metrics, and improved coordination between business functions. He performed financial analysis in support of the $975 million sale of Mobile Office Trailers to Reese Corporation whose majority owner is Callahan Capital. Ed also led the development and implementation of a Transition Services Plan that enabled the sale of Mobile Office Trailers to occur, and generated $4 million of revenue for GE. Ed worked closely with Norma Rogers, the Controller for GE TFS/ Mobile Office Trailers, increasing the rigor of the accounting for both businesses as well as driving the financial activities and due diligence related to the sale of Mobile Office Trailers.

From a leadership perspective, Ed was able to reduce the size of his organization in this role from nine to six by elevating the performance and efficiency of his team through training and coaching individuals, and identifying innovative processes. The three reductions were accomplished through the promotion of Joan Arnold to GE Energy, the resignation of Larry Gordon to join a Dallas real estate business, and the promotion of one of his Genpact (the Joint Venture partner company in India) employees.

Joan had become frustrated during her first two to three years with the company. She was not getting the training, responsibility, and experience she had hoped for when she joined right out of college. Ed took an interest in her development and she was given broader responsibilities and more stimulating projects to enable her to gain her promotion. Larry had been an employee with the company for less than a year, but he had approximately nine years of experience in government agency positions previously. Shortly after Larry was hired, his hiring manager had resigned and the position was not filled for approximately nine months until Ed was hired.

Larry informed Ed that he had been very frustrated due to the lack of leadership that he had been given and was not sure that he would continue at GE. Ed recognized that Larry's experience was probably not best suited for his GE role, but Ed took an active role in developing Larry despite knowing he probably would leave the company relatively soon. Showing such an active interest in Larry's development later played a role in helping Ed to gain credibility quickly with other TFS members. Ed enjoyed contributing to the growth of Joan and Larry and seeing the professional excitement return to them regardless of any impact on his own career.

CFO, GE Working Capital Solutions (formerly Equipment Services), Trailer Fleet Services (TFS) and Mobile Office Trailers Philadelphia, PA - 2007 to 2008

After the sale of Mobile Office Trailers the costs for TFS needed to be reduced to offset declining volumes of the business, and due to the sale of Mobile Office Trailers, there was less revenue to leverage the cost of the support functions. There were back office synergy related gains when the Mobile Office Trailers and

TFS businesses were integrated. The sale of Mobile Office Trailers eliminated these synergies.

During spring 2007 and summer 2008, Mike Harris gave Ed the opportunity to be the Finance Manager for TFS or to pursue other opportunities in GE. He preferred to move to another business, and he identified him as available for promotion in the fourth quarter of 2007. Mike Harris, Norma Rogers, the Controller, and the Finance Manager for TFS all resigned during August 2007. Ed was named CFO and given a retention plan of $100,000 to stay until January 2009 when Mike officially resigned and moved to Cigna Corporation.

Ed had a great leadership experience in this tough CFO role. He had to gain the confidence of the remaining finance team to stabilize the organization, restructure the financial responsibilities due to the resignations, increase the level of financial analysis, and integrate the business into a new GE Division (GE Capital Solutions). These accomplishments were achieved while developing a viable long-term strategy for a business whose operating income run rate turned negative in third quarter 2007. With Ed's leadership the team developed the correct operating metrics for the business and determined that the existing business was not a viable GE model. The management team recommended that the business should either be sold or the company should exit all product lines except Operating Leases.

The Finance team totaled forty-five when Ed assumed the role and eventually declined to forty-three. His direct reports had responsibility for Accounting, Tax, Accounts Payable, Auditing, Marketing/Pricing Finance, and Financial Planning and Analysis. Half of the employees were in India and were part of the Genpact supplier. One particular leadership example that Ed was proud of was his development of Charlie Dunn. Charlie had spent most of his career in other companies in accounting roles, but in his few years at this GE business he had moved into FP&A.

Charlie's challenges were to develop his operational analysis skills, to identify business issues, and to improve his diplomacy in engaging and supporting his operating teams. The other obstacle Ed confronted was a very sensitive and personal situation that Charlie was experiencing. Ed decided that before Charlie could be written off, he had to be given a fair shake and provided the coaching and training in the skills that would be required of him to meet expectations. Ed delivered the clear expectations to Charlie, initiated his coaching and training, and then transitioned the responsibility for his continued growth to Matt Kelley once he was comfortable that Matt could handle this role.

Ed prepared the detailed financial backup for his divisional leaders at the time, David Miller, CFO GE Equipment Services, and Donna Ray, President and CEO GE Equipment Services. Donna and David, who were both GE Company Officers, attempted to negotiate the sale of the business to Ellis Leasing, owned by Berkshire Hathaway, Inc., and an ex-GE TFS employee who had private equity backing. GE did not want to absorb the loss that would have resulted from the offers received from both of these parties. As a result, the exit strategy was implemented. Under this plan, TFS was re-aligned under GE Capital Solutions, and Ed's new manager agreed to allow him to look for other opportunities.

The opportunities within GE Financial Services for someone at Ed's level, and his little GE Financial Services experience, were very limited. Other GE business units had also started reducing staff or implemented hiring freezes. Ed's new manager quickly learned that the pessimistic profit projections for 2009 were driven by the retirement and early sale of operating leases during 2008. As a result, the manager asked Ed to assist him in some strategic planning in exchange for a retention and severance package.

Ed's desire was to leverage his experience in a smaller organization anyway. He wanted an opportunity to be part of a management team with responsibility for the growth of a standalone business. He wanted to find a business that had real opportunities for growth after spending the last eight years in shrinking environments. Ed agreed to the terms of his manager as he wanted to leave the business in the best shape possible. The severance would give him some extra cushion as he pursued his next career move.

QRS Associates - 2009 to Present

Ed had brokered the deal to leave GE right before the economy tanked in 4Q. In the spring of 2009, he was contacted by QRS Associates about a CFO position with a home builder in greater Philadelphia. Although he did not pursue the position, Ed's relationship with QRS led to interim CFO and consulting assignments as a 1099 employee.

Ed's strategy was to gain experience with a private equity portfolio company and as a result either turn the interim assignment into permanent roles or build his experience until the right situation presented itself.

Since May 2009, Ed has had full-time assignments, except for August and September each year in 2010 and 2011. His strategy is working as he has had three private equity portfolio company experiences. The other two assignments with pharmaceutical companies provided him with more project management and supply chain experience. The Presidents of both private equity companies where he was the interim CFO wanted to hire him, but the particular businesses did not meet his desires. He also had a great offer to be the CFO of a $160 million textile private equity portfolio company, but he had to make the tough decision to turn down the opportunity as he could not convince his family to move to Richmond, VA. His third child, a daughter, was a sophomore in high school at the time. Commonwealth Investment Partners has inquired about his interest in some of their companies, but the geographical locations were not doable.

Interim CFO, CCK Technology, Inc.
(formerly Excelsior Technology, Inc.)
Quincy, MA - May 2009 to January 2010, January 2011 to May 2011, October 2011 to Present

In May 2009, QRS Associates engaged Ed as the CFO for Excelsior Technology, Inc., then a $30 million mechanical systems manufacturer, with 25% production at a Chinese facility. Initially, the President wanted Ed to focus on developing an automated pricing system. However, Ed suggested to the President, Ronald Helms, that there was a severe deficiency in understanding the manufactured costs, so time would be better served in first straightening out the cost accounting, systems, and financial reporting. Once the costs were really understood, then the business could invest the time in automating the pricing system.

At the time Ed began his tenure, the company was facing the challenge of restructuring the business as it was starting to feel the effects of the country's economic pain. Despite lack of clarity in the costs, Ed had to convince the President that he needed to reduce costs by 30% and not 15% - 20% as he originally thought. Although there was a pretty sophisticated ERP system in place, including a standard costing system, there wasn't the financial leadership in place to provide the proper reporting and analysis and maintenance of the system. There was also a lack of controllership for the Chinese operation. Further manufacturing costs were not accurate.

Ed worked with the Controller and the IT person to interpret the cost accounting system. Fortunately, the previous owner before the sale to Royalton Investment Partners in 2008 still had thirty days remaining of part time support to the business. Ed was able to capitalize on the owner's time available before the selling date to understand other applications of the company's IT system

The Controller and IT individuals didn't have the analytical experience needed by Ed to accelerate the work needed to be done, so Ed rolled up his sleeves and developed clarity to the flow of costs. This work included the difficult task of mapping and understanding the Chinese cost accounting practices. Difficult because the English used by the Chinese was very difficult to understand, and Ed didn't know Chinese. So late night "Go to Meeting" sessions were utilized with the Chinese HR manager acting as translator. Ultimately, Ed was able to understand what they were doing and validated that there were significant gaps in the process.

As a result of understanding the real cost accounting practices and implementing rigorous analysis of other costs, Ed was able to implement a financial reporting package. The package included:

- MD&A tied to business performance
- Develop credibility between the business and Royalton Investment Partners
- Improve credibility of business forecasts
- Educate business leaders on the economics of the business
- Educate all functions on the use of the ERP system
- Improve credibility with TD Bank

In addition, Ed was able to develop an Excel based customer and product profitability model. This model was also able to calculate the changes in contribution margin from period to period between selling price, sales mix, and cost change. Although Ed's gut feeling was that decreasing selling prices and sales mix were the biggest drivers to the declining performance of the business, the model was able to validate this position with actual price and mix declines by product and customer. Roland Helm's view, prior to the availability of this data, was that there was a variable cost problem.

A permanent CFO was hired. At the time Ed left, the EBITDA margin percentage had increased to 25%. The new CFO remained in place for ten months and resigned in September 2010. Roland Helms called Ed and asked him to come back, but Ed had just started a new project. After Ed completed his project in January 2011, he returned to Excelsior Technology.

When Ed returned to Excelsior Technology, he found the momentum that he had built had stopped. A majority of the enhancements had not been maintained, most of the ideas for future enhancement had not been acted on, the Chinese processes had not been corrected, and the previous Controller had been let go in the spring of 2011. In addition, the company had been challenged with the integration of a new acquisition in early 2011 and had just closed on a new acquisition.

Ed was able to reinstitute the financial discipline, further enhance the analytical rigor, streamline processes, and educate the new Controller (Tony Brent) and new CFO hire of April 2011 (Mick Pastek). In October, Ed went back to Excelsior Technology (now CCK Technology) to further assist Mick and fine tune his understanding of some of the systems and processes.

Financial Consultant, Barnett & Wight Ltd.
North Branford, CT - January 2010 to April 2010

Royalton Investment Partners had an investment in Barnett & Wight, and Peter Reed and Mike Fenster recommended to Zaid Aman, the majority owner of Charter Oak Equity, that Ed would be a good one to help them with Barnett & Wight. The company was a $50 million consumer packaging label manufacturer that was growing significantly. Charter Oak Equity wanted management of the company to produce greater visibility of the product profitability to help enable them to make better pricing decisions in the face of the strong demand. Management also desired to have better visibility to the in-process inventory and the rate of scrap.

Ed found that there was an MRP and not an ERP system in place. The CFO, Tim Evans, was relatively new and was still learning the system. Ed first had to understand the current system by working directly with the MRP provider Label Traxx and different functional employees of Barnett & Wight. Once Ed learned the system, his first strategy was to try and work with Label Traxx to see if the system could accommodate building up the Work in Progress (WIP) inventory and release to finished goods and cost of goods sold. He reached out to other label manufacturers that used Label Traxx, and they all shared their frustrations that although the system was very good for MRP, they didn't get the inventory/cost of goods that they needed. Ed took this input and developed a presentation for Label Traxx that it was in their best interest to enhance its system. However, they passed on the opportunity.

Having learned from his experience at Excelsior Technology, Inc., Ed chose to pursue this modeling exercise in Access instead of Excel as he learned the database manipulation was much more efficient in Access. He learned Access on his own and built a sophisticated cost accounting database for the company. The database included the WIP build up, finished goods, and cost of goods sold. As a result of the database, the company could produce customer and product profitability analysis and analyze the change in contribution margin from period to period. Included in the modeling was the live interaction from the MRP data into Access, formulas to calculate the number of labels produced, formulas to calculate the amount of natural waste produced, and with supplementary machine operator data, the number of good and bad labels produced.

Processes were documented and personnel were trained on the use of Label Traxx. System enhancements were identified, including the future purchasing of equipment to interface the counts of good and bad product from the machine counters directly into Label Traxx, and also bar code/scanners to produce more timely and accurate reporting of inventory.

After Ed completed the project, Barnett & Wight eventually hired an analyst whose responsibilities included maintaining and further developing Ed's work. Sometime after the analyst was hired, Tom Evans asked Ed to come back and spend a few days with him to share some insights.

Business Process Consultant National Drug, INC.
Smithtown, NY - May 2010 to July 2010

Ed was part of a three person team of Qualitative Research Systems (QRS) Associates, including Karen Katz, to review and recommend improvements to the Supply Chain organization and processes at National Drug, US. The work included interaction with individuals of all levels across all functions of the company, facilitating cross functional working team meetings, and reporting out to senior management team.

CFO, US Truck Body
Salem, IL – 2010 to 2011

Ed became Interim CFO of the US Truck Body, a $115 million truck body manufacturer, when the former CFO resigned after only ten months. The President's priorities for Ed were to take the lead in the implementation of a $17 million revolver with PNC Bank, manage the cash position until the revolver was in place, develop an operation plan for 2011, and implement customer and product profitability.

The cash management turned out to be quite challenging as the company made a significant pre-season buy of snowplows and the invoices came due. Ed managed through the crisis by developing detailed cash receipts and payment forecasts with the Controller and negotiating directly with suppliers until the revolver went in place in late December. The implementation of the revolver went smoothly with Ed as the point person with PNC Bank and the outside attorneys. An operating plan was developed in an accelerated timeline and presented to the board.

During his short time there, Ed was able to dive into the cost accounting system and develop in Access the database to produce customer/product profitability analysis and key manufacturing operating metrics. He was also able to improve the analytical skills of the Controller through his mentoring and coaching.

Interim CFO, CCK Technology, Inc.
(formerly Excelsior Technology, Inc.)
Quincy, MA - January 2011 to May 2011

See CBT Technology description previously 5/9 2009

Business Process Consultant, Laurel Pharmaceuticals
Hagerstown, MD - June 2011 to August 2011

Ed was asked by QRS Associates to assist in a project to develop an Order-to-Cash transition plan to move activities from a third party to Lupin Pharmaceuticals as at $400 million this US division of an Indian company had outgrown its service provider. Initially he was one of three QRS resources on the project but one resource was re-assigned after a couple of weeks. The project leader left the country with two or three weeks remaining and Ed assumed the lead in presenting the final product to the customer.

The project entailed working with all levels of the organization across all functions to identify the current processes, current work products, mapping the work flow required for the in-house activity, identifying new roles and responsibilities, and developing a timeline for transition activities. During the course of the assignment it was discovered that a Systems, Applications, Products (SAP) implementation from February 2011 was still not right. As a result, the project scope broadened to include an SAP correction plan and resulting SAP/other systems requirements for Order-to-Cash transition to ensure successful implementation to support new processes.

Interim CFO, CCK Technology, INC.
(formerly Excelsior Technology, INC.)
Quincy, MA - 2011 to Present

See CBT Technology description previously 5/9 2009

Personal Data

Ed married his wife, formerly Louise Collins, in 1986. Louise graduated from Hanover College in 1984 and she is also a graduate of GE's FMP program. Louise continued to work outside of the home until they had their first of four children in 1989. Since then, Louise has been a stay-at-home mom and an active volunteer for many school programs and activities. Their oldest son is a junior at West Point Academy and majors in Public Policy. He also plays on the basketball team. One daughter, a junior at Rutgers University, is pursuing a nursing degree. She is participating in the Navy Reserve Officers' Training Program (ROTC) for which she hopes to earn a partial scholarship. The youngest daughter is a senior in high school and has accepted a partial academic/athletic scholarship to attend Boston University where she intends to major in nursing and play field hockey. Their youngest son is an eighth grader.

Despite his busy work schedules, Ed has always been active in community activities. He has been active in coaching youth sports (soccer, basketball, and baseball) for the last seventeen years. He has also pitched batting practice to the high school team, when available, on weekends and later evenings. He has been a Parents Teachers Organization (PTO) treasurer for an elementary school and has participated in the Knights of Columbus. Ed enjoys exercising and prefers competitive activities such as tennis, pickup basketball, and golf. He also jogs.

RESUME

Edward R. Garvin, Jr.
1314 Bryan Drive
Cell: 717-544-2202
Levittown, Pennsylvania 19057
egarvin@gmail.com

Executive Profile

Senior Financial Executive, with public divisional and private equity CFO experience. Proven record of success diagnosing and solving strategic problems related to commercial, manufacturing, distribution, financial, and service operations. Skilled at working with teams to grow revenues, optimize costs, and develop talent. Consistent and measurable achievements in:

Selling Price Strategy and Execution	Return on Capital and Cash Flow
Product and Channel Profitability	Strategic Planning
Cost Productivity	Business Processes Integration & Improvement

Financial skills and managerial acumen developed through GE's Financial Management Program (FMP) and enhanced by Columbia University MBA. Leadership skills developed through diverse corporate cultures of GE, Volvo Trucks, American Flooring Industries, and multiple private equity companies. Breadth of experience includes:

Planning & Analysis	Project Management
Financial Reporting	Sales & Procurement Negotiations
Controllership	Asset & Risk Management
Treasury	International Operations

M&A	Investor Relation
Working Capital Management	Board & Banking Relationships
Operations Management	

Professional Experience

QRS Associates LLC
Philadelphia, PA - 2009 to Present
Provided interim CFO and business process improvement consulting services.

Business Process Consultant, Laurel Pharmaceuticals, Inc.
Hagerstown, MD - 2011
A $400MM US subsidiary of $1.4B Singapore Limited headquartered in Singapore, China.

- Developed Order-to-Cash transition plan to move activities from third party to Laurel Pharmaceuticals, including SAP implementation.

Interim CFO, US Truck Body, Inc.
Salem, IL - 2011
A $90MM truck body manufacturer and distributor; a portfolio company of LMF Partners.

- Led implementation of $17MM revolver with Bank of America.
- Developed cost accounting methodology and analysis to implement manufacturing cost operational metrics and identify product and customer profitability.

Business Process Consultant, National Drug, Inc.
Smithtown, NY - 2010

- Identified Supply Chain process and organizational structure improvements for US Division of Swiss owned pharmaceutical company.

Financial Consultant, Barnett & Wight Ltd
Hartford, CT - 2010

- Developed and implemented cost accounting system and customer profitability model for $50MM consumer packaging label portfolio company of Charter Oak Equity and Royalton Investment Partners.

Interim CFO, Elliott Technology
Quincy, MA - 2009 to 2010 & 2011

A $35MM mechanical systems manufacturer; a portfolio company of Royalton Investment Partners.

- Identified $400K bank covenant shortfall and $900K corrective action plan driving EBITDA percentage to sales improvement from 9.2% to 25.4%.
- Developed customer and product profitability analysis to drive US and China manufacturing strategies.

GE Working Capital Solutions, Trailer Fleet Services and Mobile Office Trailers
Philadelphia, PA - 2006 to 2008, Chief Financial Officer 2007 to 2008

- Provided strategic direction, operational analysis, and controllership for a $500MM trailer equipment leasing, rental, and services business.
- Developed and implemented restructuring plan to increase Return on Equity (ROE) from 3% to 20+%

through exit of unprofitable product lines, reduction of costs, and lower investment.

- Restructured and elevated financial analysis and business acumen of Finance and Operating teams, including twenty-two finance employees in India.

Manager, Business Planning and Analysis
2006 to 2007

- Provided strategic direction and operational analysis for a $1B equipment leasing, rental and services division.
- Led execution of transition services agreement and sell side financial due diligence for sale of Mobile Office Trailer business, a $980MM transaction.

American Flooring Industries, Inc.
Pittsburgh, PA - 1998 to 2005

General Manager Finance, Americas - 2001 to 2005

- Provided strategic direction, operational analysis, and financial leadership for a $1.0B flooring division.
- Developed plan to increase return on capital from 12% to 20%.
- Produced consistent 3% to 4% annual productivity ($15 - $20MM per year).
- Achieved 3% average annual price gains ($25 - $30MM per year).

General Manager Finance, Commercial Products
2000 to 2001

- Provided financial leadership for $600MM flooring business segment.

- Identified $4MM of distribution cost savings through improved financial analysis.
- Implemented improved pricing analysis and controls to achieve $3MM annual savings.

Director, Operations Analysis - 1998 to 2000

- Provided financial consolidation and analysis for $3.4B Corporation.
- Led Operating/Strategic planning processes.
- Integrated financial organizations and business processes for two acquisitions totaling $1.3B sales.
- Developed and implemented consistent business metrics across divisions of $3.4B Corporation.
- Provided analysis for investor relations calls and wrote MD&A for quarterly and annual publication.

Volvo Trucks, Inc.
Bethlehem, PA - 1993 to 1998

Executive Director, Commercial Operations
1995 to 1998

- Provided financial leadership for Sales, Marketing, and Parts and Service for $3B truck manufacturer.
- Established terms and negotiated sales closure for new truck deals up to $100MM.
- Increased Operating profit to $160MM gain from $150MM loss.
- Improved truck pricing discipline resulting in $25MM annual selling price gains and 3% margin increases while market share improved from 11% to 12.6%.

Assistant Commercial Controller - 1993 to 1995

General Electric - 1983 to 1993

Manager, Programs and Productivity, GE Appliances
Louisville, KY - 1992 to 1993

Manager, Dishwasher Mfg Finance, GE Appliances
Louisville, KY - 1991 to 1992

Senior Financial Analyst, Mfg. Division, GE Appliances
Louisville, KY - 1990 to 1991

Financial Analyst, Commercial Operations, GE Plastics
Pittsfield, MA - 1988 to 1990

Senior Auditor, GE Aircraft Engines
Evendale, OH - 1986 to 1988

FMP, GE Power Systems and GE Installation Services
Lynn, MA and Schenectady, NY - 1983 to 1986

Education and Training

MBA, Columbia University, New York, NY 1996
BS, Business Management and Marketing
Harvard University, Cambridge, MA 1983
Financial, Leadership, and Total Quality courses, including Six Sigma
GE, Volvo Trucks, and American Flooring

COVER LETTER

Greetings Mr. Gilreath:

I am submitting my cover letter and resume regarding your "skin in the game" CFO search S#993 for the PA sweet goods manufacturer, owned by your private equity client. After reading the job specifications and listening to you summarize what your client is seeking, my experiences as an interim CFO for three private equity companies should be an excellent fit.

Concerning the "must haves", my capabilities include the development of metrics around labor reporting and ingredients/material reporting and tracking profitability by each product line, customer, and distribution channel profitability.

I personally developed return on capital models utilizing Excel 2003 and 2007, as well as Access 2007. My analytical skills include working with Sales/Marketing teams at Volvo Trucks in driving sales increase from $1.1B to $3.0B while improving market share from 11% to 12%.

The key to running the business both operationally and strategically is to have the best "fact based data" to analyze current performance and assess potential growth opportunities. In most cases I have personally developed rigorous reporting, systems, and financial management. The benefit is being the right hand sounding board to the President in working with his team to identify the short-term and long-term initiatives to improve the business performance. I look forward to meeting you to discuss your CFO search. Best wishes.

Cordially,

Ed Garvin

VP Operations Hire

Below are the Indiana Jones Bio (IJ), resume, and cover letter exhibits of Jim Thorne, a skin in the game VP Operations hire.

N.B. All names of candidates, companies and locations have been changed for confidentiality purposes. Any similarity of fictional names used to actual names of persons, employers and locales is purely coincidental.

Confidential Indiana Jones Bio of Jim Thorne, hired as skin in the game VP Operations for an old established Pennsylvania sweet goods manufacturer.

Early Background

Like my older brother and sister, I attended public K-12 schools in Hartford, Connecticut. My father was an engineer in a machine tool company and my mother stayed at home until college expenses drew her back into the work force. Besides Little League and school sports, my main developing talent was in music. I played trumpet solos in school concerts. In high school, I played first chair in the All-State orchestra and band. I was president of the band, senior editor of the yearbook, and a member of the National Honor Society. Following graduation, I played in an orchestra with students from top music schools. By then my mind was fixed on becoming an engineer and then a plant manager.

College and Army

The only college I applied to was Georgia Tech, which was also my father's and cousin's alma mater. The work at Georgia Tech was much harder than anything I'd ever experienced. However, this academic rigor is where I learned how to really apply myself at the tasks at hand. Upon turning eighteen, I registered for the draft as the law required. A few months later, I was reclassified 1A. Having watched other students being drafted out of school, I signed a commitment to ROTC which allowed me to finish college before entering the service. In the start of my senior year, having become disillusioned with Electrical Engineering, I changed my major to Industrial Engineering, a field I didn't even know existed before college. As a result, I was required to take a second junior year.

While at Georgia Tech, I was commander of the military fraternity, a Distinguished Military Graduate, the drum major of the band, president of the band fraternity, and the recipient of the A.J. Garing award for four years of exceptional band service. At the end of my last quarter, I passed the eight-hour Engineer-In-Training exam, the first step toward becoming a professional engineer. The summer before my senior year, I was fortunate to be one of six students selected nationwide by Kimberley Clark to be a summer engineer. I spent the summer in their Irving, Texas plant which produced Cottonelle, Kleenex, Viva, and Scott branded products. After graduation the following June, I accepted their offer to become a Process Engineer. With a two-year military commitment looming, I left Kimberley Clark after six months with the understanding that the position would be available for me upon my return. I then reported for active duty.

Following the active duty officer branch training, most of my classmates received orders for Vietnam or Korea. I was assigned to be Executive Officer of a training company at Fort Jackson, South Carolina. My main responsibility was to run a 400-man company of transient enlisted men during their Military Occupational Specialty (MOS) training prior to permanent unit assignments. After a year, I was promoted to First Lieutenant and appointed Battalion S-4, where I was personally responsible for $3,000,000 worth of equipment being used by 2,400 men. By the time my two year enlistment expired, I was determined to get an MBA. Still single, my plan was to live at my parents' home in Hartford, Connecticut, and attend The University of Bridgeport on the GI Bill. After a few weeks at the university, I revised my plan, sought a full-time job, and moved my graduate school classes to nights.

Work History

Curtiss Candy

As the junior Industrial Engineer at a Curtiss Candy plant in Bronx, New York, my first assignment involved using a stop-watch and clipboard to find ways to improve the company's sanitation during the third shift. Subsequent work included setting standards, monitoring efficiency, generating cost reductions, planning new products, and other fundamental industrial engineering work. It was here that I started to learn how factories operate. After a year, I was promoted to Industrial Engineering Manager with a subordinate engineer and administrative assistant. My duties expanded to include budgeting and staff accountability for cost improvements.

Within two years, I had finished my MBA and achieved Professional Engineer registration. Further, I was promoted again. My new position was Corporate Industrial Engineer based in midtown Manhattan. I worked on multi-plant projects, managed cost improvements for the three-plant company, and led a blue-ribbon task force to launch a new product line. When the new launch was approved, I was transferred back to Port Chester and promoted to Plant Production Manager. The launch was successful. Unfortunately, the product was not successful, due to its inherent stickiness which was deemed acceptable by our president, but not by consumers. I supervised two levels of managers and supervisors in the 300-employee, non-union plant, producing hard candy, mints, and molded cough drops. After three years, our production was moved to the new plant in Michigan. Like most of the workforce, my own position was eliminated. I was offered a staff position in New York, but I wanted to run a plant, not be on staff. I found a new position at Pepsi in nearby Purchase, New York.

Pepsi-Cola

My first position at Pepsi-Cola Bottling Group was Industrial Engineering Group Manager. My main purpose was to write and implement a nationwide cost improvement program. A month later, when I presented the program to the VP Manufacturing, he asked me, "If we do this, how much will we save?" I was sort of prepared for the question. I replied, "Three million dollars." He said, "Go do it." The program started pretty well in some areas, and less well in others, but after three months, it became clear we weren't going to make $3,000,000. Clearly, I had to do something. I headed to the plants. After meeting with the managers at a plant, I spent the rest of the day with each of them individually, observing and recording all the cost improvement projects they had done.

Then I flew to another city and did it again the following day. I went to twenty-four cities in twenty-six days, and returned with a suitcase full of information. Two weeks later, I visited each plant again, this time in twenty-seven days with 110 transferable cost improvement ideas, including pictures, stories, and contact information. Enough interest and improvements were generated that we achieved savings that first year of $7,500,000. The next year, we added an additional $10,500,000 in improvements.

It was during this time that I met my wife, Sara. We learned together about the transient Pepsi culture when I was transferred to Buena Park, California to be Production Manager at one of the highest volume plants in the system. Coinciding with the 1984 Los Angeles Olympics, the demand exceeded our capacity. We ran that union plant from January to December without ever shutting down for more than an hour and a half (every day, for sanitation). By the end of the year, we had shattered previous records for production and profitability. The lesson I learned here was how to manage assets and schedules for maximum throughput over a sustained period of time. My Pepsi days ended when the new Western Division Manufacturing Manager arrived, intent on replacing the current staff with people he knew from Pepsi's Purchase, NY headquarters. I held on longer than most in a position created for me, but the future was dim. Alternatively I found a position at Anheuser Busch in St. Louis.

Anheuser Busch

Anheuser Busch owned and operated its breweries, but marketed its products through independent distributors. My role was to develop distribution strategies and facility plans for the distributors on a pay-for-service basis. In less than a year, I completed projects with seven distributors and developed a system that helped the department become more productive. Nine months after joining Anheuser Busch, I was contacted by Jim Grogan, the former Engineering Director from Curtiss Candy, whom I greatly admired. He told me he was with a new company called Lark Confections in Chicago. He said, "Come up and let's talk." When I discussed the Lark opportunity with my Anheuser Busch Director, he agreed it was a good move for me and wished me well. We parted on good terms.

Lark Confections, North America

Jim Grogan was the Senior VP of Operations at this new $600 million corporation formed through acquisition of four smaller confections companies. The challenge was to become competitive with the largest and best in the industry. Appointed Vice President, Manufacturing Services, my job was to help develop the Operations Strategic Plan. I've often thought of this experience as my "PhD in Operations". We developed, presented, and implemented a five-year, $80,000,000 project that reduced the plants from eight to five, reengineered processes, modernized plants, improved quality, reduced the workforce, and saved $21,000,000. The affected plants were closed with three years' notice to employees. One plant was a large Teamsters plant in Chicago's west side. We redirected the employee teams there from working on projects like cost reductions and quality improvements to subjects like English as a second language, and personal financial planning. We inserted an outplacement center in the plant. That plant ran well during the entire run-out period, even earning OSHA's highest award for safety improvement.

At Lark Confections, I also led the employee involvement/ continuous improvement program, product change control, maintenance management improvement, Sales and Operations planning, stock keeping units (SKU) rationalization, and others. Ultimately, the top line growth tailed off with the decline of the lucrative baseball card business. One or two at a time, all senior management was replaced. Eventually, the company was sold to Hershey.

Anecdote: two years after announcing the plant closing and one year before the end date, two nearby plants owned by different companies closed after misleading their employees regarding the security of their jobs.

Neighborhood activists, including our plant, erupted over angry protests which occurred without warning. The next day, the plant manager and I met with the protest leaders at the plant. The group included a leader from People United to Save Humanity (PUSH), the bishop of the neighborhood church association (very powerful in the area), the head of Chicago's union organization a real estate re-developer, and one young man who was connected to neighborhood street organizations. I explained why the company made its decision, that it wasn't changeable, and all the things we were doing to help the people in their coming transition. Then I suggested we work together, pooling all our contacts, to try to find a party to buy the facility and keep it alive, producing something, and continuing to employ people. They agreed, and we operated without interruption or interference until the planned closing. (Ultimately, their involvement did not help. I eventually worked through a broker and sold the facility for $2,500,000.)

Lane Goodwin

After Lark, I met the new VP Engineering of a national uniform rental company, who asked me to help him modernize their 100+ industrial laundries. I also met the head of project planning for Lane Goodwin, an engineering and architectural consulting firm. I put the two companies together and stayed on as project manager. While at Lane Goodwin, I also led or participated in projects with other diverse clients including Coca-Cola (worldwide) and a large lumber operation. During this time, I learned that consulting was not my dream. Always being the outsider did not appeal to me; I missed being a part of a team. I was also on the road 90% of the time. When the opportunity to be VP Manufacturing at Foster Foods, a Chicago-based candy company, appeared, I moved on. It offered the work I liked, higher salary, and it allowed me to be at home again. Similar to Anheuser Busch, I discussed the opportunity with my supervisor. He wished me well, and we parted friends.

Fabulous Brands

When Greg Ross, CEO at Foster Foods, hired me to run four candy plants in Chicago, he told me the company might be acquired soon by a group forming a new, large candy company. Because of my Lark experience, I was okay with that. I went to work, building teamwork and improving productivity in the Chicago plants, when, sure enough, we were acquired by Fabulous Brands along with three other companies two months later. I was moved to the new corporate headquarters to run seven plants. The challenge here was to form a functioning company from disparate parts while meeting day-to-day demand. We had non-communicating ERP systems, different business cultures, mismatched similar products, redundant capacities, and we were trying to achieve "one order, one shipment, one invoice." In a company with 4,000 SKUs, the task was not for the faint of heart. In nine months, I installed plant management teams in each plant and instituted 24/7 operations.

A great deal of my time was spent ensuring orders were shipped complete and on time. Also, through weekly plant manager meetings, individual coaching, and occasional large group meetings, we started to develop a corporate culture centered on core principles and participation. Unfortunately, the new Fabulous Brands CEO, from a totally different industry, terminated the experienced candy sales managers and general managers, including my former boss, Greg Ross. Within two years, with declining sales and growing investor discontent, managers were replaced, and the company was eventually acquired by Nabisco.

Joy Snacks

Greg Ross recommended me for the position of VP Manufacturing at Joy Snacks, a $180 million family-owned snack foods company in South Chicago. The owners were rebuilding after a successful turnaround. (Remarkably, through a strange series of events, Greg Ross soon became CEO of Joy Snacks.) The 500,000 square foot plant had between 300-750 union employees, depending on the season. Technologies included powder blending and packaging, liquid pasteurizing and packaging into flexible film, and aseptic blow/fill/seal bottling. During my eight years in the company, we added liquid pouch filling, dry mix desserts, and line extensions.

My initial scope included production, maintenance, engineering, quality, planning, procurement, and distribution. By the end of the first year, when the full extent of the work needed in the plant was evident, and when both manufacturing complexity and quality requirements were increasing, the supply chain functions were reassigned to alleviate my duties in order for me to focus in the plant. We ran incompatible products alternately on the same equipment; allergen and non-allergen, Kosher and non-Kosher, sugar and sugar-free. Then we became a registered drug manufacturer requiring higher level regulatory oversight. This company was on the FDA's highest watch list for years with never a failed audit or recall.

It was at this company that I was able to complete a comprehensive program to achieve and maintain a highly productive plant after starting from a weak position. I selectively replaced weak managers, supervisors, and leads. We carefully chose their replacements, some from the outside, and some promoted from within the company. We selected operators and mechanics, and implemented comprehensive training programs. We revised incentive systems. We implemented and relentlessly performed preventive maintenance. We revised incoming, in-process, and finished product quality checks and migrated from QC to QA. We raised and maintained the level of housekeeping and facility appearance. We applied 5S in batching, greatly improving the reliability of that critical area. One of the results was a 30% productivity increase in the largest department, enough that when we acquired a competitor, we could take in its production and close the unneeded satellite plant.

When we acquired the dessert mix business, we reengineered/ simplified the process and brought it into our plant, once again closing the acquired operation. As a result of all the improvements, safety, quality, cost, and workforce morale all improved. After eight years, we had achieved substantial improvements and had a strong, well trained management team in place. When sales growth slowed, with no acquisitions imminent, the owners decided to run day-to-day operations themselves. My position and Greg's (CEO) were eliminated.

Interim Resources LLC

A former Sales VP from Fabulous Brands, impressed with the progress we made there, recommended me to Interim Resources, a boutique senior executive interim management/consulting firm, for a project they were starting. For nine months, I was part of a small team at a $260,000,000 snack food operation in North Carolina. The owner wanted to exit the business, but had run into a potentially fatal quality issue. Our first task was to recover from a failed Walmart quality audit. We had less than thirty days to correct seven critical failures and prepare the plant (400,000 square feet, 300 non-union employees) to pass the re-audit or face losing 35% of its business. The facility and organization were poor.

My partner and I led the recovery personally on the floor and through the plant staff. We cleaned and upgraded the facility, reassigned management, established SOPs, trained the employees, and passed the re-audit. Within the next three months, we were audited twice again by Walmart, and also by the FDA, State, and County. We continued to improve yields and costs. Then, with a very short lead time, we successfully developed and launched a new product for a multi-national retailer requiring installation of new lines. Within a year, the business was sold for a multiple higher than targeted.

Anecdote: after our third re-audit, we had earned Walmart's trust. One morning I received a call from Walmart's head of private label quality. She was in our part of the state with two regional managers and would stop by in a couple of hours to show them "what a good plant should look like." With no additional preparation, we hosted their plant tour and received compliments.

Anecdote: during our work, it became clear the production manager had to be removed. He was a hard-working, intelligent, nice man, but he was not effective in his role. After discharging him, I was able to help him in modest but tangible ways in his job search. Four years later, we still remain in contact, and he continues to look for ways to return the favor.

While performing this interim assignment, I was contacted by a recruiter searching for a VP Manufacturing for the nation's largest private label juice supplier. The interim work was substantially complete. I helped source and train my replacement. George Livos, the Interim Resources executive leading our team, understood and supported my move, and to this day we remain friends.

Super Juices, Inc.

As VP Manufacturing and Engineering at this $670,000,000 private company and leading supplier of premium private label beverages in North America and around the world, we provided complete product development from concept to store aisle in state-of-the-art manufacturing facilities. My first task was to improve plant productivity. Recent sales success had driven all five plants to add staffing to run 24/7 to try to keep up. Unfortunately, capacity limitations and variations in demand in the thousands of SKUs produced forced the plants into more frequent changeovers and shorter runs. Since many employees were new, the experienced operators were required to work considerable overtime. Morale in this non-union workforce was already low due to the company's historical top-down culture. To try to maintain service rates, products were increasingly produced in remote plants and then shipped long distances to the underserved markets. The whole picture was a perfect storm of rising costs, declining service rates, and poor morale.

Recovery came from focusing on productivity. Personally leading teams of operators, supervisors, and support staff, uptime and yields in the highest priority areas were addressed. As the teams gained skills, I withdrew, leaving plant staffs to lead their own recovery. Getting and using timely, relevant data, the effort naturally led to three fundamental activities: assigning employees to positions that best aligned their skills with each position's requirements; training operators, line teams, and supervision; and improving and sustaining preventive maintenance. Quality, safety, housekeeping, and sanitation were inevitably drawn in and addressed. In addition to the work of the teams, some managers, supervisors, and leads were changed functionally. As productivity improved, the scope widened to include scheduling, materials management, and upstream operations.

Within a year, four of the plants were operating on five-day schedules, generating an annual labor saving of $6,000,000. The one remaining seven-day plant was the most productive of all, and remained on 24/7 due to its market's high demand – a very good situation for the company. Since each plant was now supplying its own market, annual inter-plant freight costs were reduced by another $6,000,000. New savings continued to be realized as additional issues were addressed and upstream improvements were accomplished. Improved productivity also increased capacity, enabling additional business and new products, so the top line grew while inventories were reduced. Naturally, since savings fell directly to EBITDA, their effect multiplied when determining the ultimate value of the company.

After eighteen months, the plants were running well but Quality needed help. We were trying to become SQF certified, and the project was over budget and over schedule. (SQF is an internationally recognized food safety and quality system.) Responsibility for the plants was transferred, and I was assigned to Quality, plus three other tasks:

1. Continue management of Engineering
2. Develop and implement a company-wide employee involvement/continuous improvement program aimed at strengthening the culture
3. Set up a joint venture in China

I reorganized the Quality department leadership and implemented a Quality Strategic Plan, focusing on the important long-term and short-term priorities. I set up Super Juices Way, our own internally-developed program combining elements of Total Quality Management (TQM), kaizen, workout, lean, Six Sigma, and others. Finally, I coordinated development of a joint venture with the largest beverage supplier in China. Within eighteen months, all plants were SQF certified to Level III (the highest level). Super Juices Way was active in all locations with a steering team headed by the CEO, dozens of employee teams, and over forty trained employee facilitators. A joint venture company was set up in Hong Kong with its first subsidiary up and running in Shanghai. In 2010, Super Juices was acquired by Premium

Beverages, Inc. My position was one of many eliminated in the transition.

Personal and Family

Sara and I now live in Syracuse, New York. A University of Miami graduate, she has been a stay-at-home mom as well as a full-time employee in accounting, retail, education, and insurance. We lived in a far northwest suburb of Chicago for twenty-three years where we raised our two sons. Today, our oldest son is a Graphic Design student at Syracuse University and lives with us. Our second son is studying Architectural Science at Columbia University.

My outside activities have always been subject to business and travel constraints. I was active in the boys' organizations when they were growing up. For several years, I was a Village Trustee and headed Planning and Zoning. A few years ago I learned to fly, but gave it up since it took too much time. Recently, gym membership has been my most frequent activity.

RESUME

JAMES THORNE
18 Meridien Lane, Syracuse, New York 13207
Cell (748) 495-2204
Home (716) 442-3338
jimthorner.1@aol.com

Manufacturing & Operations Executive

Core Strengths

- Operations improvement - cost, quality, and service
- Employee involvement / continuous improvement
- New product development
- Acquisition integration
- Food, beverage, and related

Experience

Vice President: Manufacturing, Quality, Engineering, Change Management Plant Manager, Production Manager, Senior Consultant, Industrial Engineering Group Manager

Branded and private label, public and private, union and non-union

Methods

Principle-centered leadership, Six Sigma, Lean Manufacturing, TQM, TPM

Professional Experience

Super Juices, Inc., Syracuse, New York - 2007 to 2010
VP Quality, Engineering, Change Management
2008 to 2010

VP Manufacturing and Engineering - 2007 to 2008

- Recruited to improve manufacturing in $670 million private label juice and beverage company.
- Subsequently reassigned to improve quality and implement other initiatives. Super Juices was acquired by Premium Beverages, Inc. in 2010.
- Improved productivity 30% across five plants in eighteen months. Maintained output while reducing from 24/7 to 24/5 through reorganization, training, maintenance, and leadership. Saved $12 million.
- Reorganized quality department, achieved SQF 2000 Level III certification in all plants, developed and led quality strategic plan. SQF is a globally recognized food safety and quality program.
- Created and implemented employee involvement/continuous improvement program. Established structure, trained forty-one leaders and facilitators, and led corporate steering team. Saved $1 million.
- Set up a joint venture company in China to provide private brands beverages to major international retailers

Interim Resources LLC, Chicago, Illinois
2006 to 2007
Interim Manufacturing Executive Hire

- Commissioned by leading senior interim executive firm to rapidly improve failing operations at a $260 million private snack food company. Resulting turnaround positioned the firm for sale above targeted multiple.
- Recovered from failed quality audit, preventing imminent loss of company's largest customer.
- Designed, installed, and operated new manufacturing lines for major international customer.

- Reduced costs $1 million in nine months through improved maintenance and production management.

Joy Food & Beverage Company, Chicago, Illinois
1998 to 2006
VP Manufacturing

- Managed manufacturing, quality, maintenance, engineering, planning, and distribution for $200 million food, beverage and pharmaceutical company. Technologies included powdered desserts and beverages, pasteurized liquid form/fill/seal packaging, aseptic blow/fill/seal bottling, and liquid pouch filling.
- Improved productivity 30% on main lines through reorganization, training, and maintenance, creating enough new capacity to close an acquired plant. Saved $1 million per year.
- Led Lean Manufacturing, Six Sigma, and 5S programs which reduced changeover time 75%, yield losses by $650,000, and strengthened the most critical manufacturing operation.
- Developed three new manufacturing lines for new products, including pharmaceuticals.
- Integrated manufacturing of $20MM, 150-SKU dessert mix acquisition into existing operations including process improvements and $4MM capital.

Fabulous Brands, Chicago, Illinois - 1996 to 1998
VP Manufacturing

- Recruited to direct four plants as VP Manufacturing at Foster Foods. Two months later, upon acquisition by Fabulous Brands, moved to corporate staff to integrate and direct seven plants.

- Reorganized seven plants, selected plant managers and staffs, integrated supply chain and instituted 24/7 operation for new $600MM confectionery company in nine months.
- Improved productivity of major product line 67%, saving $1.3 million annually.

Lane Goodwin Engineers, Atlanta, Georgia
1995 to 1996
Senior Operations Consultant

- Brought together a 135-site industrial laundry company and a 4,000-employee architectural and engineering firm and then led the resulting reengineering project.
- Performed site visits, conducted design seminars, and applied Lean techniques.
- One of a three-man team that achieved strategic alliance status with $18 billion soft drink manufacturer.
- Led consulting team at world's largest hardwood processing operation.

Lark Confections, North America, Springfield, Illinois
1987 to 1995
Vice President, Manufacturing Services

- Number two operations position in newly-formed $600 million confections company. Recruited by a former supervisor/mentor to help develop and implement operations strategic plan.
- One of three on executive team that developed $80MM, five year plan to integrate, modernize, and consolidate plants from eight to five. Led implementation teams, negotiated with civic and government groups, and managed sale of idled assets.

- Reduced costs $21MM, increased productivity 40%, and improved quality.
- Led employee-involvement/continuous improvement process. Savings averaged $4MM each year. Scope extended to procurement, plant maintenance, and SKU rationalization.
- Created and led system to manage new product implementation and product changes in 4,000-SKU firm.

Anheuser Busch, St. Louis, Missouri - 1986 to 1987
Senior Consulting Engineer

- Designed distribution systems and facilities for independent distributors.

Pepsi-Cola Bottling Group, NY and Los Angeles, CA 1981 to 1986
Plant Production Manager - 1984 to 1986
Industrial Engineering Group Manager - 1981 to 1984

- Developed and managed 24-plant, nationwide cost improvement program, saving $7.6MM in first year, and an additional $10.4MM in second year.
- Managed 24/7 production in $4 million case plant for eleven months leading to record profit.

Curtiss Candy/ J & J, Bronx, NY and Skillman, NJ 1973 to 1981
Plant Production Manager - 1977 to 1981
Industrial Engineering Manager - 1973 to 1977
US Army, Fort Jackson, SC - 1971 to 1973
Battalion Staff Officer - 1972 to 1973
Company Executive Officer - 1971 to 1972

Education

Georgia Institute of Technology, Atlanta, Georgia, Bachelor of Industrial Engineering – 1970

University of Bridgeport, Bridgeport, Connecticut, Master of Business Administration - 1975

Professional Engineer, Connecticut - 1975

COVER LETTER

Dear Mr. Gilreath:

Enclosed is my resume for your "skin in the game" VP Operations Search #991 for an Old Established Pennsylvania Sweet Goods Manufacturer posted on Gilreath Consultancy's website.

After reviewing your detailed VP Operations job description, I believe I could "land on my feet running" in that position. I have a BS in Industrial Engineering and an MBA.

I am experienced in processing food items and have a good understanding of ingredients in supply chain as it relates to bakeries in general.

I have over twenty years in progressively more responsible manufacturing, supervisory, and managerial positions with experience in strategic planning and budgeting in companies with $60M-$100M+ in sales.

I am experienced in supply chain management, operational principles, and FDA regulatory compliance.

I am hands-on having been responsible for assuring gross profit margins are maintained in accordance with approved guidelines. I have reduced ingredient costs regarding waste and scrap by 25% and monitored for over scaling and adjusted accordingly.

I constantly track specific operational metrics (KPIs) used to report the performance of the business to the CEO and keep tabs on specific progress against company and key individuals' performances.

I am experienced at overseeing multiple locations and successfully integrating acquired businesses and realization of operating synergies and benefits. I take pride in the fact that I have recruited and retained highly qualified subordinates whom I monitor but let do their jobs. The VP Operations compensation range is acceptable and the Equity Purchase Plan is the opportunity I have been seeking.

I look forward to speaking with you about this position. Thank you for your time and interest.

Cordially,

Jim Thorne

VP Sales and Marketing Hire

Below are the Indiana Jones Bio (IJ), resume and cover letter exhibits of Mike Hartman, a skin in the game VP Sales and Marketing hire.

N.B. All names of candidates, companies and locations have been changed for confidentiality purposes. Any similarity of fictional names used to actual names of persons, employers and locales is purely coincidental.

Confidential Indiana Jones Bio of Mike Hartman, hired as skin in the game VP Sales and Marketing for Texas specialty furniture designer, manufacturer, and distributor.

Early Background

Mike is a Central Texas native born and raised in the small community of Lubbock, Texas. He comes from a long line of German immigrants whose hard work, honesty and dedication were their hallmarks. His father worked as a Controller at Johnson Mining in Freemont, Texas and provided the family with a comfortable upbringing. One of the most defining moments of Mike's young life was when his father sat him down just before his sixteenth birthday and explained that if he wanted to have clothes, a car, a college education, or anything else, Mike would need to work in order to pay for it himself. He arranged an interview with the local Alway grocery store and the rest was up to him. Mike did well on the interview and worked for Alway stores for almost ten years while supporting himself through high school and college.

Mike is proud of the fact that he was able to pay for all of his expenses along the way, but especially for his college education.

It was trying at times, but he found the experience to be self-liberating and also a tremendous source of independence. He also supported himself during this period as a professional musician, playing a steel guitar in a country band. His regular week consisted of working up to forty hours at Alway, playing music Friday and Saturday nights, along with attending college full-time at The University of Houston. This schedule left little time for anything else. Mike successfully managed each of these diverse requirements of his time and graduated with a true understanding of the challenges that face individuals both now and in their later years.

Mike's Professional Career

Sysco Corporation

Shortly after his graduation from The University of Houston, Mike's first professional job opportunity came with Sysco Corporation, Houston, TX, one of its 283 food service distribution locations. Sysco Corporation is well known as an industry leader in the supply and distribution of grocery, tobacco, health and beauty aids, and non-food products to the Convenience Store Industry, Supermarket Chain Stores, and Member Club Stores.

Mike was honored to be selected into the prestigious Careers in Professional Leadership (CPL) Program at the start of his career with Sysco Corporation. This highly competitive and challenging training program was envisioned by the company's board of directors as a way to groom future company presidents and executives. The program included an intensive regiment of positions in Purchasing, Accounting, Marketing, Distribution, and Transportation. CPL candidates were required to participate in Masters level continuing education courses from Cornell University while maintaining a grueling work schedule. Those in the program maintained positions of the highest caliber in each work area with all of the responsibilities and challenges that went with each assignment.

Mike had the opportunity to work on the start-up of a new Sysco Distribution Center in Kissimmee, Florida and was the buyer in charge of the Grocery category, the largest in Sysco Corporation. He maintained the highest divisional service level of 99.5% to customers and an overstock of less than 4% overall. This achievement was the highest rating of any grocery buyer at Sysco Corporation. Mike was the youngest at the time. He then went on to manage the Southwest Distribution Center in Austin, Texas and held positions in Transportation, Distribution Center Management, and managed the largest cigarette tax stamping operation in the nation. He was responsible for over $56 million dollars in cigarette inventory and oversaw the stocking, selection, stamping, and auditing of this large and important profit segment for Sysco Corporation. Mike's tenure at Sysco Corporation gave him the opportunity to direct and manage any key areas of a state-of-the-art grocery distribution center to include inbound receiving, stocking, inventory control, selection, and shipping of outbound freight to customers. Some of the highlights of his career at Sysco Corporation are as follows:

- Directly supervised and managed 100+ employees in a 500,000 square feet wholesale grocery distribution center.

- Planned and supervised the expansion of the grocery distribution center from 350,000 square feet to 500,000 square feet.
- Developed and implemented time studies to evaluate employee's productivity levels and accuracy to increase grocery selection and fill rates in the distribution center
- Managed and dispatched 105 commercial drivers in a fifteen state territory.
- Designed new routes for outgoing loads resulting in increased on-time delivery to customers, improved delivery accuracy, and higher efficiency in utilization of equipment.

Reason for leaving

Opportunity to gain increased responsibility from 1,800 SKUs to 57,000+ SKUs.

SW Hardware Distributors, Inc.

His next career opportunity was with SW Hardware Distributors, Inc. in Odessa, Texas. S.W., as it was known, was one of the nation's leading independent hardware wholesale distribution networks with facilities located throughout the United States. S.W. serviced independent hardware retailers in North America with a full-line of hardware products. The Odessa, Texas facility shipped and distributed hardware products to twenty-six states.

As a Distribution Center Supervisor, Mike was responsible for managing ninety+ employees in a 300,000 square feet wholesale hardware distribution center. He reported to the General Manager of the Odessa, Texas Distribution Center. His position required that he manage all inbound, receiving, stocking and selection of over 57,000 SKUs. Mike supervised distribution and shipping of these products to 2,500 customers throughout the continental United States.

During his tenure, Mike pioneered forecasting, production, sales, and inventory control reports to maintain optimum scheduling of personnel and products throughout the distribution center. These reports led to successfully planning and implementing a relocation program of all distribution center merchandise by sales per item. This ambitious program resulted in increased productivity of selection, receiving, and stocking personnel.

Reason for leaving

Opportunity to become a VP Purchasing and different product lines.

Two years later, in 1992, Mike was approached while he was employed at S.W. by the former mayor of Round Rock, Texas, and former President of a Sysco Corporation Division. He was invited to come on board as Vice President of Purchasing for the Plumbing Products Division of Round Rock Supply Corporation, a privately held corporation that specialized in supplying the Central Texas market with a full array of wholesale plumbing products to the plumbing trade and local consumers.

Mike's responsibilities included managing and directing the procurement and inventory control of the Plumbing Products division, the procurement of 4,000+ separate SKUs of commercial and residential plumbing products, negotiating with vendors, accounts receivable, and accounts payable. He also consulted for Unimex™ Corporation, a multi-national acquisitions firm and subsidiary of Round Rock Supply Corporation on capital investment and acquisition opportunities in the Mexico and South America market.

Reason for leaving

Opportunity to become Marketing Operations Manager for a new dynamic product line in a new industry for him.

FurnitureArt® Corp/Design Surface Division

Mike's greatest career challenge was about to be realized in his appointment as Marketing Operations Manager for the FurnitureArt® Design Surface Division, San Antonio, TX. He met his future manager, Mark Walters, at a Promise Keepers rally in Denton, Texas. Mike and Mark hit it off right away and he began telling Mike about his challenges as the newly appointed Director of Sales and Marketing for FurnitureArt® Design Surface Division. He was having issues with finding the right person to manage the operating segments for the category: marketing, product development, fabricating, and especially financial management. Mike gave him advice on how he should approach the challenges he faced. Before Mike knew it, they were working at his home on proposals to upper management of FurnitureArt® that same evening, and soon thereafter, Mike was on board and managing the very things in which Mark was so concerned.

His time at FurnitureArt® was the most challenging of his professional career. He was catapulted into the forefront as Marketing Operations Manager and Area Sales Manager of a solid surface company with a completely new line of solid surface products and no firm road map on how to get the products to market.

FurnitureArt® had produced a polyester blend in a solid surface product for several years but was unable to gain traction in the marketplace. Dupont Corian™ was the market leader, mainly for the creation of the solid surface category and for being formulated of acrylic instead of polyester resin.

This blend was a definite advantage in the solid surface industry and Corian had capitalized on their leadership and exclusivity position very handsomely. FurnitureArt® was well known in the Architecture and Design community as the industry leader in High Pressure Decorative Laminate. It was also a company that had a very loyal and large Independent Distributor base and enjoyed market domination in that category.

FurnitureArt® wanted to achieve the same level of success with its solid surface line and knew it was time for a major overhaul. The challenge was to take a tired line of outdated patterns and create a totally new solid surface line for FurnitureArt®. There were countless logistical issues to completing this endeavor, however, the company was dedicated to take the challenge head on.

Mike started by taking the existing thirty-two patterns of polyester blend and eliminating all but the top twelve selling patterns. FurnitureArt® then re-introduced these twelve patterns in an acrylic formulation to the marketplace. These patterns took not only the many challenges of relocating all existing sheet goods to Temple, Texas, controlling the decreasing production of the current polyester, and phasing out patterns, but then developing and producing an entire line of acrylic versions of these patterns. It was such a daunting task to phase out and re-introduce this large amount of patterns.

FurnitureArt® partnered with Artistic Acrylics of Louisville, Kentucky. Artistic had a state-of-the-art manufacturing facility of acrylic sheet products for the bath industry. They had created a line of acrylic sheet goods for the solid surface industry but had no effective method to distribute the product to the marketplace. The time was right for FurnitureArt® and Artistic to start a joint venture, and Mike was on the team to complete the task. Months of hard work, negotiations, and preparation led to the successful re-introduction of FurnitureArt® Design Surface from an outdated polyester line to a new and exciting line of acrylic sheet goods. Sales grew almost overnight and FurnitureArt® went from a small player in the industry to a strong number two to Dupont Corian™. This progress was a phenomenal achievement that put FurnitureArt® on the map to success as a leader in the decorative surfacing industry.

Mike maintained and controlled corporate and divisional expenses for the product category and established the pricing and profit margins for the full line of solid surface products to include sheet goods, sinks and seam kits. He created category forecasting models and operating plans for the product line that allowed the company to better track the expenses and sales progress with the category. Mike's days were filled with presentations and recommendations to senior management on proposed sales, marketing, production, and distribution initiatives.

He became known as the "numbers" guy for FurnitureArt® Design Surface by upper management, and gained a reputation for being a successful manager with a high level of integrity and accuracy for the items that he managed. Each day brought new and more exciting challenges. Mike was privileged to increase his level of responsibility during his tenure as Marketing Operations Manager in such areas as:

- Directly managing sales and marketing campaigns with both local and national advertising agencies
- Participating in the development of new marketing campaigns and design look for FurnitureArt® Fiji® Solid Surface and the introduction of FurnitureArt® Starstone® Solid Surface
- Development of national media advertisement programs for industry publications, consumer publications, television advertisement, radio advertisement, and current FurnitureArt® Design Surface website
- Successfully planning and implementing direct sales and distribution of FurnitureArt® Design Surface Sheet goods, bowls and seam kits to Design Surface Metro Centers and Independent Distributors located throughout the United States
- Developing return on investment models and legal contracts utilized in the review of solid surface and engineered stone manufacturing facilities located in the Northeast and South Eastern United States, China, and Korea

This higher level of responsibility also gave Mike the opportunity to travel on behalf of FurnitureArt® Design Surface to Foranzo, Italy to tour and evaluate the Bresa Stone Manufacturing facility. Bresa is known as a top producer of engineered stone product and offers a full line of machinery to manufacture and fabricate engineered stone.

He traveled to two of Italy's largest stone fabrication facilities; Marone Arrico and Master Granatello. Each of these facilities utilized the Bresa process and were large scale, highly advanced stone fabrication facilities. Next, he met with the Victor Torelli Corporation. Victor Torelli was known as a top manufacturer of stone fabrication router bits for stone fabrication equipment. He then traveled to Stephano Margarta Stone which is one of the world's largest engineered stone manufacturing facilities. His last stop was to the Trazzi facility in the Czech Republic to determine the overall feasibility of engineered stone and to determine if it was a viable product category for the United States market.

This trip and the information he gathered led him to performing an in-depth review of engineered stone products, especially the Silverstone™ product line. Mike evaluated their company assets, marketing plan, fabrication models, and go-to-market strategy. Later, he developed an analysis regarding a potential purchase of the Cambetta™ engineered stone facility by FurnitureArt® Design Surface. He met with FurnitureArt® executive management along with the former owners of the Cambetta™ facility, a group of venture capitalists who had found the facility to be above the cost/return threshold they considered appropriate. Mike developed return on investment models and market analysis of the potential product line. At the time, the Cambetta™ facility was not a viable manufacturing facility, and it would have taken what was considered to be too excessive of an investment to get the facility in full operation.

Mike also played a large part in the development of a successful supplier/purchaser agreement between FurnitureArt® and Hautou International of Korea, a large international manufacturer of acrylic solid surface products. FurnitureArt® is currently expanding their line of solid surface patterns utilizing the Hautou product line that Mike helped in making available to the domestic marketplace.

An area that needed major assistance during this time period was the FurnitureArt® Design Surface Warranty Department. Mike was sought out by upper management to take charge of the department and correct the issues that it faced. Some of the areas where he improved the operation included:

- Established audit points of consumer warranties to standardize the process
- Created a client follow-up program that measured the consumer's satisfaction level of the repair or replacement process. Utilized information to manage third party fabricators and their crews in the field
- Reduced the existing backlog of active claims in the system by 92%
- Improved the backlog of outstanding payments to third party fabricators on approved warranty repairs or replacements by 50%
- Monitored the database system to create weekly and monthly reports for accrual purposes for future warranty expenditures

FurnitureArt® Solid Surface is known for providing the customer a full-line of products and services designed to make the distributor, fabricator and end consumer satisfied with their purchase. The product line that FurnitureArt® promotes today was a direct result of many initiatives Mike helped pioneer. The product line also enjoyed successful and profitable growth during his tenure as Marketing Operations Manager to include:

- 216.75% growth in cumulative Net Dollar Sales

- 462.59% growth in cumulative Net Operating Income
- 55.33% growth in cumulative Net Profits
- Maintaining divisional expenses at 8.5% under approved operating plans

Mike was awarded the President's Award on two separate occasions during his career with FurnitureArt® Design Surface. This prestigious award is given by nomination only and is approved by the President of FurnitureArt® for outstanding performance, dedication, and service well beyond expectations.

The overall effects of MMI Corporation's purchase of FurnitureArt®, and the eventual decline of support to the solid surface product line led him to be open to other opportunities that existed in the marketplace. Being a native of Central Texas and having an extensive network of personal and professional associations, it wasn't long before Mike was approached to work in an industry that was totally different from what he had experienced in the past, but is quite successful nonetheless.

Reason for Leaving

FurnitureArt® acquired by MMI Corp. and there were drastic changes in acquired product lines and company culture.

The Personal Wealth Advisers, Certified Financial Planners®

The Personal Wealth Advisers have earned the reputation of being the premier independent investment advisor in the Texas Gulf Market. This firm has achieved a level of success not seen in the independent investment advisory market with assets under management approaching $100 million and clients located worldwide. Joe Johnson approached Mike to be his Manager of Operations. He envisioned having a strong individual to come on board to be responsible for the oversight and direction of the firm's Financial Advisors, Office and Customer Service Staff, and client accounts.

This led to the supervision of the execution of transactions and fund transfers on behalf of the Personal Wealth Advisers' clients, reviewing all internal and external documentation and maintaining communications in accordance with industry compliance standards. This position has allowed Mike the opportunity to learn an entirely new area of financial management and has broadened his operations background. He considers his time in this profession to be a positive learning experience and Mike is ready for a larger challenge where he can use his many years of management experience in the surfacing industry.

Personal Information

Mike and his wife, Donna, have been happily married for over eighteen years. They have been blessed with two children. His hobbies include playing the electric, acoustic, and steel guitar, hunting, reading, and spending time with his family. Donna and Mike teach Sunday school for the Youth Department in their church where he also plays guitar in the praise team. He serves on the Finance Committee, he is a member of the Board of Trustees, and he serves on various other committees.

COVER LETTER

Dear Mr. Gilreath:

This cover letter and resume are in response to your firm's search for a VP Sales and Marketing for a Central TX Solid Work Surface Materials Producer. I have proven experience in engineered surface materials as a versatile Sales and Marketing Director with a record of success in sales productivity and product management. I have also successfully marketed stone materials to hospitality, industrial, retail, commercial, and residential clientele. In fact, I spearheaded the growth of product sales from zero to $16M in one year with gross profits that exceeded plans by 20%.

I increased a troubled product line by 10,000 SKUs that created $15 million in new sales and grew profits by 40% while attracting 200 new customers in twenty additional states.

I improved profitability 30% over two years by focusing sales efforts on higher margin products, strengthening pricing discipline, and shifting toward branded product lines versus private label. My references will verify my team building skills and abilities in strategic planning, sales forecasting, and market analysis that has given my former employer a competitive edge in the surfacing industry.

Lastly I am seeking a Sales and Marketing management opportunity with the potential to put some of my skin in the game. I will appreciate the chance to visit you in person to discuss my background and experience in more detail. Best wishes.

Cordially,
Mike Hartman

Here are the SITG gross earnings of each of the above mentioned four C-Level executive hires:

The above four C-Level skin in the game candidates in this chapter were my hired search candidates who each invested some of their own funds in the equity of their employers. The CEO invested $100K and his equity earned over $1 million dollars gross at the exit five years later, less taxes. Part of his earnings came from qualifying for his annual merit stock options which the CEO earned each year he led the company until its sale (or liquidity event).

The CFO invested $60K skin in the game and his equity earned $750K gross at the company's exit five years later. Part of his earnings came from his portfolio company's annual stock option plan distributions. That plan was automatically paid if the CFO was still employed at the plan's distribution date.

The VP Sales and Marketing invested $50K skin in the game and his equity earned a total of $670K gross at the company's exit 4.3 years later. Part of his earnings included his annual merit stock option plan. The stock options were earned each year except the third year when the VP Sales and Marketing didn't qualify for them based on not reaching his yearly objectives.

The VP of Operations invested $75K skin in the game and his equity earned $490K gross at the company's exit five years later. Part of his earnings came from his portfolio company's annual stock option plan. That plan automatically awarded additional equity options if the VP Operations was still employed at the plan's distribution date.

Chapter 7

Organizing Your References Before Launching a *Skin in the Game* C-Level Job Search

After forty years of headhunting, I consider reference checking to be the key ingredient in 90% of my successful total C-Level hires. This was true in my Fortune 500 retained generalist searches ending in 1986, and in my skin in the game retained searches for PEGs for the past twenty eight years. I have taken courses on power interviewing of C-Level candidates. I once helped two different GM candidates be hired based on my overall "gut" judgment in the early eighties. Both were fired within a couple of months after they were hired. I finally realized I can't judge C-Level candidates by my gut feelings. I hadn't been aggressively checking enough key references of my C-Level candidates with whom I had good chemistry and rapport.

In the "old days" I was trained to contact a few references on each qualified and interested finalist job candidate. If their references were acceptable, I would schedule to meet each of my final two or three C-Level candidates for dinner and a cocktail, beer, or wine. During dinner I would conduct a quasi-interview. The next day, if I still felt strongly about each candidate, I would review my notes and write a twelve page report for my client as to why I thought Joe Candidate was a good fit for their job search.

I noticed my clients would tend to firmly reject at least one of my referred finalist candidates, sometimes two out of three. Other times, job offers for a couple of different searches were extended to my finalist candidates. Being hired was subject to additional key reference checks by the client with unsatisfactory results. They weren't terrible, just not strong enough to warrant hiring these candidates. About that time, I remember seeing a magazine ad by a large investment fund. The more informed our clients are about their investment funds, the better investment decisions they make.

Since 1990, I require my qualified and interested SITG job search candidates to okay my checking at least a dozen of their key references. That's before they meet my PEG clients. My written reference checks then become part of my candidate binders mailed to my clients. I am known for doing that, but it has produced better candidate-client interviews and a quicker hiring process. Since 1990, I discontinued candidate dinners and those personal reports. Now I only meet C-Level search candidates for breakfast interviews.

I have had my C-Level candidates undergo various client psych testing procedures, including one psychologist doing eight hours of testing and interviews in one day. A few of my SITG C-Suite Executive candidates weren't given a snack, or coffee or lunch. Just water. This is part of the stress situation applied by the client's psychologist. I asked that psychologist, "What went wrong with the candidates they recommended to clients after testing? Those eventually fired three to six months after being hired?" He called it a scientific anomaly and kept on psych testing for their clients.

Candidate reference checking has always worked well for me, my clients, and my hired candidates. I highly recommend SITG C-Level job seekers pay attention to the care and treatment of their reference.

I would bet you a few five pound Maine lobsters that many qualified and interested CEO, CFO, and VP skin in the game job candidates end up being turned down due to their known and unknown reference problems. It doesn't mean the candidate's references were bad. Those contacted just couldn't give the candidate's C-Level job candidacy a strong endorsement. The PEG hiring authority might have decided to call a few contacts known to the firm, who had some connection to the candidate's former employer. The candidate was never told. It means those references called were not the candidate's "key" references such as the candidate's former bosses, company owners, or direct reports. They might have been a former company board member or investor known to the PEG who didn't see the candidate's day-to-day accomplishments. Another reference problem can develop when a job candidate's key references are called unawares by a PEG Partner. If they haven't reviewed the SITG job description ahead of time, their supportive, well-meaning reference to the PEG Partner can come across as unconvincing.

As a general rule, unprepared references don't like to be put on the spot by a PEG hiring authority asking point blank, "Will Joe do a good job for us as COO?" If the answer is, "I think he would." The next reference question is, "Can you give me some specific examples of why you feel that way?" What's the problem? The reference hasn't seen Joe's resume in eight years, back when he was Joe's boss. Skin in the game candidates must email their key references their resume as soon they produce one, right before executing their SITG job search networking campaign. You should also email a PEG job description for which you are a candidate after the first interview to your key references. Then they are prepared in case they receive an unexpected call from the PEG hiring authority.

You may not believe it, but every so often, one of my SITG job search candidates gives me a key reference of his to contact. This is always towards being one of my three confidential final search candidates. I call the reference, who is the former Chairman of the Board and former boss of my candidate, Hank. Then that reference immediately asks one point blank: is this between you and me? If they want it that way, yes. Typically, the references want to be sure what he tells me will never get back to his former subordinate President, my SITG candidate.

"Okay," he says. "What do you want to ask me about Hank?"

"Would you re-hire him as President?"

"No."

"Why not?"

"Hank, at board meetings, promised profits, told you what you wanted to hear, but delivered company losses. His A player subordinates constantly turned over. They wouldn't work for him."

"How did Hank keep his job?"

"He personally handled our three biggest customers and he ended up selling some unused company real estate in Texas to a big conglomerate for a whopping financial gain."

What will your references say to a PEG Partner interested in hiring you? I say, show the PEG hiring authority your written references during your first interview. I have found that PEGs will accept a candidate's several written references if they are solid and from executive titles above yours. If so, usually the PEG Partner won't do any additional reference checking.

There are ways for A player C-Level candidates to help offset potential "vindictive or unfair references". You need to organize your key references in advance of your SITG job search networking campaign. Discover those who will provide you with supportive written references, those who will remain neutral (company policy) and those who will be uncooperative (don't return your emails or your voicemail messages).

How are the candidate's references typically handled if he is the PEG C-Level job candidate of a retained search consultant (headhunter)? The majority of retained search firms do not handle SITG C-Level searches exclusively in the lower middle market ($10M-$100M in sales). That's been my market for over twenty-five years and my C-Level candidate screening is due diligence-oriented. You will be an "evidential candidate", who is a future portfolio company investor. Take a due diligence approach for SITG interviews with PEGs.

I was a generalist retained search consultant for fifteen years before concentrating on PEG C-Level hiring, and I have many headhunter friends, including a handful for over twenty-five years.

Most headhunter generalists side with their candidates who don't want their key references contacted until they meet the client to see how their mutual chemistry matches. Their candidates claim they want to learn more about the portfolio company's business and the job. In this highly competitive 2015 job market, there are many capable C-Level candidate rivals available. Job candidates need more than a super resume and winning personality to be hired. They need to become evidential candidates. Avoid being "one and done". PEG hiring authorities want proof. Be sure you have it with you at your PEG interview.

Generalist headhunters typically do their serious reference checking when their candidate is a finalist. That's around the time the client says, "If his references check out strongly, we will make him an offer." Then the scrambling begins to locate the candidate's key references. Good luck on their reaching the candidate's strongest ones. The candidate's "poor" references don't have to say the candidate did bad things. They may answer certain reference questions such as, "Is Frank a strong CEO leader?" a little vaguely like, "I guess so". Or the headhunter might rattle off a long CEO job description he is trying to fill to a key reference of the finalist candidate.

Then he asks, "Do you think Frank can handle that job?"

"The headhunter is hitting me with all these CEO job requirements and job responsibilities at once. From what I know of Frank, he's never had multi-plant full P&L before, but I guess he could handle that CEO job."

If that headhunter's PEG client wants to call Frank's references himself, I wouldn't bet Frank would be hired. The lesson here is that the skin in the game C-Level job candidate has to take control of his own references.

How to Ideally Handle Your References

While I think of it, never list your references on your resume. Never.

From the moment you decide to pursue a skin in the game C-Level job, you should begin assembling a comprehensive "reference posse" list of at least a dozen or more references. An SITG candidate needs key positive written references at the highest and most informed level, related to his employment history. To be considered a serious SITG C-Level job candidate, your reference list must not be mostly supervisors, temporary help, plant hourly employees, employees reporting two rungs below you, the HR Manager or US Secretary of State, John Kerry.

SITG C-Level job candidates must list references who can confirm parts of their resume claims. You need references aware of your work habits, management style, accomplishments, and results. Include former bosses, former employer company owners, subordinates and peers, customers, consultants, vendors, board members, and investors. Be sure to list your former company CEO, President, and CFO if they are familiar with your work experience. This is what I call your "reference posse".

I propose you be a pro-active SITG job seeker and have key reference letters with you at PEG interviews. The same goes for your networked referral meetings who don't know you and are trying to determine if they will refer you to one of their well-connected M&A professionals.

At least you should attempt to acquire written references from your key references. If the candidate and the PEG Partner sense a good job match by the end of the candidate's interview, the candidate can leave his copies of his reference letters with the PEG Partner. Otherwise, just when the candidate is on the verge of receiving a job offer, or needs them the most, some of his most compelling references can be suddenly "out of pocket". They go to Kenya on vacation, move to Costa Rica, or have passed away. Decide now to get your references in writing, once and for all. Notice most LinkedIn profiles list recommendations including some I call "mini-references" from others as well as endorsements.

Don't be afraid of contacting your references about them each giving you a written reference. Their references are for you to have in your valise for important networking referral meetings and PEG job interviews. Your first step is to produce a factual resume containing your accomplishments that your key references will verify. Afterwards, you should email your resume to each reference on your target list. Go back at least ten to fifteen employment years. The more the merrier. I'm serious! References where you currently work are presumably off limits (unless you get a job offer, subject to the PEG hiring authority speaking to your current boss). Remember, if you're still employed, indicate it at the top of your candidate resume.

Next, if you are being considered for a SITG C-Level job with a PEG, email each of your targeted references an edited job description. Explain that you have signed a non-disclosure agreement with the PEG, and had to keep specific company identification information confidential on the job description you emailed your references. As a routine search assignment precaution,

I always create an edited job description for public disclosure of the SITG C-Level search assignment.

Some SITG job searchers won't get as many written references as they expected from their key references. Some will avoid your request due to company policy. Others will agree to give you a verbal reference if they get a call from a PEG. However, if you have a good to great C-Level employment track record, you will receive more supportive references in writing than you expect. You have to ask. Explain that you are embarking on an SITG C-Level job search campaign to join a PEG portfolio company. You also plan to buy a small percentage of its stock with up to $100K of your own funds. You are networking with your contacts and other avenues for referrals to PEGs or to M&A professionals who might refer you to PEGs. In this poor economy and highly competitive job market, you need written references in support of your resume statements. They are a key part of your "show and tell" exhibit folder for presentation in meetings with networked referrals and in your PEG interviews.

Written key references confirm you are an evidential candidate, increasing your SITG job search credibility. Remember, you are networking with friends, family, colleagues, and business contacts and creating a chain of networked referrals. The further away you network from your well-known contacts, the more likely your networked referrals become virtual strangers. They don't really know you, only what your mutual referral told them and the resume he emailed. This is valuable potential contact. Some of these referrals are well connected in the M&A sector. Such people protect their important relationships and only connect a referral if they impress them. Having written key references as part of your "show and tell" at networked referral meetings gives more credibility. Your verbal and informative exhibits impress. You are a strong SITG C-Level candidate.

If there is a headhunter involved in your SITG C-Level PEG candidacy, already having supportive written references can only make his job easier and save time during the client referral process. You can re-contact your written references, sending them a copy of the edited job description for which you are contending. Tell each key reference why you feel that job seems to be a match with your past achievements and abilities. When either your headhunter or PEG Partner contacts your written references, you have prepared them for such a call. That helps all concerned.

You are only asking each of your references to vouch for those accomplishments and metrics listed in your resume. At the same time, you will appreciate if each would email you a two paragraph reference on company letterhead. Even snail mailed to you would be vundebar! Wonderful!

Do you call or email your references first? I suggest emailing them and attaching your resume. I have found that many references appreciate having a job candidate's current resume to refresh their memories about dates, titles, duties, responsibilities, and results. Inform your references that you are gearing up your SITG as a (C-Level job title here) job search networking campaign. Ultimately, you plan on investing your own money in the equity of the portfolio company a PEG owner hires you to help grow. Millions have been made from similar skin in the game investments and C-Level jobs in PEG portfolio companies. That's why you'd appreciate a few reference paragraphs in writing to show the PEG at your initial interview. It makes you an evidential candidate and could lead to more interviews and an SITG job offer.

Let's say the SITG job seeker's organized networking efforts result in positive interviews with a referred PEG. There is good mutual chemistry and an apparent C-Level job as well as mutual interest going forward. What typically occurs next?

For Candidate A, utilizing his Multi Packet Portfolio (chapter 10) of several written references and other informative exhibit items, it's time for the PEG to discuss an SITG job offer. Another scenario is you are one of two finalists for the job. Based on my own experience, if Candidate A provided four or five written reference letters, including two or three from key references, the PEG Partners will not pursue contacting more references. However, you have to set a high standard as an evidential candidate for PEG job Candidate B to meet or exceed. I'd bet my lobsters on Candidate A being hired.

For Candidate B, who presented his resume, interviewed well, and dropped impressive names of M&A professionals, the PEG Partners are impressed but ask for some references. Here is where any SITG candidate can be at risk in this promising employment situation. Odds are, Candidate B has C-Level experience in a similar industry to that of the PEG's portfolio company with the C-Level vacancy. Executives don't move from, say, clean room brain surgical instrument manufacturing to private label children's underwear manufacturing. So this PEG must have their own contacts within the same industry to check out Candidate B.

Regarding Candidate B's reference list that he gave the PEG, typically if the important references on it aren't given a heads up, they will not be properly prepared for such a call from the PEG. Also, the important references on such a list aren't emailed a copy of the job for which Candidate B is being considered. The references may want to discuss the PEG call with Candidate B or the unprepared key references on Candidate B's list may not be reachable on the first call. This often leads to phone tags. Such circumstances do not help any SITG job candidate. This occupies a lot of the PEG Partner's valuable time. As a result, this PEG Partner may never reach an SITG job candidate's most knowledgeable and vital references. Another potential disadvantage is such delays may lead to the PEG Partner delegating Candidate B's reference checks to the firm's principal or MBA associate. This could be like Don Quixote filling in for Zorro! The lesson here is for SITG C-Suite executive candidates to always prepare their key references for such situations.

I have not known PEGs for routinely having tons of patience. Generally speaking, if there are other SITG job rivals to your candidacy under consideration, one candidate's reference checking delays are a rival candidate's opportunity. In the case of Candidate A, who was hired, the more a PEG knows about the SITG candidates, the better his final decision.

You may prefer to check LinkedIn for profiles there of your key references including former employer, company owners, bosses, peers, subordinates, board members, investors, consultants, vendors, and customers. LinkedIn has a tutorial on how to solicit someone to give you a recommendation that you can list on your own LinkedIn profile (see chapter 8).

Go to: https://help.linkedin.com/app/answers/detail/a_id/96/ft/eng

Dealing with Problem References and an Inconsistent Job History

Securing an SITG job with a PEG portfolio company is very challenging, even if your references claim you can walk on the Charles River. After you land the C-Level job, it remains constantly demanding under tight control. You almost have to know the status of your Key Performance Indicators on an hourly basis. That's why so many of my hires earned millions at their liquidity events for their stock ownership. Whatever your past C-Level employment record, you must have functionally proven yourself enough times and achieved measurable results that contributed to your company's profitability. That's the name of the game in the PEG world; results and evidence. Achieving, spearheading, or strategizing consistent profits, growth, turnaround, and efficiencies.

The trend in hiring in the biggest PEGs ($1B + average deals) is CEO, CFO, COO all day interview sessions, answering the same questions asked in different ways multiple times. I developed a modest due diligence-oriented vetting approach in trying to produce interested and qualified SITG C-Level hires.

Does your background have "a dark side"? Do you have many frequent job changes? Do you have problem key references from your past bosses or superiors, owners, or investors? If you can't deal effectively with your employment "dark side", you are wasting your time trying to land a PEG SITG C-Level job.

I was fired as a VP in a Boston Personnel office of over forty-eight recruiters early in my career in Boston in the late sixties. I landed on my feet when the VP/GM of a Stamford, CT branch recruited me to relocate there. Great turn of events for my career. Lesson: don't sulk, move on with vigor.

If your career has a "dark side", avoid leaving out jobs in your resume and LinkedIn profile. Avoid giving yourself elevated job titles to your real ones. Don't create new employment dates. Don't give yourself a phony MBA degree. Any of the above will eliminate your PEG SITG job candidacy. Once your false information is discovered, even after you get hired, it will get you immediately fired. Search firms lose clients if and when such incidents occur. Spend your time rebuilding your evidential candidacy.

At this point in your career – know thyself. You must decide what are the ideal job titles and situations for you to produce targeted results? Can you grow a business profitably or can you play a significant functional role in doing so? There are no shortcuts in preparing for your SITG job search. Start writing your Indiana Jones Bio and proceed from there.

I want to make it clear that I have not promoted unqualified candidates for my skin in the game executive searches. Neither have I ever indulged in touching up a candidate's X-rays on their references and resume. If you check my references, clients will tell you my attitude is, "When in doubt, knock them out". That doesn't mean I haven't placed successful candidates who have had their dark sides. I have found that most references want to be fair in providing their confidential input on my candidates. I always ask references, "What's the worst thing you could say about our CFO candidate, professionally speaking? Can you tell me anything that you would want to know about this candidate if we were doing this skin in the game CFO search for you?" Can you withstand your references' reply to that question and remain a viable job candidate?

Go back fifteen employment years. List your job history chronologically. Write down the accompanying job title(s) and your proudest accomplishments in each employer. Write the most important hierarchical titles from the top down in each employer. Take your time. Think about them. Are you missing any important title per each employer? Who in each company can you attempt to receive written references from to verify your key accomplishments there? You need a reference mass from each of your employers within the past fifteen years.

Master Reference List Hierarchy per Employer:

- Company Owner(s)-Name(s)
- Board Members-Name(s)
- Investors-Name(s)
- Bankers-Name(s)
- Your Direct Bosses-Name(s)
- CEO-Name
- CFO-Name
- HR-Name
- Functional Department VPs-Name(s)
- Direct Reports-Name(s)
- Vendors-Name(s)
- Customers-Name(s)
- Consultants-Name(s)
- Auditors-Name(s)

Who in each hierarchy list will give you a **definite** bad reference per employer going back fifteen years of employment? Place an X next to each **definite** bad reference title/name per employer. Is each **definite** bad reference true per hierarchical list per employer? On a scale of one (false) to ten (fact) rate the truthfulness of each **definite** bad reference per employer. Can any other titles/names on your list offset each **definite** bad reference per employer? On a scale of one to ten, rate each other title/name on your lists as a potential offset to your definite bad reference per employer.

You might go back twenty years instead of fifteen years if your employer accomplishments during the extra five years warrant going back.

Looking at each hierarchical list per employer, consolidate your best potential reference titles/names and decide from which ones you will solicit written supportive references. Do the same with each hierarchical list per employer and consolidate **definite** bad references titles/names.

You may have been placed by a headhunter with an employer where you expect definite bad references, but are not absolutely certain. You might ask that headhunter if he will check your reference there with the source of the definite bad reference. I have done this a few times to help clarify the type of reference my former candidate(s) will receive. It's worthwhile because only one reference was verified as definitely terrible. An HR VP once asked my opinion about the best type of reference to give for someone let go by the company but not for "cause". I answered, "He just wasn't suitable for our type of operation." She was happy with that.

You have to build a case for what you have done well for your past employers and who you can use as references to help you prove it. You have to be able to recognize a job opportunity that seems to fit you well and then go after it. First, make sure you have covered your unfair bad references with supportive written references to offset the damages.

Before you have begun networking meetings and networked referral meetings as well as PEG interviews, prepare your Multi Packet Portfolio. It should contain your key written references and what I label "atta boys". These can include past written complimentary job performance appraisals, any written recognition from company PEG owners, board members, customers, or industry association recognition. It could be a photo of you and your team opening a new plant in China in the company newsletter. It can be a past non-proprietary company Excel spreadsheet showing your positive financial turnaround involvement in a formerly money losing portfolio company. You should follow the chapters in this book that apply to your C-Level job function.

Most routine "bad references" I uncover can be overcome. They relate to politics, personality friction, professional jealousy, or, in some cases, personal vindictiveness. After you have organized your written supportive references evidence to offset a few bad references, consider these suggestions below.

Provided you have the job qualifications, you might increase your odds of a PEG hiring you for an SITG C-Level position located in the "boondocks". Not in your top ten locations but it might rebuild your career. You might consider a VP Sales job with more travel than you planned. Ask about consulting opportunities with a PEG. They might need an interim to help get one of their portfolio companies ready to eventually sell to a financial or strategic buyer in a year or so. They might need an interim COO for one of their portfolio companies. Something for you to consider where you can land on your feet running. Do well and that could lead to a full time SITG gig!

Remember, always offer to be a reference for your own willing references unless they were truly bad performers. What goes around comes around.

Chapter 8

Fine Tuning Your Presentation

Preparing for M&A and PEG Networking Meetings, and PEG Interviews

You must prepare your presentations before you start networking or skin in the game job interviewing. Then you should practice your verbal elevator pitch and face-to-face "show and tell" until you are comfortable and confident in your presentation.

I am a firm believer, educator, and long-time user and provider of selected "show and tell" material as part of all my SITG candidates' presentations. I recommend select exhibits for M&A and PEG networking meetings and PEG interviews. Let's say through your networking efforts, you have been referred to the President of the local Association for Corporate Growth (ACG chapter). His job is being an M&A consultant. For you, this is a major networking coup. This ACG chapter President must have a potential goldmine of referrals including ACG connections. Treat this like an SITG job interview. Do your research on him and his employer. Book a meeting with him for coffee. Follow the procedures I have outlined in chapter 9, such as making sure his referral source emailed this reference your resume and CC'd you in the emailed introduction. Then decide what select exhibit items of yours would support your qualifications and employment results. Buy a pocket folder of your appropriately chosen exhibits that you can give to this solid networked referral at the end of your meeting. Review my suggested list of exhibit documents to consider your options. How to use them in your networking meeting is covered in chapter 9.

PEG Partners are a tough audience. Presume for the moment the fact that the PEG Partner is accustomed to conducting exhaustive due diligence on all potential acquisitions. He will not automatically believe your resume and verbally stated accomplishments. He will probably doubt some of the results you achieved in your last job. You'll be asked why you aren't still employed there. If you are not an accomplished interviewee with a less than enthusiastic PEG interviewer, it's time for some "show and tell" about you. Let's bring out some metrics achieved, some profit numbers, and some company turnaround evidence. Now, watch your interview atmosphere improve!

I urge you to think about any complimentary letters, emails, industry awards, military honors, solid performance appraisals, and Excel spreadsheets that would enhance your credentials, credibility, and life/career accomplishments. Every A player C-Level executive I have ever screened for one of my retained searches has some of these complimentary items that I call "atta boys". Thoughtful selection of the right items to present will elevate your networking meetings. These items will also enhance your PEG exploratory meetings and face-to-face PEG job interviews.

Don't you envy that physically fit, highly presentable executive job candidate? The image of "clothes make the man"? He presents a resume full of credentials, noteworthy accomplishments, and striking results. He makes a great impression in networking sessions and lands promising referrals from these meetings. His elevator pitch just blows people away. Imagine, Stanford University graduate, number one in his MBA class, and also number one in his Cornell University BSBA class. His interviews with PEGs are so solid that a few of the hiring authorities are urgently trying to open up SITG job opportunities for this lad within their portfolio companies.

The above job search candidate's little secret is he looks you in the eye, and he charismatically lies about some, or even all of his credentials and accomplishments. He looks the part, why not act the part? The trouble is he has plenty of company playing this game.

While I worked in New York City as General Manager of Weidemann Consultants Executive Search, I fell for the glib talker phony more than once before I smartened up. I would bet you two lobsters that as a candidate you will compete with candidates misrepresenting part of their background to get hired. To me, a job candidate doing a little lying is like being a little pregnant. I paid the price in lost clients and credibility. I went by my gut feelings regarding a few impressive appearing and sounding candidates which I thought were a perfect match for my searches. Instead of checking them out thoroughly, I helped get them hired. Soon after, they got fired.

For the past twenty eight years, I have specialized in skin in the game hiring. Now I don't trust what any search candidate tells me. My reputation rests on my credibility and the honesty of my hired C-Level executive candidates. My motto remains, "When in doubt, knock them out." Every time I check my candidates' references, I email the reference a copy of his resume and an edited version of the SITG job search that the candidate is seeking. My email tells each reference that no matter what he tells me about Mr. So and So, even if he truthfully murdered someone, it remains between us.

Nothing will come back to the candidate. If you say he walks on the Charles River, the information will only be between you, me, and my private equity client.

I have often been really surprised and also disappointed by prospects that appear very promising. In almost every skin in the game search assignment, I uncover deception on the part of an impressive sounding candidate. Examples include: one VP Sales candidate's resume on LinkedIn had more employers listed than the resume copy I used for my search. One candidate couldn't locate his University of Chicago MBA Degree. I did verify that there were several people with my candidate's exact name who were confirmed, but not specifically his social security number. Another candidate couldn't locate his Purple Heart to bring to our interview, not the colored paper award. Two years ago, one of my COO search candidates provided me with a couple of positive reference paragraphs on separate company letterheads from two of his former bosses. The trouble was the candidate wrote his own reference letters, which I routinely uncovered. The biggest fraud committed over and over throughout my career has been candidates lying about their MBA or Masters degrees. It still bothers me to hear a grown C-Level executive fraud crying while apologizing to me on the phone for misrepresenting his MBA, "No one has ever checked until now."

I pride myself on producing qualified job candidates. Hopefully you will become one from reading this chapter. The most sought after candidate for my clients throughout my search career has been the qualified and interested job candidate. The more the PEG hiring authorities know about their C-Level job candidates, the better informed their final selection.

Perfecting Your Three Minute Personal Elevator Pitch

As a skin in the game job seeker and networker, you need to be able to communicate your search objective. This objective includes targeted job title, your mini-bio, and in a nutshell, your functional value proposition to a PEG. Notice that the elevator pitches below are no-nonsense, factual, and full of protein, not fluff, and no exaggerations. An elevator pitch is not something you give to a PEG job interviewer. It is for use in a network setting, one-on-one, or in a small group environment at an M&A function.

The candidate's elevator pitch should be compact, clear, and informative. After writing the elevator pitch, it is necessary to rehearse it and practice presenting it often to colleagues, friends, and family until the candidate feels comfortable and confident communicating it. Avoid a machine gun delivery or sounding like Poll Parrott. Be sure to hit the main points of one's background in the presentation. Hopefully it will enable the audience to easily grasp credentials, qualifications, desired job title, and equity purchase mission. The candidate will probably network with a number of connections who don't know many details about the candidate's job. The elevator pitch could result in their referring an M&A contact that leads towards a PEG Partner meeting.

I am trying to keep you from giving an elevator pitch full of fluff, smoke, and braggadocio. You may have to write a dozen elevator pitches before it sounds right. Remember, if it's the truth, it's not bragging.

Here is a CEO elevator pitch example for you to adapt to your own qualifications and experience:

"Hello, my name is Gordon Jones. I am networking for full P&L skin in the game job opportunities with private equity firms. As a CEO or multi-site COO, I am well experienced in improving manufacturing operations that produce engineered products for commercial, aerospace, and defense markets. My former employers include United Technologies, Barnes Group, and Parker Hannifin. Utilizing LEAN and continuous process improvement, my teams generate long-term results. I have an MBA from Boston University and a BSMA from West Point. I am seeking to buy equity in the portfolio company I join to help grow so I can share in the equity value increase at the company's eventual sale to a financial or strategic buyer. Thank you for this opportunity to introduce myself and my background."

Here is a CFO elevator pitch example for a candidate to adapt to his qualifications and his experience:

"Hello, my name is Joe Barnes. I am networking for CFO skin in the game job opportunities with private equity firms. As a proven Financial Executive, my experience evolved from Plant Controllerships with Union Carbide Chemicals & Petrochemicals. Later, as a Multi-Plant Business Unit Controller with GE Plastics, I had full P&L and balance sheet management for up to five manufacturing locations. At GE Energy, I was Finance Director for their power generation business. I am now CFO with a $220M Hispanic Food manufacturer/distributor. My background ranges from the shop floor to senior management of C-Suite companies. I have a BS Accounting and Executive MBA from Marshall University. I am a CPA in West Virginia and a Chartered Global Management Accountant. I was awarded GE's Six Sigma Green Belt Certification in 2002. I am pursuing an opportunity to join and buy equity in a portfolio company. I want to share in the increased equity value of the company's eventual sale to a buyer. Thank you for this opportunity to introduce myself and my background."

Here is a VP Sales and Marketing elevator pitch example for you to adapt to your own qualifications and experience:

"Hello, my name is Ben Rabinowitz. I am networking for VP Sales and Marketing skin in the game job opportunities with private equity firms. I have a twenty-three year record of achievement in the medical device arena as an experienced Sales and Marketing Senior Executive. After graduating from Cornell with an MBA in Marketing in 1988, I joined a $1.5B Boston Scientific Division where I spent eleven years in various sales management roles selling coronary stents and catheters for interventional cardiologists. After being promoted to Group Marketing Manager of Stent Development, I became Cardiology Director of Vascular Marketing, establishing market leadership for five surgical products generating $400M in sales. I then became Medtronic's Global Marketing Director, Implantable Cardioverter-Defibrillator Devices & Leads for three years. I am currently Vice President of Surgical Specialty Products, US Sales, for a $375M Division of C. R. Bard, Inc. I am pursuing an opportunity to buy equity in a portfolio company. I want to share in the equity value of the company's eventual sale to a buyer. Thank you for this opportunity to introduce myself and my background."

Here is a COO/VP Operations elevator pitch example for you to adapt to your own qualifications and experience:

"Hello, my name is Mary Shaw. I am networking for COO/VP Operations skin in the game job opportunities with private equity firms. I have been a global operations and supply chain executive for most of my twenty year career in the U.S. and Shanghai. I have led and developed high performance teams in the specialty foam, silicones, and plastics advanced materials industry. After achieving a BS Chemical Engineering Degree from Tufts University and an MBA in Operations from Rensselaer Polytechnic Institute, I joined DuPont Corporation in Process Engineering. Two years later, I moved up to Extrusion Department Manager. A few years later, I became Manufacturing Operations Manager for a $50M plastics, polymers and resins plant serving automotive parts Original Equipment Manufacturers (OEMs). There, I improved all key operations metrics including gross margins and maintaining positive cash flow. Then, I joined Celanese Corporation for a GM position in their $60M global silicon business serving OEMs, aircraft, automotive, electronics, and industrial markets. Four years later, I was promoted to VP Manufacturing Operations for this high volume automotive part business with Celanese Asia in Suzhou, China. There I spearheaded multi-million dollar revenue growth and significant cost savings implementing Six Sigma and Lean Manufacturing initiatives. I recently completed a five year assignment as VP Operations for a $525M Celanese US global manufacturer of specialty materials solutions for telecommunications, automotive and consumer products markets. Now, I am pursuing an opportunity to buy equity in a portfolio company so I can share in the equity value increase at the company's eventual sale to a buyer. Thank you for this opportunity to introduce myself and my background."

In chapter 9, I introduce the uninitiated candidates to the powerhouse M&A institution called the Association for Corporate Growth (ACG). If it turns out that your networking effort through your friends and referrals have little or no connection with the M&A sector, you may find yourself giving your elevator pitch to fellow attendees of the fabulous ACG monthly breakfasts. They are a phenomenal networking opportunity for making the right mergers and acquisition PEG and PEG service provider connections. The candidate's articulated elevator pitch delivered smoothly and informatively at ACG M&A related events will be well received. Practice, rehearse, and practice your elevator pitch. A solid presentation will bring the candidate closer to his objective of meeting or getting introductions to PEGs.

The more the candidate networks with solid contacts, the more referral chains of contacts develop. The further out in the referral chain one networks, the less likely one knows the referral source and the less likely they know the candidate. If the presentation is solid, the more likely one will keep the referral chain going until there is a worthwhile PEG introduction. You may not have many M&A contacts with whom you are networking, but your solid presentations to referrals who are virtual strangers to you will bail you out in the networking game.

I face the same networking challenge in trying to develop new PEG clients. Unless a person knows me well or is out of a C-Level job, when they meet me at a social event, they ask, "What do you do for work, Jim?" Years ago I would say, "I'm a headhunter." You could see the lack of enthusiasm in their demeanor and the person invariably walked away. Now, if people learn I am a skin in the game headhunter whose hires often end up millionaires, they usually show keen interest. In all of Gilreath Consultancy's literature and website, I list client references and some client names. Those names cut to the chase and get my target audience's attention. I have my own elevator pitch I give at the Association for Corporate Growth events. I'm not afraid to drop client names, show client reference letters, or mention some of my more successful skin in the game CEO hires like the late Al Samuelsen. Al made $11M from his invested equity and merit equity options, as CEO of a former successful Metapoint Partners acquisition in New Hampshire.

I suggest SITG candidates prepare select exhibit material to use, as needed, to bolster their resume statements and verbal claims. These exhibits are for networking and PEG referral meetings, and for PEG job interviews. This key exhibit material will require a little creativity and thought about what items you might include in their exhibit folder. Afterwards you should practice presenting various exhibits to your spouse and friends.

SITG candidates are showing some of these exhibits to reinforce their presentation credibility. The SITG job candidate must be selective regarding key "due diligence" items he files in his pocket folder. Next he should (practically) memorize his exhibit items and their filing sequence in the pocket folder. Here's an example: Ricky Jay, the world class magician and world famous playing cards trickster, can fool even fellow magicians with his wizardry. Ricky said he initially would spend eight hours a day with a deck of cards practicing tricks over and over until he could perform them automatically without thinking.

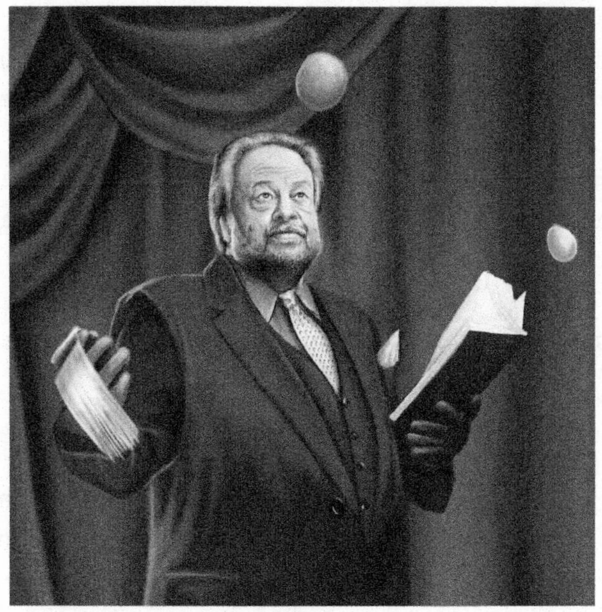

Do you think you will fumble around looking for papers in your pocket folder during a PEG networking session? Not if your few exhibits are key and not if you practice presenting them. Use your research on the PEG to match your best exhibit items to their preferred acquisitions. Rehearse the networking meeting in your mind.

A few specific examples of exhibits assuming you are the candidate:

As you mention plant layouts you reconfigured years ago as COO of XYZ company, you might have photos from a news release or an employee newsletter showing it saved your employer millions of dollars and enabled the company to add a third shift. You might have successfully folded in several acquisitions of former fragmented competitors and after your portfolio company was sold, the PEG's Managing Partner wrote you an "atta boy" letter with your liquidity check.

The latest dynamic in business contexts is to tell the person, "I'm on LinkedIn if you want to check out my background." I realize you can list some of this exhibit information on your LinkedIn listing, but I feel it's more effective if you are meeting with someone and that you hand them a document that reinforces what you were just speaking about.

My Suggested List of Item Copies for Your Career Folders:

1. **College/University Degree(s)** - Every search has prospects lying about their MBA degree. If your diplomas are very large and framed, take a photo of each diploma, load the photo into your computer and make eight and one half by eleven size reproductions. They work fine.
2. **Certifications (CPA, CMA, Lean Six Sigma, Green Belt, Black Belt etc.)** Same as above.
3. **Honorable Discharge from Military and Military Honors (Purple Heart)** - I'd almost bet you a lobster that the PEG hiring authority is a veteran.
4. **Resume (marked confidential if employed)** - Your LinkedIn resume may be abbreviated compared to your full length version.
5. **Completed Self-Rating Quiz** - Self estimate your level of expertise versus the job description you are being measured against if you are in a job interview with a PEG (see chapter 10 on Self-Rating Quiz details and example).
6. **Copies of your reference letters marked Confidential** - Include any "atta boy" letters. These would be sincere

and noteworthy compliments from heads of customers or vendors. Maybe these letters would be from the President of an acquired company, or little known activities from non-profit or community work, industry or association awards, or recognition. Use one or none as you see fit, perhaps to reinforce subject matter in a meeting conversation.

7. **Any positive former employer performance appraisals of yours marked confidential** - Appraisals would include any 360 degree performance appraisals that were positive overall.
8. **Any non-proprietary Excel spreadsheets of metrics, KPIs or financials in support of your claims of great results you achieved or helped your teams produce at one or more past employers marked confidential** – A good example of the claims are when my search candidates rate themselves 10s - or even 11s or 12s on their self-rating quiz. I want to see numbers, metrics, or financials. You have, no doubt, accomplished above average results in your current or past job functions. A claim is applicable even if it goes back five years or more. If you happen to have an old non-proprietary spreadsheet showing "Before and After" results you achieved, show and tell. The more your interviewers witness some of these exhibits, the stronger impression you leave. Tell 'em, then show 'em. You'll impress 'em.
9. **Any relevant illustrated former employer product, company, and media or PR literature. E.g. a company newsletter showing you with the COO of your newly opened Shenzhen, China manufacturing facility** I am not experimenting with these exhibit suggestions. All of my search candidates have had three ring binders

furnished with some or all of these exhibit examples and a few more. Clients review these binders carefully for the most part and are impressed. For a typical Gilreath Consultancy skin in the game search assignment, we average three candidate binders referred per hire.

10. **Your "For Your Eyes Only" Indiana Jones Bio** It's your call whether you leave a copy of your Indiana Jones Bio with the PEG Partner after a successful skin in the game job interview. If you have been told you will be having a second interview with another Partner from the PEG, you could give the Partner who just interviewed you your entire exhibit file including the Indiana Jones. Mark it "For Your Eyes Only".

I typically suggest the SITG candidate buy a dozen or so Esselte Oxford Blue Poly 8-Pocket Folders - Letter Size - 9.1 x 10.6 x 0.4. (office products stores sell these; so does Amazon.com). You can easily file up to ten career exhibit items, suggested above, per pocket folder. If the SITG candidate doesn't have that many exhibits, he can select a pocket folder with fewer files. The purpose of this pocket folder is "due diligence" items in support of your resume statements, your degrees and certifications, written references, and any other key "atta boys".

You will probably have a satchel grip, briefcase, or valise with you containing your career folders. Use them for your upcoming networking meetings and PEG exploratory sessions through your networking referrals. Ideally exhibit folders are your due diligence ammunition for PEG job interviews. The proof is in the pudding; pictures are worth thousands of words. Trust me, the proper contents of this career folder will strengthen your presentation and impression on the PEG Partner. One of our long-time PEG clients stated that Gilreath's candidates are 80% hired when we review their career binders and interview them. Using your pocket folder exhibits in your networking meetings will enhance your credibility with the contacts you are meeting. The results will be an increase in valuable referrals. Using the pocket folder in PEG job interviews could greatly increase your hire ability. My skin in the game search philosophy is, "The more factual information our clients receive about C-Level executive job candidates, the more informed their hiring decision."

Let me mention the obvious to you as a reminder. Hopefully, as a result of your networking, you will end up competing for one or more C-Level skin in the game job opportunities. If you have any competitors, even if a headhunter refers them, they will not have presented to the PEG the due diligence information and exhibit material you are supplying. Another point to keep in mind; I have found over the years that a PEG is instinctively impressed when a C-Level executive wants to work for them as well as buy equity in the portfolio company. Not every job competitor will so readily embrace the skin in the game concept. I remember one Midwestern VP Operations job applicant of mine, on learning he would have to buy $70K worth of portfolio company stock if he were hired, was shocked. "You expect me, after I'm hired, to invest my hard earned money in company stock and fall in with strangers?" It is in your favor when applying for the job if you completely endorse the skin in the game concept.

Become a Member of LinkedIn

LinkedIn (www.linkedin.com) is the world's largest business-oriented social networking service launched on May 5, 2003; it is mainly used for professional networking. According to LinkedIn's PR, there are 100 million+ registered members in the US out of 313 million members globally. LinkedIn is an outstanding networking tool to find bios of many of your own job search networking connections. You'll locate many M&A industry private membership groups and PEG Partners with whom you might connect either through networking or through the direct cold calling approach yourself. LinkedIn allows registered users to maintain a list of contact details of people they know and trust in business, as well as network potential connections to skin in the game job opportunities through your contacts. You can also do research and get free advice and information on LinkedIn. I recommend *LinkedIn for Dummies*, 3rd edition by Joel Elad, MBA, $24.99. It will give you a nice foundation about using the features of LinkedIn and building your profile.

A basic LinkedIn account is free, and joining LinkedIn is easy for anyone who wants to create and maintain a professional profile online without the cost.

- Build and maintain a large, trusted, professional network
- Find and reconnect with colleagues and classmates
- Locate and connect with your key references
- Request and provide recommendations
- Create a professional presence on the web
- Request up to five introductions at a time
- Search for and view profiles of other LinkedIn users
- Receive unlimited InMails
- View 100 results per search

- Save up to three searches and get weekly alerts on those searches

To get started, open your web browser and go to LinkedIn. You see the initial LinkedIn home page. In the "Get Started" section in the middle of the page, provide your first name, last name, e-mail address, and a password in the boxes provided. To help you get started using your free account and to learn more about LinkedIn features and functionalities, you can view any of their free pre-recorded online Learning Webinars (http://help.linkedin.com/app/answers/detail/a_id/530/~/linkedin-learning-webinars). Click on the session in which you are interested. I recommend the following three LinkedIn prerecorded webinars: "Creating an Online Presence on LinkedIn Part I", "Engaging with Your LinkedIn Network Part II", and "LinkedIn Premium: Getting the Most out of Your Premium Account".

Once you're ready to begin aggressively networking your M&A contacts and their PEG contacts and contacting some LinkedIn member targets cold, I recommend you eventually upgrade to a LinkedIn Talent Finder Premium Account. I have used it since 2006 for $119.95 a month. It is cancelable monthly. With such a Premium account, you can search for up to 700 profiles each time you search for targets, filter and send InMails to reach anyone on LinkedIn, get hundreds of additional search results, and see more information about who has viewed your profile, among other useful features. Make certain you research LinkedIn Talent Finder Premium Account by name in the Premium Help Center.

First thing's first. You have to read this book cover to cover following the chapters in sequence, planning your skin in the game job search campaign. Timing is important. No use having M&A networking and PEG appointments before you are well organized and prepared to be at your most effective job searching. Avoid ready, fire, aim! LinkedIn membership can play an important aid and timesaving role in your skin in the game job search effort when the time comes.

Why *Skin in the Game* Suits You

You are a skin in the game job search candidate. You want to put some of your own dollars in the equity of your potential new employer, if the risk/reward ratio seems worth it. The PEG company owners are conducting due diligence on you. They need to hire a key executive like you to turn around one of their failing acquisitions. Meanwhile you are conducting due diligence on them and their portfolio company to determine if you are a good match.

You are knowledgeable about their business, their industry, and their products and markets. You have some insight into the challenges, Capex requirements, and a winning growth strategy. The job will last for five or so years if all goes as planned before the liquidity event occurs. It could be your biggest payday, and the biggest payday for the management team, if growth targets are reached.

What do you think of the stock valuation price? How about the management team? They also have skin in the game. It's a good sign, encouraging going forward, if the PEG ownership has done a number of successful deals in that industry. Your wife is your close partner. Good, because the family will have to relocate to where the business is headquartered, perhaps down south. Company sales are $30M, EBITDA is $4M. A number of fragmented competitors need to be acquired at the right price and integrated into the parent company. You have been looking for such an opportunity for years. The PEG owners want you to invest $100K for 3% of the company and merit annual stock option plan could increase your equity holdings. What could go wrong? You spoke with others in your function from a few of their other portfolio companies. The salary is average and the bonus potential is fair, but the PEG has shown you their financial projections of three estimated EBITDAs. One exhibit shows below targeted EBITDA results, the second exhibit shows targeted EBITDA results. The third exhibit shows exceeding targeted EBITDA results.

The PEG ownership is considering a few other candidates, but you have a solid career folder including key references that have very positive attributes to say about you and the PEG. You have to want the skin in the game concept and you have to be flexible on job location if the deal is attractive. Having your career folder well stocked with your references assures you as a leading candidate, especially if skin in the game employment suits you.

Chapter 9

Networking

If you go to your public library or a national bookstore like Barnes & Noble, there are dozens of books on general networking. These books will help you to build your network referrals including headhunter contacts. However, no books, of which I am aware, focus on networking for SITG C-Level jobs with PEG's portfolio companies. Only evidential SITG C-Level job candidate networkers should apply. Networking for a risk-oriented PEG C-Level job is a narrow focus. There are standard C-Level jobs in the Fortune 1000 companies even though the job market is competitive. Such jobs pay a salary and provide stock options. I did retained searches in that employment sector for twenty years. I met many capable managers, including a number of my search hires, who became victimized by company politics or mergers, divestitures, and downsizings. In come the new regime and their entourage. The executive dominos start coming forth from two levels up. Last in, first out. Welcome to downsizing.

The SITG candidate wants a more exciting risk reward scenario with a PEG portfolio company. He'll need to do some serious networking to meet the right referrals that will lead to PEG interviews and an SITG C-Level job hire. Then he can invest some of his own money in the stock of his new employer as part of his job offer. It's quite different than, say, looking for a retail store department manager's job purely as an employee.

Who Is the Ultimate Target with Whom You Are Seeking to Connect?

The SITG candidate's ultimate networking target: middle market private equity groups. They acquire companies with sales to $150M-$200M. A lot of profits are made by lower middle market PEGs who typically acquire companies up to $100M in sales. PEGs often need and hire qualified and interested SITG C-Level executives who have worked in similar industries. There are different PEG "models" but all are financially driven. A number of PEGs tend to acquire underperforming companies, which often are $200M in sales and under in familiar industries where they have had success. PEGs ideally seek an Investment Rate of Return (IRR) of 25% or more on their investment. Favorite slow growth industries for middle market PEGs are manufacturing, business services, chemicals, consumer products, and retail. PEGs buy companies in which they highly frequent but have a plan to drive rapid growth and profitability.

The PEGs almost always bring in their own CFO after an acquisition and are not afraid to change out the CEO and other C-Level executives, either. By the same token, PE firms have the right to remove underperforming CEOs—and they are quick to assert that right when necessary

I know firsthand because I have handled a number of what Gilreath Consultancy terms "stealth CEO replacement searches". These incumbent CEOs were not recruited by me. This involves using our best efforts to conduct highly confidential searches to replace unwanted incumbent SITG CEOs the PEGs wanted removed from their respective portfolio companies as quickly as possible. Once their replacement CEOs were hired based on our search results, the incumbent CEOs were terminated to their great surprise.

In spite of my "due diligence" screening system for SITG C Suite executives, I have experienced a few CEO terminations. One was within 2 months of his being hired as SITG CEO to run a lower middle market PEG owned private label confectionary products business in MA. This CEO hire had separated from being a CEO of a consumer products company in TX under unknown circumstances. I was unable to check a reference from the Chairman of that company because of a legal Non-Disclosure Agreement (NDA) between my CEO hire and his former boss there. My PEG client agreed to hire this CEO after reviewing the 3 ring binder I assembled on this SITG candidate. Short story, my CEO hire had apparently been caught red handed, continuing to provide consulting to his former clients after he was hired by my PEG client. Meanwhile he had never gone house hunting in the area towns and hadn't booked many industry and client related appointments at a major confectionery trade show. My PEG client decided meeting with this guy did nothing to improve this CEO's productivity or attention to the CEO job duties at hand. He was soon fired and my client PEG refunded the candidate's $100K skin in the game check. Luckily, I was referred to a better qualified CEO candidate, a former CEO who had just left a SITG situation after his PEG's company was sold.

The SITG candidate's networking should ultimately lead him to PEGs owning companies providing familiar products or services and employing similar systems and procedures in related industries and markets where he has been a successful C-Level performer. It would be fortuitous if you happen to get networked to a Limited Partner. Often, a Limited Partner invests in more than one PEG fund simultaneously, so you increase your likelihood of other opportunities.

There are middle-market PEGs seeking to partner with SITG executives interested in acquiring the business they are managing.

The SITG candidate has to network these referrals to increase such opportunities. There are PEGs seeking to partner with an SITG CEO experienced in certain industries to acquire a business that the CEO can help lead and grow. As an example, I know Post Capital Partners in New York City, a private investment firm, that invests in small and lower middle market businesses. They seek companies with solid fundamentals and attractive growth prospects with primarily repeat and recurring revenue models. I have referred a few SITG CEO prospects during the past ten years to what they call their Executive Partnership Program. Through it they do "Executive First" Searches in partnership with talented CEOs to find a company to buy together. Post Capital Partners also pursues Management Buyouts and Growth Capital Investments in partnership with talented CEOs running strong businesses. Mitchell A. Davidson, Managing Director, is my main contact: mdavidson@postcp.com. Tel: (212) 888-5700 Ext 204. Fax: (206) 339-2815.

Networking for M&A Titled Connections Will Lead to PEGs

Target the Mergers and Acquisitions sector professionals. They are specialists involved in various aspects of buying and selling businesses and joining companies into one surviving entity. Below, I list titles and mini-job descriptions of various Merger and Acquisition services. M&A encompasses a wide variety of tax-free and taxable stock transactions from Leveraged Buyouts, asset acquisitions, joint ventures and mergers, and spinoffs. Most M&A professionals are service providers to PEGs. Some have enjoyed long standing mutually rewarding relationships with them. The SITG C-Level job candidate might be introduced to PEGs, depending on the strength of their PEG connections. It also depends on the relationships of your networking referrals to any of these M&A titles.

How Does the SITG C-Level Job Candidate Begin Networking?

Order a few hundred quality business cards (not the cheap looking versions) as soon as possible. You will need them to hand out at every networking opportunity, especially at an Association for Corporate Growth (ACG) regular networking event. Put your name, address, LinkedIn website address, your email address, and cell phone number. On the back of these business cards print in all caps: SEEKING A SKIN IN THE GAME (*YOUR TITLE HERE*) JOB OPPORTUNITY WITH A PRIVATE EQUITY FIRM'S PORTFOLIO COMPANY. Always have a minimum of 10-20 of these business cards with you.

Typical networking advice by "networking experts" suggests that you should begin by networking for SITG job opportunity referrals through what I call your "collegial circle". These contacts include your friends, family members, church members, colleagues, former company bosses, peers, associates, your barber, clothier, gym manager, tailor, and college, and university alumni. C-Level job search networking in general is very hard work. Networking is not a part time endeavor. It requires consistent effort, zeal, strategic and tactical planning, organization, rejection tolerance, fortitude, sound execution, and determination. I call networking to the above "congenial group", the "leaving no stone unturned" approach. If networking this group fails, there are other more promising networking approaches I suggest later in this chapter.

Get Started Networking on LinkedIn

Establishing your networking profile is a lot easier, more productive, and timesaving if you join LinkedIn. Then view the free LinkedIn tutorials to get familiar with the basics.

https://help.linkedin.com/app/answers/detail/a_id/530/~/linkedin-learning-webinars

LinkedIn is a great resource for networking through referred connections to your targeted PEGs listed there. Another option, if necessary, is for you to connect on LinkedIn directly with desired PEG targets. However the most productive way would be through a monthly membership like my Premium-Recruiter Lite account costing $119.95 monthly, cancelable within one month. Joining and using LinkedIn for networking immediately makes networking easier and quicker. Locate the majority of your referrals on LinkedIn and view their bios before you speak with them. Use LinkedIn to track down your references and fellow alumni too. You can research for M&A service providers and PEGs to cold contact or network with through your connections. If you connect with someone on LinkedIn, your mutual LinkedIn connections will automatically appear. They represent additional networking connections.

During your networking activity, your network referred contacts can check out your LinkedIn bio while you're on the phone with them. After you become a LinkedIn member, put the LinkedIn symbol on all your emails under your name. Anyone you email while skin in the game job searching can click on the LinkedIn symbol, and they will land on LinkedIn. Then they can click on your name or photo and be taken to your site.

Reminder: pick up the 3rd edition of *LinkedIn for Dummies* by Joe Elad, MBA for $24.99.

Networking Your Contacts and Their PEG and M&A Referrals

Hopefully you have a time management tool to keep you organized in order to schedule and track phone calls, appointments and follow-ups, and establish time management, to do lists, and set priorities. I use Outlook. Some networkers use Day Timer or Planner Pads. Others use contact management software such as ACT or Goldmine. Whichever you use, be sure to organize and keep track of your networking activity.

Starting with your "congenial group" of contacts, email each of them your resume and the purpose for this networking missive. If you happen to meet up with some of them while doing errands, shopping, bowling, taking your family to the local pizza shop, or to any other social encounter, tell them to expect an email soon about you becoming an active SITG job candidate.

You are executing a networking campaign starting with your "collegial circle" including this person. Hand him a business card and say you look forward to chatting with him after he gets your email and reviews its details.

The SITG Candidate's Intro Networking Email to His "Collegial Circle" Members

Put the email together in your own words after reading my suggestions and examples. Use regular email. Your email should cover:

1. Make your PEG SITG C-Level job networking pitch for referrals. Your networking pitch is that you are seeking to be hired by a PEG to work as a (title sought) for one of their appropriate portfolio companies and put some skin in the game for company equity.
2. Attach your resume marked CONFIDENTIAL- STILL EMPLOYED, if needed.
3. Mention you have a LinkedIn profile.
4. Explain about PEGs. They acquire companies using substantial debt in a leveraged transaction and incorporate an operating plan with rapid growth and profitability.
5. It would be ideal for the CEO candidate to be referred to Level **I** through their networking contacts such as a PEG's General Partner, Managing Partner, Partner, Operating Partner, or a Principal or Limited Partner.
6. Mention the value of Mergers and Acquisition professional referrals connecting you to PEGs.
7. A referral to M&A professionals is a high percentage way to be networked to PEGs. They are "specialist" PEG service providers. Attach my list in your email of Mergers and Acquisitions sector titles and their job summaries for your contact to review for possible networking referrals to you. If you don't have an individual's email, phone him and obtain his email and then follow the previous email instructions. Ask each contact to review your

resume so they are more familiar with your background. Do they have any questions? If so, answer them. Then ask them if they can think of anyone who can give you as a referral from the attached M&A professionals list.

8. Attach a list of ten M&A sector titles and their job summaries from my Master M&A professional titles list below.
9. Each of the following M&A sector titles should know many PEGs. You will definitely meet some or most of these M&A titles (and PEGs) at high powered Association for Corporate Growth networking events.

Jim's Master List of M&A Professionals

Headhunters

Network your contacts for retained search consultant connections that represent middle market PEGs. Hopefully such headhunter referrals are conducting a C-Level search that is a match with your background. The two best things a headhunter can do for you is complete 8-12 professional reference checks on you in writing, provided by you. The next is to get you an interview with a PEG.

Mezzanine Lender

A lender of debt with warrants involving subordinated collateral that is negotiated to return 20%. The Mezzanine Lender is able to convert their debt to equity ownership if their loan is not paid back in time or in full.

Investment Banker

An Investment Banker helps companies raise either debt or equity capital. They prepare the private placement memorandum designed to protect both parties from making a bad investment. An Investment Banker also provides M&A advice for transactions.

Commercial Banker

Commercial bankers are a frequent M&A partner, providing senior debt to fund an acquisition. They would typically have a large number of PEG networking contacts.

Venture Capitalist

A Venture Capitalist (VC) is a risk-oriented investor and provides equity, not debt. A VC might invest equity in a novel technology or a business model in high technology industries, such as biotechnology and IT. The loan recipient typically does not have access to traditional lenders because it is usually a startup with very little hard assets. Unlike PEGs who raise their target investment to fund before acquiring a company, VCs generally take a minority interest in a (technology-related) company and often undergo a series of fund raisings. Many of these companies often run out of funds before their product goals are achieved. I have known of angel investors to provide seed money for a VC company developing a disruptive software marketing idea.

Limited Partner

A Limited Partner has a share of ownership in one or more "partnerships" but takes no part in managing any partnership. A Limited Partner receives a share in profits and losses of the partnership, but is not liable for any amount greater than their original investment in the partnership.

M&A Lawyer

An M&A lawyer advises a company on the legal ramifications of a sale, merger, or acquisition. They typically interface with other attorneys simultaneously on similar transactions. Each lawyer specializes on a wide variety of individual issues from Real Estate (RE), to benefit plans, tax, labor, the Employee Retirement Income Security Act (ERISA), compensation, etc.

M&A Partners of CPA Firms

M&A Partners of CPA Firms offer PEGs and companies a full range of M&A and financial advisory services including accounting, auditing, tax, and strategic input.

M&A Consultants

M&A Consultants frequently under the aegis of investment banking offer PEGs their specialized expertise in matters of valuations, financial opinions, and forensic services and strategy involving divestitures, acquisitions, sales, and mergers.

M&A Turnaround Specialists

M&A Turnaround Specialists are hired by a company's board, its bank, or creditors to devise emergency initiatives and execute plans to hopefully help put the company back on its feet. These services might even involve preparing the company for sale or liquidation.

The Turnaround Management Association (TMA)

The Turnaround Management Association (http://www.turnaround.org/About/Facts.aspx) is a global non-profit comprised of turnaround and corporate renewal professionals in forty-nine chapters in the United States. It is recommended that you attend one of the local TMA breakfasts, luncheons or cocktail events near you for the opportunity to mingle and network for PEG or M&A referrals and connections. Exchange business cards, but don't hand out your resume. It's considered "tacky". This is a great opportunity for practicing giving your elevator pitch.

Ask each referral source to introduce the SITG candidate to their Level **I** and Level **II** referral by mutual email showing a CC to the candidate's email listed. See example by Pete below.

If your contact, Pete, has a referral for you, ask for his referral's phone number and email address. What's the next step? Pete could email his referral your resume introducing your name and stating his relationship with you. He would CC your email address in this introductory email. For example:

"Hi Joe, meet Howie Jones. Howie, meet my friend, lawyer Joe Berg. Attached is Howie's resume. He was my former college roommate, golfing buddy and best man at my wedding. Howie is seeking a skin in the game CEO job opportunity with a middle market private equity group. Joe, I remembered that you have done M&A legal work for years in that sector. I'll leave it to Howie to follow up with you for a brief chat. Thanks, Joe."

Whenever the networking candidate is given a referral's name, he should learn whether it is a Level **I** or Level **II** contact from the referral's source. Level **I** (PEG) referrals must receive your highest follow-up priority. The SITG candidate should ask for the name of the individual's PEG or employer and his email address. It's important to learn the source's relationship to the referral and the referral's office location. Once the networking candidate is given this information, he should quickly do research on each referral. Print out their LinkedIn profile and make notes on the back. A SITG candidate should avoid prematurely speaking with any referral. First he should conduct basic LinkedIn research on the referred individual and his PEG or M&A employer. Using Google as a backup, if necessary, would be productive. Check for ACG Membership.

The candidate should use his LinkedIn membership to locate and research profiles of any individual referrals and their PEGs or M&A service providers, or other employers. While researching the profiles of any individuals on LinkedIn, review any potential recommendations to those individuals by professionals at PEGs or from M&A service providers. The candidate might convert such advocates to networking contacts in follow-up conversations with the individual referrals connected with them. I will be surprised if LinkedIn lacks information on your targets. As a research backup, the candidate can Google any referred PEG websites by name.

The same goes for M&A referrals and their company's websites. Once there, click on "Team" for bios on a specific Partner or staff member referral. Staying on the PEG's website, the candidate should click on the PEG's portfolio and review their current and former holdings. Hopefully this PEG's industry preference will be a good fit with the candidate's background.

Now, returning to our example of Pete introducing Howie by mutually addressed email to his Level **II** referral attorney friend, Joe. Beforehand, Howie should have learned about Pete's relationship with Joe, gotten Joe's last name, his company's name and location, his phone number, and his email address. Howie should have done some research on Joe's individual LinkedIn profile. He should also have located Joe's law firm's LinkedIn profile. Again, if LinkedIn didn't have adequate information on Joe or his law firm, Howie should use Google as a research backup. Check if Joe is an ACG Member.

If the SITG C-Level candidate doesn't receive an email or a call from Joe by the next day, he should call Joe for a brief chat. Joe's secretary could be helpful on that call. If Joe's got a busy schedule that day or is out of town, the candidate should leave a low key voicemail. Request the chance for a brief chat once Joe's back in his office. If the call would be long distance for Joe, your voicemail could ask Joe to email you the best time for you to connect with him by phone. Leave your email address just in case.

Set of Procedures Candidates Should Follow when Given a Level I or Level II Referral while Networking

The SITG candidate should complete the following steps before verbally connecting with any referral from his networking activity:

- Know whether this new contact is a Level **I** or Level **II** referral. Unexpected examples of a Level **I** referral include an SITG candidate's restaurant manager acquaintance who knows a PEG Partner as a regular customer. The Partner often brings PEG Limited Partners and other guests to the restaurant. Some Level **I** and Level **II** referrals do not work in the M&A sector but they have jobs that bring them into frequent contact with PEGs or M&A professionals. For example, I recently met an M&A lawyer at a Lexus Dealership while talking over coffee in the customer's waiting area.
- Be sure your referral source mentions you are actively networking for a SITG C-Level job with a middle market PEG.
- Learn the source's relationship to the referral and the referral's PEG or M&A firm name, office location, email address, and phone number.
- Quickly do research on each referral. Level **I** (PEG) referrals should be the highest priority. Conduct LinkedIn research on the referred individual and his PEG or M&A employer. Use Google as a productive backup, if necessary. If this PEG referral is an ACG Member, make a note of it.
- The networking SITG candidate should ask each referral source to introduce him to the Level **I**/Level **II** referral

by mutual email showing a CC to the candidate's email listed. See above example by Pete.

- If a referral source doesn't want to introduce the Level **II** candidate to the referral by mutual email, get the referral's full name, company name and location, email address, and phone number. The candidate should ask this referral's source if he can use his name when he contacts this individual. In any event, learn the source's relationship to this referral and conduct your research on his background. The candidate should check for any mutual commonalities with this individual and also note whether he is an ACG Member. Now you can email this person your networking introduction. Explain the source of his name and purpose of you contacting him. Always include your resume and list of M&A titles in your email. Ask for the best time and date for you to have a brief chat. In the upcoming ACG segment, I explain to check with all M&A referrals about their potential ACG involvement and how you should network with them for their ACG contacts.
- After the SITG candidate connects with a referral from his networking effort, he should email a thank you to the source of each of his referrals. Do not drag the latter into any contact difficulties you might be having with their referral(s). Your segue is that you've been introduced by email along with the resume attachment to your networked referral. You asked him for a referral, and he gave you one. Now, you're on your own!

Making Your Initial Contact with a Level I Networked PEG Referral After He Received an Introduction Email from Your Mutual Connection Who CC'd You

Allow the Level **I** PEG referral twenty-four hours to review the introductory email and your attached resume. Presumably you have done your LinkedIn or Google research on the PEG contact, and checked out the PEG's website and their middle market portfolio companies. If your background fits well with this PEG's industries' focus, you should try to meet up with him. The SITG candidate can be a good fit with certain PEG's portfolio companies. Your background is not only a match with their industry preferences, but with certain products, customers, markets, OEM lean manufacturing needs, IT system needs, and logistics efficiencies. All of these synergies warrant you trying to meet the PEG and see where it leads.

Twenty-four hours after your referral source's email to his Level **I** contact, you can email this PEG referral. Use his regular email, not his LinkedIn email, unless that's all that is available. I find PEG Partners do not always check their LinkedIn email as frequently. Let him know you appreciate your mutual contact's email introduction. Focus his attention on your resume's listed experiences in industries similar to his PEG's holdings and other synergies in your background. Remind this PEG referral that you are seeking a skin in the game C-Level opportunity. If you can invest up to $100K, mention it; otherwise skip mentioning an amount.

You could end your email by requesting a time for both of you to chat, and leave your cell phone number under your sign off.

Then wait for his return email. Otherwise, make a follow-up call in a day or two. Early morning calls are ideal.

If you call and need to leave a voicemail, say you appreciate your mutual contact's email introduction. Then gently press for an early morning meeting next week, if possible. How about 7a.m. at a nearby coffee shop to his office for thirty minutes? Leave your cell phone number and end the call.

This PEG referral might call back or email you that there is no current need for someone of your current title and background within their holdings, but he will keep you in mind. You could mention on the return email that you would appreciate an early morning thirty-minute meeting over coffee (or alternatively a late afternoon meeting). If his PEG office is fairly local, there's no travel or time issue, but if the PEG referral is holding fast and doesn't agree to meet you, ask him if he can think of another PEG peer with whom you might network.

If the PEG Partner gives you a name, his referral's PEG and his contact information, thank him and ask if you can mention the PEG Partner referred you. Next, ask if he is active in the local ACG chapter. If yes, is he planning to attend the upcoming ACG C-Series breakfast? If yes, you will be on the lookout there to shake his hand and say hello. If he is an ACG Member, does he know the chapter President or any of the chapter officers or board members to whom he could refer you? Again, if he gives you names, thank him and ask him if you can mention he referred you. At the end of this conversation, thank this PEG referral for his time, interest, and helpfulness. "Please keep me in mind if a skin in the game C-Level opportunity develops for which I could interview."

Email the source of this PEG referral as soon as possible, mention how you benefitted, and express your thanks. Get in the habit of always thanking sources of your referrals and the referrals themselves. Even if you get a referral from your referral, always email them your thanks.

To the reader, my suggestions on how you deal with Level I PEG referrals might seem assertive or overly tenacious. If a PEG Partner is with an operator firm they negotiate deals for a living. Operator PEGs want to be involved in running their acquired portfolio company, whereas the Supervisor PEG's modus operandi is to trust the acquired company's management team. Their deal PR sheets typically mention the acquired company's solid management team as one of the attractions of acquiring the company.

The operator PEGs are typically ready to close acquisition deals; if they fit their "sweet spot"... they make their pitch. Let the chips fall where they may. C-Level executives can't foresee how many PEGs will have as many synergies with the SITG candidate's background as this one. If I asked an SITG candidate's PEG referral what he thought of my advice based on my experience, he would be impressed. At the least, he would keep the SITG candidate in mind for upcoming opportunities.

Based on the SITG C-Level candidate's resume emailed to the PEG referral, and the candidate's phone chat with the PEG referral, he agrees to meet the candidate at the Provence Café this Friday at 7a.m. for coffee.

Meeting a Level I PEG Referral From Your Mutual Connection After You Followed Up His Intro Email and Your Resume

This example is the SITG candidate's networking meeting with a PEG Partner referral at the Provence Café for coffee. You have been connected to this PEG referral by someone with whom you've networked that he respects. That's a good start to a face-to-face networking meeting.

A thirty-minute networking coffee with a PEG Partner will fly by. At this point it's not a job interview, but the SITG candidate should treat it as one. I have observed that most PEG Managing Partners play their cards inside their vest. Occasionally, they have decided to replace a C-Level executive from one of their portfolio companies on a downward EBITDA trend. It's not yet an active search with their preferred headhunters. If they hear about a promising potential C-Level executive hire through their network, they will take action. It's happened to me occasionally. Instead of the search, I am often asked to check such a C-Level individual's references (for a fee).

I have found that PEGs will often refer C-Level candidates they have met and by whom they have been impressed. The same goes for highly recommended C-Level executives recommended to them by respected PEG peers. PEG Partners have established relationships with other PEGs with whom they have made successful deals. They often recommend highly regarded C-Level referrals to their preferred headhunter(s).

Many are ACG Members and socialize with their peers at various ACG dealmaker events including networking breakfasts, luncheons, and cocktail socials. They also solicit trusted colleagues about confidential C-Level hiring needs. This is the confidential hidden PEG job network. Why pay a headhunter a $90K search fee in a job market perceived to be overloaded with qualified candidates in many older, slow growth industries? Lower middle market PEGs are not all equal regarding SITG. Some will only consider qualified SITG C-Level candidates for their vacancies. With others SITG is optional, and still others only offer a stock option plan.

Bring your brief case to your coffee meeting with the PEG Partner. That will hold your duplicate set of key exhibit items you want to hopefully show the PEG Partner, or leave with him at the meeting's end. Check out chapter 8 for a list of potential exhibit item options from which to select key items. Be selective. Choose a limited number of exhibit items for best impact relevant to the PEG's business. Consider your background's match with various product classes, markets, and industries the PEG Partner's portfolio companies are in. You are waiting for an appropriate moment and subject matter discussion to use a solid relevant exhibit piece preferably of metrics, numbers, and EBITDA results relevant to your experience and results achieved.

At any thirty-minute coffee with a PEG Partner, follow the PEG Partner's lead by answering any questions he may have about your resume. Ask him if his PEG is currently in an acquisition mode. Ask about the current business climate. Look for an opportunity to state why you are seeking a skin in the game opportunity. Explain why you are interested in his PEG, based on your research and background match. The PEG Partner may reiterate that they have no need for your C-Level background at present.

Even though this PEG has no full-time vacancy matching your qualifications now, mention any of the following you agree with, as a means of joining their PEG:

- You are willing to relocate.
- You would consider an interim C-Level position with one of their portfolio companies.
- You are open to handling a consulting project for the PEG until a full time SITG C-Level opportunity unfolds.

This will help keep you in mind and gives the PEG Partner options for which to consider you.

You might show the PEG Partner an Excel spreadsheet exhibit item relative to the conversation subject matter being discussed, or you might not show any during your networking meeting as time flew by. What is the best reference letter you can show this PEG Partner (if any)? Has any name popped up during this meeting of a mutually known executive who might coincidentally be a good reference of yours? If yes, be sure to mention this individual, even if you don't have a reference letter from him yet.

In any event, at the end of your networking coffee meeting, say something like, "Mr. Hynes (PEG Partner), I know our mutual contact, Joe Allen, who sent you my resume, has known me for thirty years, and endorsed my character. However, he and I never worked together. So, I collected several exhibit items related to my career in a folder to leave with you. They include some reference letters from a few of my former bosses. These other confidential items support statements in my resume. Hopefully you will keep me in mind for a future SITG job opportunity." If you are invited to meet with this PEG partner again and others at the PEG's offices, expect to be asked to sign an NDA(Non-Disclosure Agreement). You won't learn anything of a confidential nature unless you have signed the PEG portfolio company's NDA. Show it to your lawyer if you have concerns.

Meanwhile, ask him if there is anyone he can think of with whom you might network towards a possible SITG job opportunity? Ask him if he is active in the local Association for Corporate Growth chapter. If yes, what does he like about it? Express your interest in ACG. Does he know the chapter President, chapter officers or board members you might connect with? If he gives you a referral and contact information, thank him. Then ask if you can use his name in making contact with this referral.

If you have your preparation routine down cold, you will experience more productive networking meetings with referred M&A professionals, and PEG Partners. When you speak, look into the person's eyes. What most impressive "metrics" exhibit or two might you pull out of your briefcase to reinforce your accomplishments related to this PEG's businesses? You have done your research on this PEG's holdings and this PEG Partner's background. That will help you present influential exhibits related to his PEG's industry preferences matching your valued background. Practice for your highlight exhibit moment when you will be asked, "Describe your greatest business related accomplishment?" It's "show and tell" time. If you have a written reference from your former boss or someone in authority at the time of your greatest accomplishment, pull that out of your briefcase as well. If the PEG says he will keep you in mind for an appropriate C-Level job opening in their portfolio companies, that's the signal for pulling out your "due diligence" pocket folder for him to take with him. It will be good to have if he wants to show your file to another partner. Get into the habit of marking your sensitive documents CONFIDENTIAL. It sets the tone for trustworthiness.

You may have your iPad with you and can quickly flick to an exhibit item relative to the discussion you are having or the question the PEG is asking. In that case you can tell your referred PEG Partner that you will email him links to the exhibits you've shown on your iPad. Consequently, it would exclude you needing a pocket folder and copying select career exhibits to give this PEG Partner. However, if this PEG Partner wanted to refer you to a PEG colleague or PEG peer of his, the pocket folder is compact "due diligence" on you and your career. It's a handy "show and tell" and may lead to another PEG referral and SITG job opportunity.

Making Initial Contact with a Level II Referral

This **Level II** contact would be a referred M&A professional. After you have been referred, make a habit of implementing the following routine:

- Learn from your networking source of his relationship with this referral. If you were given the referral's cell phone number, that's a positive indication. Maybe you can also tell of their relationship from the email in which you were CC'd from your source to this referral. For me, the closer their relationship, the more assertive you can be with your follow up with this referral in terms of soliciting PEG contacts.
- Before you follow up, check out this referral's name and company affiliation on LinkedIn or Google. It is more efficient if you print out his profile on one page. You may be more comfortable showing a show and tell

document from your iPad, iPhone or laptop to a PEG hiring authority. I prefer paper in such situations.

- What did you learn from your research on this M&A sector referral and his current and former employers? Do you know anyone who recommended him on his LinkedIn profile page? Are there any mutual connections listed on his LinkedIn profile?
- At this point, you might decide to follow up this referral with a phone call. If you connect with this individual, introduce yourself and your mutual contact who referred you. "As you may know, I am seeking to be ultimately hired by a PEG to work as a (title sought) for one of their appropriate portfolio companies and put some skin in the game for company equity. Do you have any questions about my credentials, background and experience listed in my resume?" Answer his questions. If you have any other mutual connections to this referral that might reinforce your competencies, by all means, bring them up now. Does he know any PEG Partners? Yes, but most of his M&A consulting firm's relationships are between his boss, the CEO, and the General Partners or Managing Partners of the PEGs. Is he an ACG member? You are looking into possibly joining ACG. Does he know the chapter President, officers or board members? If yes, how about meeting for quick coffee some morning or late afternoon?
- From your prior research on this referral, his employer, his office location, his possible ACG connection and from this discussion you should be evaluating whether to try to meet him. In this case he could be a promising source of valuable referrals. Try to meet with him for coffee near his office. He says he's out of town for a week.

- Can he think of a PEG Partner to whom he might refer you?
- Can you arrange to meet at the upcoming monthly ACG breakfast in ten days?
- Ask if there is anyone else in the M&A community that comes to mind whom you might network with.
- Put the ACG breakfast on your schedule after making a reservation. Register right away before the breakfast is sold out.
- Make notes of the summary results of this networking referral follow-up conversation in a file.

Meeting with Referred Level II M&A Professionals for Coffee, Lunch, or Cocktails

There are "networking experts" who advise networkers to meet with any of their contacts and fill up their social calendar. I feel the SITG networking candidate should be selective about meeting almost all their connections face-to-face while networking. Most of my own "collegial circle" of contacts haven't got a clue about what skin in the game hiring is all about. If you ask some, they'll say, "Jim's a headhunter!" You are better off cold networking with PEGs on LinkedIn or from Dealmaker Portal's website.

At this stage, hopefully you have emailed each member of your "collegial circle" your intent to pursue a SITG job with a middle market PEG. You have explained your ultimate targets PEGs key titles and job definitions there. You have given your "collegial circle" a list of ten examples of target Level II M&A professionals, and their job descriptions. Lastly you have emailed them your resume.

You will meet some of these contacts in your normal activities at work, at local retail establishments, health care facilities, church-related events and at social events, at restaurants, bowling, golfing, at the beach, etc. All will thank you for emailing them your resume and details of your SITG job search and asking for their help in your networking campaign. They also received the titles and job descriptions of your Level **I** and Level **II** networking targets in your email. Bottom line: can they provide any worthwhile contacts from their own networks? Don't be surprised if your collegial network starts referring you to registered stock brokers, investment planners, and advisors. That's what many collegial networks think when you mention investing in company stock.

As you run into individuals from your "collegial circle" while you are mutually out and about town doing normal activities, whoever says they can't think of anyone, hand them your business card with thanks. Ask them to keep you in mind and contact you as soon as they have a referral. At that time you will learn their relationship to the referral and get some other details. Others you encounter will say they don't know any contacts in M&A and PEGs. Hand them your business card with thanks.

Still other contacts from your emailing will phone you with, say, a well-connected M&A referral, or the President of the local ACG chapter. Try to meet them for coffee or lunch to discuss their referrals. If you receive enough good networking referrals, you will be busy following up CC'd emails mutually introducing you to each. Then comes rapidly researching these referrals and their PEG's business or M&A employers. I advised you use LinkedIn primarily for doing your research. Hopefully you have joined by now. Always conduct research before you email, phone, or meet with networked referrals.

Optimistically, your coffees and luncheon meetings with networked referrals should lead to PEG meetings or job interviews. In addition your follow on referrals from your initial meeting should also increase. Then subsequent coffees and luncheon dates with referrals from your initial referrals should keep you productively occupied. Remember to thank all who have given you referrals.

Getting Involved with the Association for Corporate Growth

Now comes the time for the SITG job candidate to expand his networking effort, big time. While he is networking his "collegial circle" and following up their worthwhile referrals, he is soliciting promising referrals from referrals. Simultaneously the SITG job candidate should become involved with the Association for Corporate Growth.

One powerhouse organization to definitely encounter PEGs and Mergers and Acquisitions professionals is at the Association for Corporate Growth events. You should check out the websites of the national chapter in Chicago, IL, and the website of your nearest local ACG chapter. After you become acquainted with ACG, try to connect with ACG members within your networking contacts. Then plan on joining your ACG connections at the next fabulous ACG monthly C-Series breakfast hosted by your local ACG chapter. Each breakfast features a noteworthy speaker of interest to the middle market growth focused community. It is just one of the many super high powered networking events for PEGs and M&A professionals seeking deals, cutting edge information, and contacts.

The Association for Corporate Growth (www.acg.org) is based in Chicago, dedicated to sound corporate growth. Founded in 1954, ACG is a global organization with fifty-six chapters and over 14,000 members. Doing business is at the heart of the ACG membership experience. Chapters in the U.S., Canada, Europe, and Asia bring dealmakers together to help them achieve their business and professional goals.

ACG is a trusted and respected resource for middle-market dealmakers and business leaders who invest in companies. ACG provides members with powerful business-building resources including, face-to-face events, online tools, structured networking opportunities, exclusive member benefits, and leading-edge market intelligence.

75% of ACG members report that they have done business with fellow members including my wife and business partner, Diane. We were active ACG Members for over ten years and learned a lot about M&A through attending ACG sponsored presentations. Gilreath Consultancy was a Bronze Sponsor of both the 2008 and 2009 Annual Growth Conferences. We have met many leading middle market dealmakers at various ACG events and we have made many lasting M&A related friends and acquaintances as ACG Members. In fact, most of Gilreath Consultancy's PEG clients are ACG members. Our annual *Search Beacon* newsletters have featured a number of ACG members among our diverse list of M&A professional contributors. In September, 2007, I had the honor of addressing the ACG Buyer's Roundtable of the Boston ACG chapter, discussing skin in the game job searching.

The SITG job candidate should use LinkedIn to connect with local ACG members within his networking contacts and referrals. I did a LinkedIn advanced search of my contacts for Greater Boston ACG members and turned up 137 connections. A LinkedIn advanced national search count of all ACG members in the US totaled 1,365,726. All ACG sponsored networking events are "platinum" productions in terms of their organization, sponsorships, educational topics, and expert presenters. In addition, menus, food, libation, and servers are always "five star". ACG breakfasts/lunches and all events are also held in first class locations. These are high powered networking experiences, unlike any other association events I have ever attended.

The ACG annual membership fees vary by chapters and run between $425 for Boston, $550 for Connecticut, $595 for San Diego.

If the SITG C-Level job seeker's networking efforts haven't produced a local ACG chapter contact as yet, he should still check out the closest ACG chapter to him. Then try to attend their C-Series monthly breakfast as a non-member by going to its registration site and signing up. These ACG C-Suite monthly breakfasts officially run from 7a.m. to 9a.m. EST/EDT but informally run longer. They typically sell out quickly.

The SITG C-Level candidate may not be a great networker personality, but it helps if he attends an ACG networking event with an ACG chapter member, officer, or has a local ACG chapter board member introducing him to fellow attendees. With that in mind, he should Google for the local ACG chapter board member titles and their contact information.

Then the SITG job candidate should email/phone the board Chairman, then chapter President and other board members until he connects with a board member that will meet him at the next ACG chapter C-Series breakfast meeting. He can explain he is interested in possibly joining this local ACG chapter and is networking for a SITG C-Level job opportunity with a PEG. He has heard that the C-Series breakfast is a terrific networking event and registered for the upcoming one. Can he meet this board member there, introduce himself and learn more about this ACG chapter? A PEG SITG C-Level job candidate should qualify for ACG chapter membership as a future investor in his employer's equity, (if and when he decides to join ACG). Naturally it would be better to meet up with your own ACG member contacts and their networking referrals and introductions. However, this is a good exercise for the SITG job candidate overcoming not knowing any ACG local chapter members yet.

Each ACG breakfast features a guest speaker, frequently an expert on a topic of interest to association members. The tables are set for ten attendees each. Be sure to offer and receive business cards from everyone at your table; they will generally be doing the same. My best advice at the monthly ACG breakfast is to arrive early with 100+ of your business cards and no resume. Try to exchange them all with fellow participants. Don't sit at a table too prematurely. All around the room are hundreds of businessmen and women exchanging cards and handshakes, many discussing LBOs or M&A opportunities, or potential deals.

Mingle, go with the flow, shake hands, introduce yourself by name, and mention it's your first ACG breakfast. You are seeking a skin in the game opportunity to help grow a portfolio company profitably in your sweet spot which is OEM engineered products manufacturing, or whatever. That short explanation is about all the time you may have to give your "reason for being there elevator pitch". Always offer your business card and try to get one in return. That's almost as important as your pitch. Typically, job hunters aren't greeted with open arms by attendees but you are looking to invest up to $100K in the equity of your next PEG owned portfolio company when hired.

Reminder: have your email address, your cell phone, and home phone numbers printed on the front of the business card. On the back of each of your business cards print the following words: seeking a skin in the game (job title here) opportunity.

Do not bring any resumes with you.

The coffee urns section at each ACG breakfast is where members put on their name tags. It's good to position yourself in that vicinity. That way you can address the member by their name tag and exchange cards with each. Make your "elevator pitch". Be on the lookout for name tags with ribbons designating a local ACG chapter officer who is circulating. Introduce yourself to him and deliver your "elevator pitch".

An icebreaker question the SITG job candidate can always ask as he mingles into an animated group of participants is, "How do you like ACG networking events? I am thinking of becoming an ACG member."

These monthly ACG breakfasts always have a number of PEGs in attendance. They tend to mill around with each other. Observe their name tags, join in their circle and exchange business cards. They and other ACG member attendees did not attend this breakfast to meet C-Level job seekers, per se. The sooner you can get the words out that you are "seeking a skin in the game job opportunity" to invest some of your own money in your new employer, the more likely a PEG will exchange business cards with you.

The monthly C-Series breakfasts are just one of many super high powered networking events for M&A and PEG professionals and business owners. As an ACG member for many years, I can vouch that ACG sponsored events are constantly well attended and world class in all aspects. Everybody who is anybody in the M&A middle market sector attends ACG networking events. Especially those seeking to close deals, expand knowledge, and develop contacts active in middle market growth. Become involved with ACG as soon as possible and step up your networking efforts there. For most SITG job seekers, ACG could be the difference maker to attaining their ultimate hiring objective. ACG sponsored events are the Emerald City of M&A networking!

Following Up the First ACG C-Series Monthly Breakfast With a PEG Partner With Whom You Exchanged Business Cards

If you have a mutually productive discussion at the ACG breakfast with a fellow attendee, be sure you have exchanged business cards. Ask them if they'd care to set up a meeting in a day or two for coffee at a place of their choosing. They may request you email them your resume and they'll get back to you. Research them and their firm on LinkedIn or Google as soon as possible in advance of meeting with them. Once again, check out those who have given them recommendations, as well as taking note of their connections for possible mutual contacts.

Once back at his home office, the SITG job candidate should sift through the business cards he's received at the ACG breakfast. He should prioritize following up every one and especially keep a separate pile of the PEG's business cards. Follow up the PEG highest titled Partners' business cards first. Start researching one PEG Partner at a time using LinkedIn. Print out each Partner's LinkedIn profile sheets. Magic marker highlights of interest to you, including names and backgrounds of people who recommend this PEG Partner, and listed connections for any mutual contacts or affiliations. These magic marker highlights can be referred to in your follow-up email to this PEG Partner. Summarize your highlights and staple it to his LinkedIn profile copy.

Next Google this partner's PEG. Check out their listed current and former portfolio company holdings and what type and investment size of acquisitions they focus on. How do your background, qualifications, and interests fit with this PEG's holdings and interests? Even if it is not a match, following up with this PEG Partner may yield a worthwhile PEG referral for your efforts. Remember, your target PEG is in the middle market or lower middle market, where ACG members reside. Large market PEG deals in the billions will not be interested in your up to $100K investment for any stock in their multi-billion dollar acquisitions. Have your PEG Partner research information in front of you, as reference material, when you email him and speak with him on the phone.

Once the SITG job candidate has completed his research on the PEG Partner and PEG, he should email him with a copy of his resume. If you are a match with this Partner's PEG, consider the following:

"It was a pleasure making your acquaintance at the C-Series ACG breakfast. I appreciate receiving such a welcoming greeting and your business card, as I am a first time participant at an ACG event." (If your research on this Partner or his PEG showed areas of mutual connection, mention those you feel might enhance your mutual relationship a little.)

"As I mentioned, I am seeking a skin in the game C-Level job opportunity with the right PEG. I am impressed with your LinkedIn profile and your PEG. Based on my research your PEG has acquired some companies whose industries, (industries, markets, product classifications, or customers) match my qualifications and experience. Attached is my resume and a reference letter from Joe Moore, an investor and board member of Vesuvius Metals, my last employer. The company has just been merged with Reynolds Metals and my position was redundant. In my resume, you'll note my overall background and experiences fit with a number of your acquired companies. I am hoping we can meet some morning soon for a coffee at a shop near your office for a brief chat. I will call your office tomorrow to follow up this email and I look forward to meeting you for coffee soon".

If he declines your coffee by email, but says he will keep you in mind, mention (if it applies) that you would relocate, consider an interim C-Level position with one of their portfolio companies, or that you are open to handling a consulting project for the PEG until a full time SITG C-Level opportunity unfolds. Lastly if there is no positive reaction to your coffee meeting request or additional employment options you will consider, email him asking if he can think of anyone he might refer you to. If he emails you a name and their contact information, ask if you may use his name as a referral. Finish by asking that he keep you in mind if a SITG C-Level opportunity develops. Thank him either way.

If you are not a match for this PEG, consider the following:

"It was a pleasure making your acquaintance at the C-Series ACG breakfast. I appreciate receiving such a welcoming greeting and your business card, as I am a first time participant at an ACG event. As I mentioned, I am seeking a skin in the game C-Level job opportunity with the right PEG. I am impressed with your LinkedIn profile. I did a little research on your PEG, Wellington, Frost LLC and noted your recent successful health care related software acquisitions. I realize that my C-Level background in the design and manufacture of artificial joints, limbs and stents is not a fit with your target acquisitions. Hopefully you don't mind that I attached my current resume in the event you think of the name of a PEG colleague or M&A professional I might network with. I will consider an interim C-Level assignment with a PEG whose holdings are more in line with my background and experience. I appreciate your time and interest. Thank you. Best wishes."

Following Up the First ACG C-Series Monthly Breakfast With M&A Professionals With Whom You Exchanged Business Cards

Mergers and Acquisitions cover a wide variety of professional niches. Many M&A professionals will list tombstones of deals they helped consummate on their websites. In researching those who exchanged business cards with you, look for those M&A websites that list some of the PEGs these M&A specialists have had as clients. Prioritize the business cards of M&A professionals in terms of following up first with anyone whom you seemed to enjoy a good rapport. Maybe someone who has mutual contacts with you who seemed interested in a follow-up get together.

Research the LinkedIn profiles of each M&A professional who gave you their business card. Look for any of their background information that connects with your own. Note in their LinkedIn profiles the names and affiliations of those who recommended each individual you are researching. Pay attention to listed connections at the bottom of their LinkedIn profile.

I suggest you photocopy the LinkedIn profile of M&A specialists and mark with a highlighter areas of his background that connect with your own, and note the identities of people who give him recommendations. Then Google each company of the M&A professionals you exchanged business cards with. Keep this information together with any notes for future follow-up.

Research their PEG clients for PEGs whose preferred types of acquisitions and their current and former portfolio companies match areas of your own background. Look for similar industries, technologies, markets, customers, and product classifications. You should end up with a research file on each M&A professional. This includes copies of their LinkedIn profile, excerpts from their company website, and information about any of their PEG clients with any portfolio companies that are a fit with your own qualifications and experience.

Email each M&A professional that it was a pleasure to make their acquaintance and exchange business cards. Mention it was your first ACG C-Series breakfast and you are seriously considering becoming an ACG member. Explain your SITG job search mission and that you have taken the liberty of attaching your resume for them to learn more about your background.

For those M&A specialists who list PEG clients (based on your research) with holdings that fit your qualifications on their website, mention you would appreciate the chance to grab an early morning coffee at a coffee shop near their office early next week. If you don't hear back in a few days, phone them to nail down the coffee meeting (if you become coffee'd out, rotate decaf tea, apple juice, and chocolate milk to also avoid a diuretic effect). Plan to bring your "show and tell" folder with your resume and a select few key items to help reinforce you being given a PEG referral by your new well connected contact. I don't normally suggest you leave any of your "show and tell" items with an M&A professional, unless he wants to show one of your documents to one of his PEG clients.

It's okay to ask if he'd like a copy of your resume to present to one of his PEG clients. If he agrees to refer you to a PEG Partner, ask him for the referral's full name, employer and location, as well as details of his relationship with the referral. Get their office phone, cell phone (if possible) and email address. Then ask if he would email this referral introducing you with a CC to you, suggesting you follow up with this referral. If not, you will follow up with this potentially valuable PEG referral on your own using my example of how to do so earlier in this chapter.

Following Up the First ACG C-Series Monthly Breakfast With Businessmen With Whom You Exchanged Business Cards

Review the business cards you have collected, minus those of the PEG Partners. For those you exchanged with businessmen, not in the M&A sector, you can do a quick LinkedIn check of each businessman's profile there. Check out their employers as well, either on LinkedIn or using Google. I suggest photocopying each person's profile and research information, and using a highlighter to call attention to mutual background connections. Keep your copies and notes together in a file for future reference. Some may have attended the ACG breakfast because they are seeking to meet PEG Partners, investment bankers, or other M&A specialists. Any of these businessmen may be looking to sell or merge their company or make an acquisition if they are either owners or senior executives of the business.

With that in mind, email each businessman your thanks for meeting and the opportunity to make their acquaintance and exchange business cards. If your research on this man or his company showed areas of mutual connection, mention any you feel might enhance your mutual relationship a little. Then explain your SITG job search mission and that you have taken the liberty of attaching your resume in this email so that he might learn more about your background. Ask him if he can think of anyone it might be worthwhile for you to network with. If so, would he email that person's contact information and his relationship to this referral? If not, then thank him for keeping you in mind if he becomes aware of a good possible referral for you. Thank him for his time and interest.

Monitor Major ACG Networking Events in the United States by Other US ACG Chapters

Each ACG chapter hosts a number of ACG events by invitation only, as well as sponsored networking social gatherings for which you pay a charge and register. If you are traveling to other states and can time your trip to a major ACG networking event in that state, register for serious out of town SITG C-Level job networking.

Below is a partial excerpt from ACG's INTERGROWTH 2015, Orlando, Florida registration site.

Example: A WHO'S WHO OF GLOBAL MIDDLE-MARKET M&A. *There's no better place to grow your network and business. Don't miss out on this perfect collection of top deal making professionals from all levels and sectors of the industry. The InterGrowth schedule is designed to drive connections from the beginning of the conference until the end with a variety of events, including networking breakfasts, keynote lunches, breakouts and executive roundtable discussions. Plus there are plenty of informal meeting opportunities throughout.*

Make ACG a main resource for networking for SITG C-Level job opportunities. ACG brings together every segment of the business growth community. Check the ACG.org headquarters website in Chicago, IL to see details of the latest major three-day networking event hosted by one of the ACG chapters.

If you are traveling to a major city in the US, Google ACG chapter in a specific city for any three-day networking events. If you attend one, you will meet a cross section of middle market

M&A professionals including PEG Partners. You might even end up playing golf in a foursome with a PEG Partner. My advice is for you to become involved with ACG as soon as possible. It will bring you closer to your SITG C-Level job and the PEG Partner who could make it happen.

Reconnect With Your College/University Alumni for Networking Events and Opportunities

Believe it or not, in this competitive economy and job market, C-Level job applicants including skin in the game job seekers are successfully reconnecting with their college and university alumni. They are contacting the President of the Alumni/ Alumnae Association and securing a list of names, especially of their MBA graduating class members and getting back in touch through email and phone. One of the most respected colleges for entrepreneurial MBA graduates is Babson College, Wellesley, MA (www.**babson**.edu) and their organized MBA alumni activities, programs and resources are truly world class. I know because I post all my C-Level SITG searches on the Babson MBA Alumni job board. Also, I have placed a few highly qualified Babson alumni in successful skin in the game CEO positions during my forty plus year career.

I have also had success posting CEO searches on *my Tuck's* alumni portal. Dartmouth Tuck has a powerful source for Tuck alumni of prominent PEG contacts on the Advisory Board of their Center for Private Equity and Entrepreneurship (cpee.tuck. dartmouth.edu/alumni).

Coast to coast there are numerous quality colleges and universities that are world renowned, especially their cutting edge

MBA curriculum. Particularly if you earned an MBA, get back in touch with your alma mater. Some have specialty groups organized by major interests such as M&A. There might be former MBA classmates of yours in a position to help your SITG C-Level job search. I suggest you explore your alma mater's website and the alumni center and get back in touch. Do it now while it's fresh in your mind.

Searching for SITG Headhunter Options

A middle market PEG with a C-Level executive vacancy at one of their portfolio companies will sign an exclusive search agreement with a retained search firm. They would like candidates from their industry or related industries, typically willing to put skin in the game. For those SITG job hunters looking to connect with headhunters who handle skin in the game C-Level searches or who specialize only in handling those assignments, I know of no lists of exclusive SITG headhunters. However, Gilreath Consultancy does specialize in skin in the game C-Level searches.

If you Google headhunter lists, retained search lists, or executive recruiter lists, many such list websites are not current and none that I know mention skin in the game headhunters. My advice: don't waste your time with them. My search on LinkedIn for US headhunters turned up 2,004 results. If you only research LinkedIn for headhunters in certain states, there may be a more manageable number for you to locate any retained search consultants listing middle market PEG clients. The Association of Executive Search Consultants (AESC) members are strictly retained search firms.

Here's my caveat: stay away from contingency recruiters, period. You do not want your resume in the hands of a typical contingency recruiter, compared to a typical retained search consultant. Only deal with retained search firms referred to you from your collegial circle, from your networking referrals, or from search consultants with AESC member firms. Another option for you to consider is Blue Steps (https://www.bluesteps.com), a service of the AESC, that charges a flat fee for a number of services including exposing your resume to 8,000 top quality search firms. I presume some of those firms handle SITG C-Level job searches. Their one-time charge is $289. Check out their website and determine if you need what they are offering. You may want to search LinkedIn for headhunters with PEG clients first such as Cook Associates. This is a good will referral from me as an alternative to researching retained search firms that handle skin in the game searches, onesey, twosey. I have no connection with Blue Steps and have never dealt with this organization myself.

Websites for Researching PEGs and Their Portfolio Companies for Free

While the SITG job candidate is networking, he will hopefully be referred to one or more PEGs at the Partner level. I have suggested he use LinkedIn or Google to research PEGs and their referred Partners. Beginning his networking campaign, he will be researching referred individuals and their PEGs. Then if he ends up having no connections to a PEG Partner nor any networking contacts to refer him to one, what should the SITG job candidate do? He can start cold networking instead of cold calling these PEG Partners, because he is one LinkedIn member contacting another member. LinkedIn's self-definition is that it is the world's largest professional network. To cold network a PEG

Partner, the SITG job candidate can either click "Connect" or "Send" an InMail on each Partner's LinkedIn profile (similar to emails). He can send a limited number based on his LinkedIn account level.

On the other hand, there is an in depth-website called Dealmaker Portal (http://www.dealmakerportal.com/) offering a Directory of Private Equity Firms, Investment Banks, Lenders, Law Firms, Accounting Firms, Deal Brokers, and Consultants. Your ultimate PEG networking targets – middle market PEGS and lower middle market PEGs are on Dealmaker Portal. You'll also find generic M&A professionals with whom to network, there. This website is easy to use, super informative and offers a vast number of PEG Partner cold contact networking opportunities for the SITG candidate. He can research up to 3,841 private equity firms for free using this site. Dealmaker Portal provides each PEG's name, logo, website address and a small map, email, phone number, and fax number. Before you click on View Website, there is an industry focus summary for the SITG job candidate to decide if this PEG's acquisition preferences and their portfolio companies are a good fit with his background. If he has further interest, he can click "View Website" and click "Team" for names and titles of specific cold networking targets.

I have personally always used cold contacting as part of my business development/networking/branding campaign. Here's how I would I would rate the effectiveness of reaching your researched PEG contacts cold.

Ivory bond paper, your business card, and envelope, 1st class stamp.

Targeted individualized emails, 3" blast emails to targeted PEGs (see page 278 on Bob Bronstein).

Cold Contact Networking SBICs

At its most basic, a Small Business Investment Company (SBIC) is a PEG that raises capital from Limited Partners, but also has access to long-term, low cost money from the Small Business Association (SBA) to supplement the Limited Partner (LP) capital. Interest has to be paid on the SBA money semi-annually so most SBIC's tend to focus on mezzanine or other current pay types of investments. SBIC's invest in qualified U.S. small businesses, generally meaning they have tangible net worth of less than $18MM at the time of investment, and they have at least 50% of their assets and employees in the U.S.A.

I have been hired by two different PEGs who were also SBIC licensees. One SITG search was for a CEO of a $15M provider of a variety of custom cut and finished tool steel. The other search was for a SITG CFO for a $40M distributor of building materials delivered to contractors on construction job sites. Each PEG has been vetted by the SBA office of the US Government, passed rigorous testing, and been licensed to have access to SBIC funds. These investments consist of loans, debt securities with equity features and equity for up to 10% of the total invested capital amount in each of their small business acquisitions or Leveraged Buyout investments.

SBIC invested companies may seem too small for many SITG C-Level job candidates but the SBIC guidelines say a company can't have a greater tangible net worth than $18M at the time of the investment. Many companies with hundreds of millions in sales don't have close to $18M in tangible net worth (not counting good will). One of my SBIC clients has acquired a few companies with sales of $200M.

This directory website link is: https://www.sba.gov/content/sbic-directory . It will provide the SITG job candidate with the contact information needed to research each SBIC Licensee by state. Each listed SBIC provides the following categories:

- SBIC firm name
- Managing Director
- Office address
- Suite 400
- City, state and zip
- Phone number/fax number
- Email address
- Investment criteria
- Investment size range
- Preferred minimum
- Preferred maximum
- Type of capital provided
- Funding stage preference
- Industry preference
- Geographic references
- Description of firm's focus

You might consider cold contact networking the Managing Directors or whoever is listed as the contact title in this Directory of SBICs for PEGs in your state. This directory is set up more for small businesses in search of SBIC funding and PEG investing than for being approached about a skin in the game C-Level job with one of the SBIC's portfolio companies.

The value of cold call networking with listed heads from the SBIC's Directory of SBICs is these are PEGs who borrow funds from the government and include that money with their own funds and use the money to invest in very worthwhile companies with higher sales and EBITDA potential. The SBIC may be a mezzanine investor. That means they would influence the company's board and maybe even have a seat on the board but don't have stock control of their invested company. That's okay. If the SBIC is impressed with an SITG C-Level job candidate, it could bode well if they referred you for a skin in the game hiring situation.

First, research this SBIC/PEG's SBIC Directory listing of their portfolio company holdings, mezzanine investments, and acquisition preferences. Then go on their PEG website. If they jive with your background and experience, you should contact the head of each SBIC, whose title is listed in the SBIC Directory. If you reach the SBIC listed Partner by phone, and your elevator pitch is well received, it may lead you to a face-to-face meeting with the SBIC/PEG. I think the mentioning of the caller seeking a SITG C-Level job opportunity and risking some of his own money in the stock of one of this SBIC company's holding will be well received.

Remember, you want to milk the cow until it's dry. In other words when you are communicating with a PEG Partner, and he has no SITG C-Level job currently, what do you do next? Keep milking. Would he mind if you emailed him your resume together with your strongest reference letter(s) you have in your "show and tell" file? Secondly, can he suggest another PEG contact to which he might refer you? (Keep milking). Yes? No? What about a member of the local ACG chapter? (Keep milking). "Maybe after you look over my resume and reference letter, you might think of a PEG referral? Thank You. Goodbye." (Dry cow).

I phoned one SBIC Partner on his listed phone number and reached his secretary.

"I am writing a book and have a question for Mr. Gray about how SBIC skin in the game C-Level hiring practices differ from PEG skin in the game C-Level hiring practices."

"He's busy right now. Here is my email address. Email me what you want to speak with the Partner about and I will get back to you."

The SITG job candidate must be prepared to deal with a secretary or voicemails. Good luck with that! Always ask yourself, "What is my plan B?"

The SITG job candidate might be better off emailing his resume, and attaching a copy of his strongest reference directly to the SBIC listed Partner. Include your "pitch" to him if your research shows your credentials and background are or seem to be a good fit with the SBIC's holdings or with their mezzanine invested companies. Again, your "pitch" is that you are seeking a skin in the game C-Level job in a portfolio company where your credentials and experience are a match.

Just as earlier in this chapter, when you were following up with a networked PEG Partner referral, you should wait a day or two and call this SBIC Partner. Review my above paragraph about milking the cow when you get a PEG Partner on the phone. If you would consider an interim C-Level job or a consulting project until a full time skin in the game C-Level position develops, ask how likely the latter might happen anytime soon?

A good example if the SITG job candidate is a qualified CEO, COO or CFO, any time you are speaking with a PEG Partner and there is currently no full time SITG job, ask if they might need help getting one of their portfolio companies ready for an exit. If your background and experiences make you a good fit for helping prepare a portfolio for exit, that may give you the PEG hiring opportunity you have been seeking. Once your interim job is finished, the PEG might have a full time need or they might refer you to other PEGs seeking a fulltime C-Level skin in the game hire. It never hurts to ask. Milk that cow. Otherwise the PEG will face hiring an interim CEO, COO or CFO, a niche consulting firm, or a Big 6 accounting firm to help. It might be cheaper to hire an interim like you.

Remember, research all referrals and their employers on LinkedIn first, then Google. Photocopies save time and you can make notes on the back and use yellow highlighters on key bio, and research information you want to remember.

"Blast Mailings" to Targeted PEGs and Select Top Headhunters

Below is my general attitude on whether the non-branded educationally and average employer-wise, out of work and maybe senior aged SITG C-Level job candidate should undertake having a mass mailing done of their resumes (and cover letters) to thousands of retained search consultants.

If you peruse headhunter websites, most claim that they can present interested and highly qualified C-Level executives for their retained searches, who are gainfully employed and not actively looking for a job. There used to be an old saying that

Macy's wanted Gimbel's managers. I routinely ask clients at the start of a retained search if there are any off-limit targets. There have been instances where my client has an agreement with their main competitor not to steal managers or executives from each other. I always ask if my client is in any employer associations of competitors and related industries. They would give me an association members' directory. The trick for me was not to get any of my client's main competitors feeling that they were raiding competitors (all socializing golf and drinking buddies at their association events) for managers and executives or a key superstar of theirs. Over lobster dinners I would receive assurances that whatever happened to their candidacy on my search, all our dealings would be confidential. If they were hired, naturally they approached me first to see what the COO job market was like for multi-plant operating room orthopedic surgical instrument designers and manufacturers.

So, if the SITG C-Level job candidate doesn't have a branded MBA education, or hasn't worked for the leading employer in their industry and isn't still gainfully employed, he will not be at the top of the pile of a search firm's candidate list for a client PEG's retained search.

Those STIG C-Level job candidates who lack necessary collegial and other well-connected contacts, sufficient quality referrals and adequate patience, a natural flair, or endurance to conduct a successful networking campaign might consider one of my favorite attention getting and quick results-oriented tools: a "blast mailing". Many times during my long headhunting career, I have done various types of blast mailings that were successful. It's just you and your audience using an accurate USPS or emailing list and the right "pitch". No middle men!

If I were a betting man, of all the potential skin in the game hiring channels I describe in this book, a proper blast mailing could be the most successful way for you to be hired for a SITG C-Level job by a PEG. You must have an influential cover letter and resume and a well assembled target list with accurate, targeted addresses and titles to read your missives.

Do email blasts to targeted PEGs, VCs and top retained headhunters really work in career transition?

By: Bob Bronstein,
President, Profile Research LLC,
bob@profileresearch.com,
215-643-3411- 800-776-0927

My friend, Bob Bronstein (Harvard undergrad, Wharton MBA), is the President of Profile Research LLC outside Philadelphia, PA. Since 1990, Profile Research LLC is the Premier Resume Distribution Service for serious job seekers. I asked Bob, a wizard of "blast mailings" for his opinion on this subject:

> We are often asked if email blasts work in career transition. After all, in this difficult economy, when hiring authorities' desks and email inboxes are piled with resumes, what value is there to another resume or email? So why bother adding to your expense to contribute another resume to the pile?
>
> The economy is clearly improving and hiring is on an uptick.

Before dealing with the issue of email blasts, we hasten to say the best way to find your next position is by networking. And networking is not just contacting the people you know in your field. It's contacting and staying in touch with everyone you know AND everyone they know. We often say, "There are five opportunities for networking every day. They are called breakfast, lunch, coffee, cocktails, and dinner. Fill two of them daily." That's ten people a week. In one year, you will have 500 people scouring the markets for you.

Remember the old joke, "How do I get to Carnegie Hall? Practice, practice, practice!" The analog in employment is, "How do I get my next position? Network, network, network."

Yes, networking is slow. It is tedious. And there is a limit to how much coffee a person can drink. But there is no substitute for networking.

Realistically, some people are good at networking and some are not and some never will be. Even bad networking is better than no networking at all, but email blasts have the advantage of expanding your network in a hurry.

An email blast is an add-on to any networking program and NOT a substitute for it.

Okay. Lecture delivered. Now on to the subject at hand.

DEFINING TERMS

For clarity, let's define some terms.

When we say email blasts we mean broadcast email, not individual, well-researched letters. (We like individual, well-researched letters, but the cost and time involved is prohibitive.)

There are three possible targets for EMAIL BLASTS:

Retained Only Executive Recruiters (sometimes called "headhunters")

Private Equity Groups (PEGs)

If requested, Venture Capital Firms

WHAT is an Executive Recruiter?

Retained Only Executive Recruiters (often called "headhunters") are hired by PEGs on a retained exclusive basis to fill C-Level executive jobs. Often the hired candidate's job offer requires that he/she invest up to $100K of their own money in the stock of the PEG's portfolio company where they will be employed. The objective is to help grow the company and increase the value of the company's equity when it's sold.

Targeting Retained Recruiters and VC/PE firms

Our data allows us to select those firms that could be looking for you. We can target by industry, by skill, by investment preference. And it only takes a few minutes of conversation to set up the parameters for each client.

How should you contact them?

Contact Retained Search Consultants and Venture Capital Firms and PEGs by email because it's what they want and it's less expensive than postal mail. Conversely, if you are in the group of people who make their initial contact on high-rag stationary, spend the extra money with the VC/PEGs. (The retained recruiters WANT the emails!)

Do email blasts work? (Finally, the point of the chapter).

The answer is, "Sometimes".

And it depends upon three variables.

In our experience (more than twenty-five years), there are three issues determining the success of any campaign:

1. What's the marketplace for people like you on the day you go to market?
2. What are your credentials?

3. How well are those credentials presented?

Let's deal with these in reverse order.

Presentation is important! You only get one chance to make a good first impression. If you are really comfortable with your ability to produce a quality resume and cover letter, that's fine. Some people can. Many people can't. You will write a resume three or four times in your career. A professional may write a resume three or four times a week, every week. Seek out a good professional writer to a least critique your resume and pay them to assist you if you are in the least bit uncomfortable with your own writing skills (see recommendations in chapter 3).

Secondly, your credentials are your credentials. You can't change your credentials today. (You can highlight the good stuff and de-emphasize the not-so-good stuff, but you are who you are; credentials speak for themselves and the PEG and Retained Search Consultant will figure that out quickly.) Further, most people hire with a set of credentials (both explicit and implicit) in mind. If you fit, you are in the running. If you don't fit, you're not. And you can't change that.

Which brings us back to the first point, "What's the marketplace for people like you on the day you go to market?" PEGs are either looking for people like you, or they are not. That is, if you're hot, you're hot. If you're not, you're not.

And the only way to find out if you are hot is to go to market.

We are often asked for a hit-rate in the email blasts world. In our judgment, there is no reliable number for a hit-rate because of market volatility. Your experience today has no relationship with someone with similar credentials six months ago or three years ago. Some clients have had so much response they have had to turn off the phone. Others have heard nothing. Certain people have been swamped with interviews. Others face great silence. Email blasts work when the market for your skills is active and it doesn't work when no skin in the game C-Level jobs are out there that fit your credentials.

In our electronic world, geography almost becomes irrelevant. A retained recruiter in Key West could be working on an assignment in Seattle, and a PEG in California could be hiring in Connecticut.

There is a small side benefit in a quiet market. Your resume will get entered into recruiters' and VC/PEG's databases and when a position does come along they will keyword search their files so you may get a call. Several of our clients have gotten calls as much as two years after their email blast campaign.

In this dynamic marketplace, things change rapidly. So the marketplace may be better thirty days from now. It will certainly be different.

A final word about spending money on your job search. Your career is arguably one of the most important segments of your life. It supports your family and your psyche. Most of us have never had to spend money on career transition. Yet, we suggest that spending on your career transition has the best return of any investment you can make. Simply calculate the return on investment (ROI) of employing professionals to help you shorten your job search by as little as a week. (At a $200,000 salary level, that's a $4000 return and a 52x ROI. A year. Every year.) If you balk at paying for resume preparation, interview training, salary negotiation, email blasts assistance, etc, do some arithmetic. We have. And frankly, for most executives and professionals, almost any amount of spending pays off handsomely.

We will add a final thought. In career transition you are making a very large sale; the earnings for the balance of your career. Professional help is available in many ways. Use it wisely.

Chapter 10

Skin in the Game PEG 1st & 2nd C-Suite Job Interviews

If this is your first PEG job interview, be sure you implement the steps below every time you have a lower middle market (up to $50M in sales $2M+ EBITDA)or middle market (up to $200M in sales, $10M+EBITDA) PEG C-Level job interview. Make a file to keep this information in. I am assuming this job interview with a PEG Partner is not through a headhunter. If it is, keep my due diligence hiring approach in mind. All headhunters do not operate similarly. So I'll assume this job interview is the result of your networking efforts as outlined in my chapter 9-Networking. Depending on the PEG's size, normally a PEG Partner would interview a CEO or a CFO for one of the PEG's portfolio companies. A PEG Partner does not usually interview Chief Sales & Marketing (also VP S & M title) or Chief Operating Officer (also VP Operations title) job candidates, as the portfolio CEOs would be responsible for the first interviews. I am using the title PEG Partner to represent other PEG titles I have worked with. Besides the title PEG Partner, any of these tiles might typically interview an SITG CEO or CFO job candidate such as General Partner, Operating Partner, Managing Director/Partner, Vice President/Principal, Chairman, or President. In any event, if you are fortunate to be referred to a PEG Partner and have a 1st interview for a job with a portfolio company, take advantage of this.

Preparing for a PEG C-Level Job 1st Interview from Networking Referral:

Obtain the name and location of the portfolio company and the C-Level executive job specifications to review from the PEG Partner or its headhunter.

1. Research the PEG's current and former portfolio holdings, the "team" on the PEG's website, and especially the Partner who will be interviewing you.
2. Review your LinkedIn research on the PEG Partner's profile for any mutual contacts, employers, university professors, or M&A consultants.
3. Research the PEG's portfolio company needing the C-Level job filled for which you are interviewing. Note how long the PEG has owned it. If it's over three years, you'll want to ask the PEG Partner in your job interview how long the PEG intends to own it.
4. Select appropriate show & tell items that will impress the PEG Partner, especially reference letters (see chapter 8, line c).
5. Check the dress code. Usually it's business casual; dress shirt, dark blazer, and no tie.
6. Ask for a copy of the Confidential Information Memorandum (CIM) or the Financing Memorandum, also called the Confidential Descriptive Memorandum. Each is a very detailed disclosure document provided on the company to potential company buyers in a private equity transaction. The CIM is drafted by the seller's M&A advisory firm or investment banker and used in a sell-side

engagement to market a business to prospective buyers. A number of my PEG clients consider the CIM to be a sales document. The Financing Memorandum prepared by the PEG buyers includes everything a CIM would have but will also include the price and how the deal is going to be structured, including the debt financing. They are very similar documents. The Confidential Descriptive Memorandum below provides much, if not all, a typical Confidential Descriptive Memorandum or Confidential Acquisition Financing Memorandum would contain. Additionally, there would be actual data next to each heading as well. As a potential SITG stockholder, if you are hired by this PEG, you would be receiving the same confidential information as all other investors in this portfolio company.

CONFIDENTIAL ACQUISITION FINANCING MEMORANDUM

Table of Contents

EXECUTIVE SUMMARY

PEG's Portfolio Company Title (background & history)

Management & Personnel (functional breakdown)

Markey Overview (industry overview-market trends-market share-end user markets)

Competitors

Financial overview-5 year historical financials.

Future opportunities.-current strategic thrust-international-new products

Legal and Environmental

Senior and subordinated financing structure

Ownership and outside investor biographies

Historical annual financial information

Transaction sources and uses of opening balance tables

Projected financial information tables

APPENDICIES
Letter of intent cover letter
Portfolio company product brochures.
Portfolio company audited financial statements.
Article on portfolio company's industry leading position.
Company Brochure

You will be asked to sign a non-disclosure agreement before a portfolio company's memorandum or financial statement summaries are shown to you. NDAs particularly involving technical companies can be lengthy and pithy. Here is a simple NDA example used by one of our longest lower middle market client PEGs. You should check the NDA with your lawyer before you sign it and then email it to the PEG Partner. You may receive the CIM and the last three years' summaries of the portfolio company financials during your interview.

Non-Disclosure Agreement Example:

Acme Technologies, Inc.
172 University Avenue
Pittsburg, PA 15219

July 10, 2013

Mr. Jeff Collins
19 Bennett Place
Baltimore, MD 21202

Dear Jeff:

Re: Non-Disclosure Agreement

In connection with our discussions relating to your possible employment and/or an investment (the transaction) in Acme Technologies, Inc. (the company), you have requested that the company disclose to you certain confidential and proprietary information relating to the business, affairs and finances of the company. The company is willing to disclose such information to you, but only on the terms set forth in this letter agreement.

We agree as follows:

1. As used in this letter agreement, the term "confidential information" means all information (whether written or oral) provided to you by or on behalf of the company relating to the company and/or its affiliates or the transaction, except information that:
   a. You can demonstrate was known to you prior to such disclosure, as evidence by documentary or other physical evidence predating the date of this letter;
   b. Was public knowledge at the time of such disclosure, or becomes public knowledge after such disclosure, through no action or omission by or on behalf of you; or
   c. Is lawfully disclosed or made available to you by a third party, which, to the best of your knowledge after due inquiry, has no obligation to the company to maintain the confidentiality of such information.
2. You will maintain the confidentiality of all confidential information and hold it in trust for the exclusive benefit of the company. All confidential information will remain the exclusive property of the company, and will be used by you exclusively for purposes of the discussions referred to above.
3. Unless previously authorized in writing by the company, you will not use confidential information for any other purpose or for the benefit of yourself or others, and will not disclose it to anyone. Any further dissemination or disclosure of such confidential information will be made only if previously authorized by the company in writing and provided in each case that such disclosure is

conditioned on the agreement by the person to whom you provided confidential information to keep it confidential in accordance with the terms of this letter and further provided that you hereby agree to be responsible for any breach of this agreement by such person.

4. Without the company's prior written consent, or as required under securities or other laws, you will not disclose to any party (i) the fact that any confidential information has been disclosed or made available to you, (ii) that discussions or negotiations are taking place concerning a possible transaction between the parties, or (iii) any of the terms, conditions, or facts with respect to any such possible transaction, including the status thereof.
5. You will promptly deliver to the company, upon request, all documents and other tangible media that contain or reflect confidential information (including all copies, reproductions, digests, abstracts, analyses, or notes) in your possession or control, and will destroy any related computer files.
6. The company does not make any representations or warranties, nor shall it incur any liability, in respect of any information (including confidential information) provided to you by or on behalf of the company, including without limitation with respect to the accuracy or completeness of such information. Nothing contained herein shall be construed to be an offer of employment or to make an investment in the company.
7. If you are required by law to disclose any confidential information, you will provide the company with prompt notice of such requirement so that the company may seek a protective order or take other appropriate action

and/or waive compliance with the terms of this letter agreement to the extent of such required disclosure. In the absence of such a waiver, if you are, in the opinion of your counsel, compelled to disclose confidential information upon pain of liability for contempt or other censure or penalty, you may disclose such confidential information to the relevant court or other tribunal without liability hereunder, but such information shall remain confidential under this letter agreement after such disclosure.

8. In consideration of the disclosure to you of confidential information, you hereby agree not to directly or indirectly solicit for employment, any employees of the company or its affiliates for a period of one year from the date hereof;
9. Provided that you shall not be prohibited from conducting a general solicitation of employment (or from hiring any employee of the company who responds thereto) not specifically targeted at employees of the company.
10. You acknowledge that any breach by you of your obligations under this letter agreement would inevitably cause substantial and irreparable damage to the company, and that money damages would be an inadequate remedy therefore. Accordingly, you acknowledge and agree that the company will be entitled, in addition to any other available remedies, to an injunction, specific performance, and/or other equitable relief to prevent the violation of such obligations.
11. Either you or the company may at any time terminate discussions with the other that are the subject of this letter agreement, for any reason or for no reason, and

the provisions of this letter agreement will survive any such termination.

If the foregoing is acceptable, please sign one copy of this letter agreement (the other signed copy is enclosed for your records). This letter agreement will then constitute an agreement governed by the internal laws of the State of Pennsylvania. (without reference to principles of conflicts or choice of law).

We look forward to productive discussions and to working with you.

Very truly yours,

Acme Technologies, Inc.

____

Name: John Braddock
Title: Chairman & CEO

AGREED TO AND ACCEPTED: _______________

Date: ____________

Mr. Jeff Collins
19 Bennett Place
Baltimore, MD 21202

Before your skin in the game interview with the PEG Partner, email or FedEx to him the following items (CC the headhunter, if there is one):

1. A copy of your confidential Indiana Jones Bio which you completed with help from chapter 4 in this book. Explain in the cover sheet that it is a due diligence version of your biography in support of your resume.
2. A copy of the SITG C-Level job description together with a completed copy of your self-rating quiz (SRQ). Explain that you broke down the key C-Level job requirements and rated yourself one to ten. You also commented on each rating, and where possible, provided one or more professional references in support of your C-Level job ratings. (If you need to call any SRQ reference first, indicate that on each reference and omit their contact phone number on the SRQ).

Below are self-rating quiz examples for each SITG C-Level function-CEO, CFO, COO, and VP Sales and Marketing

Rate your qualifications against the C-Level job requirements. After you rate yourself against each job requirement provide a short explanation for each of your ratings. Then, if possible, include at least one name, title, and contact information per quiz number of which reference would support your rating. Omit any reference phone/email contact information if you want to contact the individual first.

Completed retained search: PEG SITG Chief Executive Officer self-rating quiz example based on an actual PEG SITG

CEO job description. *All actual names and data have been edited for privacy.*

SITG CEO Candidate: Harvey Goldstein

Edited Client Company Summary

Well-established Midwest-based multi-location designer and manufacturer of high quality specialized industrial branded products to satisfy the requirements of its diverse customer base and end markets. Current global sales of $120MM were expected to double in five years internally and externally through additional complimentary mergers and acquisitions.

Checklist - Rate yourself on a scale of one to ten on these points related to these critical President and CEO specs.

Take your time (24 hours) and reflect about your responses before you make them your final answers. Thank you.

1. Must be degreed ideally with a technical degree. __9__

Candidate comments:

M.S. Management (Sloan Fellow) Stanford Univ., MBA Univ. of Maryland, BA Economics Univ. of Delaware.

2. Has solid P&L multi-plant manufacturing operations management experience including Continuous Improvement, KPI measurements, Lean, SS, Six Sigma, Kaizen, Value Stream, etc. __8__

Candidate comments:

Entire career is with manufacturing companies. Direct responsibility includes: plant manager for IMT, Cedar Rapids, IA truck plant. GM responsibility for two plant parts manufacturing company (Acme, div. of International Trucks, Naperville, IL), Responsible for three tire plants and fifty 200 employee average branch operations at Union Tires, five plants at Carlisle Companies and sixty manufacturing and distribution facilities at Hellickson Corporation. Skilled in Lean, Six Sigma, 5S, The Toyota Manufacturing System (Hino Diesel Trucks, div of Toyota) – Continuous Improvement, Value Stream mapping at Hellickson Corporation, and used KPIs in all assignments. Kaizen at Freightliner and Hellickson Corporation.

Reference: Mark Eccles, Chairman of Hellickson Corporation, 249-444-0897, markeccles@rhellicksoncorp.com

Relationship: I reported directly to Mark during my five years at Hellickson Corporation as President and CEO.

3. Has effective leadership skills, challenges subordinates, holds direct reports accountable, a "can do attitude" and is collaborative by nature. __9__

Candidate comments:

Results-oriented leader that engages the team into a strategic planning process supported with tactical plans after achieving alignment with my board of directors. I use a high performance leadership style whereby the "servant leader" approach ensures direct reports have the resources necessary to accomplish objectives that are linked to our overarching organizational goals. KPIs are then used to monitor interim results toward goal achievement and to assist the functional leaders with their own progress toward operational excellence.

Reference: Mark Eccles, Chairman of Hellickson Corporation, 249-444-0897, markeccles@hellicksoncorp.com

Relationship: I reported directly to Mark during my five years at Hellickson Corporation as President and CEO.

4. Manage direct reports including: the VP of Sales and Marketing, CFO, VP of Operations, VP of Research & Development (R&D) and Engineering and VP of Human Resources. __10__

Candidate comments:

Have had P&L responsibility since 1994 (twenty years) with Sales, Marketing, CFO, Operations, R&D, Engineering, HR reporting directly to me.

Reference: Claude Phillips, CEO (retired 2007) Carlisle Companies, 615-581-2775 home, 615-883-6001 cell, claudephillips1@comcast.net

Relationship: I reported to Claude while I was President of Carlisle Companies.

5. Has been around M&A transactions to know what investors are looking for, uses candid conversation, and is comfortable making effective presentations to banks and boards. __8__

Candidate comments:

My last two assignments have been with private equity backed companies, where a rollup strategy was encouraged. At Hellickson Corporation we acquired an eight location service network out of a bankruptcy and a manufacturing company privately held whereby an owner was retiring and we needed the strategic acquisition to expand our product line and customer base. At Carlisle Companies we acquired intellectual property rights to a new product and refined the product, tested and certified it, and launched it as a major-league homerun winning the Chairman's Award in 2006 and resulting in a $92 million first year sales result.

At Hellickson Corporation, our PE firm did not have an open fund and my CFO and I needed to renegotiate our credit facility to fund our growth and acquisition strategy. I was directly involved in those relationships. I am very comfortable with the bank relationship aspect of my CEO role.

Reference: Harry Colson, Chief Financial Officer of Hellickson Corporation, 249-576-3390, hcolson@hellicksoncorp.com

Relationship: Harry reported directly to Mark Eccles, Chairman with a dotted line to me as President and CEO during my five years at Hellickson Corporation.

6. Provide leadership, strategic guidance, and vision to expanding multi-location manufacturing, distribution, and outsourcing company on a full P&L basis towards planned global strategic growth to $200M+ while monitoring overall operating performance against company's goals and objectives. __10__

Candidate comments:

I have a solid track record of doubling top-line revenues and tripling EBITDA in a two to four year period in several assignments in both public and private equity backed companies, in companies ranging from $100 million to $1 billion in size. All companies had multi-plant manufacturing structures and complex distribution systems, and channels including company branches, direct sales force, dealers, and distributors. Extensive supply chain experience at Freightliner, Carlisle Companies, and Hellickson Corporation.

Reference: Claude Phillips, CEO (retired 2007) Carlisle Companies, (995-581-2775 home, 714-883-6001 cell, claudephillips1@comcast.net

Relationship: I reported to Claude while I was President of Carlisle Companies.

7. Mutually establish goals with each direct report and monitor results, incorporating any organizational issues

into specific performance objectives, and challenge subordinates holding direct reports accountable. __9__

Candidate comments:

In the last two assignments, I developed the Incentive Compensation system for the company, secured board approval and deployed the programs to our entire company. We developed monthly and quarterly tracking systems for goal attainment and incorporated the process into our semi-annual Performance Review Process. My Fortune 500 company experience all had established and mature performance systems that provided a solid foundation for my private equity/smaller company experiences.

Reference: Mark Eccles, Chairman of Hellickson Corporation, 249-444-0897, markeccles@hellicksoncorp.com

Relationship: I reported directly to Mark during my five years at Hellickson Corporation as President and CEO.

8. Be highly effective in identifying and capitalizing on cost, quality and service improvement opportunities while demonstrating understanding of the business strategy and financial metrics necessary for success. __9__

Candidate comments:

Operational excellence has been a major key to our financial success, not only to achieve the income statement and balance sheet objectives, but also to improve throughput. At Carlisle Companies, for example, we changed our business model from "build to stock" to a "build to order" process and eliminated

$22 million of finished goods inventory, eliminated a warehouse and double handling of finished units. We deployed the same approach with our Hellickson Tank Trailer division allowing us to eliminate potentially surplus and obsolete inventory. We improved our product quality with the use of 3D engineering tools that eliminated manufacturing errors at Hellickson Tank Trailer.

Reference: Albert Swift, Chief Operating Officer of Hellickson Corporation, 249-223-9949 cell, 249-324-3343 office, hswift@hellicksoncorp.com

Relationship: Al reported to me as President and CEO, **Hellickson Corporation.**

9. Work with the CFO and all functional VPs to assess current operating performance against plan, and understand the critical financial issues and opportunities for the company, specifically cash flow, capital structure, working capital, pricing, margins, expenses.

Conduct a comprehensive operational review of all related functional activities including processes, systems, new programs, existing methods, and procedures. Develop necessary tactical and strategic plans and time tables to address any major issues. __9__

Candidate comments:

Hellickson, Carlisle Companies, Union Tires and International Trucks were all very metric driven companies. As a Division President, General Manager, or CEO, these dashboard and process skills have been developed and refined at these world class manufacturing companies. My hands-on approach has allowed me to be a highly responsive leader without getting mired in the "weeds" at a level that was too detailed at the correct level to be highly effective in identifying trends and issues before they became major problems.

Reference: Skip Waters, former COO International Trucks, Retired, 432-715-9879 cell, 432-656-9448 home, skipwaters@earthlink.net

Relationship: I reported to Skip as Plant Manager, International Truck Parts, Naperville, IL plant.

10. Work with CFO on developing and measuring key indicators, automating business processes, and improving decision making information. __8__

Candidate comments:

My two recent private equity backed company roles were process and KPI "starved" companies. The CFO, Division Presidents, and I worked collaboratively to develop meaningful tools to measure results, trends and processes. In many cases we were dependent upon "tribal knowledge" and needed to transition into a "process driven" organization. We deployed these processes into everything from weld processes to material handling to the way in which we introduced orders into the company in the sales to engineering order entry's spec'd in process.

Reference 1: Harry Colson, Chief Financial Officer of Hellickson Corporation, 249-576-3390 office, 249-223-6005 cell, hcolson@hellicksoncorp.com

Relationship: Harry reported directly to Mark Eccles, Chairman with a dotted line to me as President and CEO during my five years at Hellickson Corporation.

Reference 2: Frank Hammill, Chief Financial Officer of Carlisle Companies, 615-299-6364 cell, 615-3974525 office, frankhammill@carlislecompanies.com

Relationship: Frank reported directly to Claude Phillips, CEO, Carlisle Companies and indirectly to me, as President of Carlisle Companies.

11. CEO should determine his or her individual primary goals and objectives to be accomplished in collaboration with the board of directors including available resources, time, budget, people, necessary steps and technologies, and devise an appropriate plan that meets mutual consensus. __9__

Candidate comments:

I have used a fact-based current situation, market forecast and strategic objective process with my board to develop CEO objectives that then "cascade down" into the organization to ensure we have alignment from ownership, to leadership, to shop floor activities. We have made great strides to ensure we do not have conflicting goals. I experienced that at Union Tire and it led to sub-optimization and poor results; i.e., higher costs, missed deliveries, high inventories, and a tremendous degree of frustration for customers and dealers.

Reference: Wade Brown, CEO of Union Tires, 803-522-3770 cell, 803-878-3490 office, wadebrown@uniontires.com

Relationship: I reported directly to Wade Brown as Vice President, Commercial Tire Systems, during my three years at Union Tires.

12. Has lived and worked in small town environment and will relocate to within reasonable commuting distance of Midwest headquarters. Experience in a unionized plant is preferred. __9__

Candidate comments:

Most recently was President and CEO at Hellickson Corporation based in Springfield, IL, including manufacturing plants, three unions and the balance union-free. We renegotiated all three labor agreements moving from three year to five year contract periods at highly favorable terms to the company including reducing the number of work rules, job classifications, and increasing the proportion of health care expense sharing on the part of our team members. I currently live in a suburban area of Springfield and have a history of long commutes into rural markets for my employment.

13. President and CEO base salary range and merit bonus plan are acceptable. __7__

Candidate comments:

I view compensation as a multi-part package including base salary, annual bonus, stock options, co-investment opportunity, and benefits (auto allowance, 401k, medical, etc.). I am flexible on any parts of the overall package. I am looking for my next engagement to have a much higher investment and compensation at-risk component to reward the future performance that we can deliver to the shareholders.

My most recent compensation was:
Salary: $450,000
Bonus: 50% of salary with a range of 0%-200% of target
Stock Options: 2.0%
SITG Investment: $250,000
Benefits: Auto allowance $1,800/mo., 401k match (safe harbor plan), medical and dental, life and LTD insurance plan.

Completed retained search: SITG Chief Financial Officer self-rating quiz example. All actual names and data have been edited for privacy.

SITG CFO CANDIDATE: BRUCE CLAYBORN

Edited Client Company Summary

Our portfolio company client is a leading designer and manufacturer of service industry machinery for commercial and industrial use in ninety countries worldwide. Sales are between $50M-$60M and this growth-oriented company is profitable and has been for most of its existence. This company is preparing to unveil two major new products this year. It currently employs over 350 corporate, engineering, and manufacturing professionals at its facilities.

Checklist - Rate yourself on a scale of one to ten on these points related to these critical Chief Financial Officer specs.

Take your time (24 hours) and reflect about your responses before you make them your final answers. Thank you.

1. Undergraduate Accounting__10__ or Finance Degree______ (either worth 10); CPA a plus (worth 10) MBA a plus (worth 10). __10__
2. High personal ethics and business integrity verifiable through reference checks. __10__

Candidate comments:

I carry my ethics and integrity with me every day. I value them as priceless and will not compromise them for anything or anyone.

Reference: Paul Morrow, CEO and Chairman, Acme Seals Corporation, 312-399-2221 cell, 312-555-4424 office, paulmorrow@acmeseals.com

Relationship: I reported to Paul as CFO, Acme Seals Corporation, for five years.

3. Minimum of several years CFO line experience including IT management, ideally with some experience in a growing a private equity investor-owned manufacturing company with $100M+ in sales. ___10___

Candidate comments:

As CFO of American Industrial Applications (AIA), the focus was on growing the business in a challenging marketplace and reporting on a regular basis to our private equity investor owners. Acme Seals, prior to its acquisition by 3M in October 2010, was highly leveraged to an asset-based lender. Our lender behaved in many ways like a private equity owner. Acme Seals continues to be a high-growth business, with sales increasing 10%-15% per year. My responsibilities for IT management date back to International Tool Works (ITW) starting in 1993 and continue through today.

Reference: Steve Handel, Chairman and CEO, American Industrial Applications, 203-239-5651 cell, 203-995-4894 office, stevehandel@hostway.com

Relationship: I reported to Steve as CFO, American Industrial Applications, for two years.

4. Job Cost accounting knowledge and experience developing metrics around labor reporting and material reporting, and tracking profitability by each product line, customer, and distribution channel. __10__

Candidate comments:

The bulk of my professional experience is in manufacturing sold directly to OEM's as well as to distribution. Kotonics, Inc. (water treatment equipment) primarily sold on a project-by-project basis, so identifying and tracking costs and profitability on a job cost basis was key to understanding the business. Kotonics also had a strong spare parts business to service the projects that had been sold.

Eversall Electric is very strong on tracking product and customer profitability and identifying where products and customers are in their life cycle. Acme Seals Corporation tracks product line profitability daily.

Reference 1: Martin Stein, Chief Financial Officer, Eversall Electric, 314-777-5331 cell 314-487-5221 office, martinstein1@eversolelectric.com

Relationship: I reported to Martin Stein as Group Controller, Eversall Electric Machine Components Group, for four years.

Reference 2: Louis Corcoran, Chief Financial Officer, Kotonics, Inc., 617-229-5449 cell, 617-465-1801 office, louiscorcoran@kotonics.com

Relationship: I reported to Louis Corcoran as Group Controller, Kotonics, Inc. for three years.

Reference 3: Nick Kotas, President, Acme Seals Corporation, 312-444-2771 cell, 312-664-8855 office, nickkotas@acmeseals.com

Relationship: As CFO, I handled special projects for Nick over a five year period including a product profitability study by customer.

5. Experienced preparing board reports and informational packages, and conducting business studies and performance analysis. __10__

Candidate comments:

I prepared board reports monthly for AIA as well as quarterly bank covenant packages at AIA and Acme Seals Corporation.

Acquisition analyses were performed while with Eversall Electric.

Monthly performance analysis and commentary have been performed since my days with Glowpoint Lighting. I also prepare a weekly "dashboard" report of operating metrics covering key indicators such as sales, orders, backlog, profitability, human resources, and working capital.

Reference 1: Steve Handel, Chairman and CEO, American Industrial Applications, 203-239-5651 cell, 203-995-4894 office, stevehandel1@aia.com

Relationship: I reported to Steve as CFO, American Industrial Applications, for two years.

Reference 2: Nick Kotas, President, Acme Seals Corporation, 312-444-2771 cell, 312-664-8855 office, nickkotas@acmeseals.com

Relationship: As CFO, I handled special projects for Nick over a five year period including a product profitability study by customer.

Reference 3: Martin Stein, Chief Financial Officer, Eversall Electric, 314-777-5331 cell, 314-487-5221 office, and martinstein1 @ eversallelectric.com

Relationship: I reported to Martin Stein as Group Controller, Eversall Electric Machine Components Group, for four years.

6. PC literate with substantial working knowledge of MS Office and key financial management programs. __10__

Candidate comments:

I am highly PC literate. I taught myself Microsoft Access at Glowpoint Lighting, and soon became a resource for the company's help desk personnel. I work with MS Office (Excel, Word, PowerPoint, and Outlook) daily. Every employer has had a different operating system – I have quickly learned how to effectively utilize these tools to improve productivity.

Reference: Louis Corcoran, Chief Financial Officer, Kotonics, Inc., 617-229-5449 cell, 617-465-1801 office, louiscorcoran@kotonics.com

Relationship: I assisted Louis Corcoran as Group Controller, Kotonics Inc. putting in a Windows XP operating system.

7. Have played an integral role in the assessment and integration of acquisitions and other growth strategies. __10__

Candidate comments:

With Eversall Electric I worked on a number of acquisitions ranging in value from $1 million to over $350 million. My role at Dycon Systems was focused on integrating this acquisition into Eversall Electric.

Reference: Martin Stein, Chief Financial Officer, Eversall Electric, 314-777-5331 cell, 314-487-5221 office, martinstein1@eversallelectric.com

Relationship: I worked as CFO, Dycon Systems, with Martin Stein integrating my former employer into Eversall Electric and became Group Controller reporting to him.

8. Aggressive driver of accountability. 10

Candidate comments:

I am a firm believer in clearly communicating goals and expectations, measuring progress along the way, and evaluating the end results. I give my direct reports support (e.g. training) in striving to accomplish their goals. They get full credit for their successes, and I hold them accountable for shortfalls. This philosophy has resulted in replacing and upgrading some positions (accounting clerks as well as controllers) to ensure the company's success.

Reference: Philip Reiss, Retired President, Dycon Systems, 617-338-2939 cell, 617-228-4663 home, philiprl@ hotpoint.com

Relationship: I helped turn around the Finance, Accounting and IT departments at Dycon Systems, reporting to Mr. Reiss for three years before we merged with Eversall Electric.

9. Successful track record implementing budgeting processes, financial management reporting, financial and accounting regulatory compliance, and negotiating debt funding. 10

Candidate comments:

I have implemented budgeting processes that build from the bottom up to achieve upper management goals for sales and income. Some businesses have allowed these budgets to be shared at an operating department level. This resulted in tremendous buy-in from the production level on up, and pushed accountability for cost control throughout the organization.

Reference: Nick Kotas, President, Acme Seals Corporation, 312-444-2771 cell, 312-664-8855 office, nickkotas@acmeseals.com

Relationship: I built a budget from scratch with help from our auditors, E&Y, and reported to Nick Kotas during that time period.

Reference: Sam Parro, CPA and Partner in Charge, E&Y, Chicago, IL, 312-222-6761 cell, 312-234-7890 office, samparrol@e&y.com

Relationship: I worked with Sam on the new budget format for Acme Seals Corporation.

10. Has directed all efforts to manage the current accounting system and implemented any upgrades or replacement IT systems. __9__

Candidate comments:

I have had IT responsibility at Dycon Systems, Eversall Electric, and Acme Seals Corporation. I evaluated the business needs versus the "nice-to-haves". I initiated the process at Dycon to replace their IT system (promoted to Eversall Electric corporate role before this project was completed). Acme Seals Corporation works with a modified package that has been customized to meet the needs of the business. In a cost/benefit analysis, we are implementing an add-on reporting package to create better reporting at a fraction of the cost to upgrade the entire system.

Reference 1: Nick Kotas, President, Acme Seals Corporation, 312-444-2771 cell, 312-664-8855 office, nickkotas@acmeseals.com

Reference 2: Martin Stein, Chief Financial Officer, Eversall Electric, 314-777-5331 cell, 314-487-5221 office, martinstein1@eversallelectric.com

Relationships: Both Nick and Martin will attest to my having directed all efforts to manage the former current accounting systems, and implementing any upgrades or replacement IT systems on time and within budgets.

11. Identifies ways to reduce costs of raw materials and products, monitor material intake, and set minimum and maximum inventory levels. ___8___

Candidate comments:

I work with purchasing and production planning personnel on sourcing some materials from overseas (Asia), bulk pricing, lead times, and production requirements for a focused business within Acme Seals.

Non-materials cost cutting includes business reorganizations at Dycon Systems and Acme Seals, as well as ongoing reevaluation of various operating expenses (credit insurance premium, telephone, etc.).

In my three and a half years with Acme Seals, sales have increased 45%. Accounting personnel to handle the increased transactional volume have increased zero. In that same period, we have gone from taking three weeks to close the books, to reporting results to 3M in three days.

Reference: Norman Roselle, VP Supply Chain, Acme Seals Corporation, 312-797-5563 cell, 312-305-1194 office, norman rl@acmeseals.com

Relationship: As CFO, Acme Seals, I worked closely with Norman on sourcing of some materials from overseas (Asia), bulk pricing, and improved lead times.

12. Leading the effort to ensure proper cash management and liquidity in the business while maximizing profitability. Identify opportunities to accelerate billings and collections. __10__

Candidate comments:

Cash is king. We control cash by carefully managing receivables, inventory, payables, and capital expenditures. Cash is tracked and reported daily. We work with the sales team to resolve any receivables disputes in a timely manner. Similarly, we work with purchasing to gain favorable payment terms with our vendors.

Reference: Louis Corcoran, Chief Financial Officer, Kotonics, Inc., 617-229-5449 cell, 617-465-1801 office, louiscorcoran@kotonics.com

Relationship: Maintained a low Days Sales Outstanding (DSO) figure as Group Controller reporting to Louis during my entire employment period at Kotonics. A big part of my annual bonus was based on a low DSO annual average.

13. Has acted as a sounding board to the President while taking the lead on managing and improving all areas of reporting, systems, and financial management. ___10___

Candidate comments:

As the Controller for Dycon Systems, the general manager requested that I be a member of the Business Management Team and the Sales Management Team. Working together, the team members set the goals and implemented the strategies that helped Dycon grow from $25 million to $100 million in sales in three years.

With AIA and Acme Seals, I worked daily with the CEO and COO on various initiatives to grow the company and restructure costs.

All these efforts required an improved and comprehensive reporting system to track progress and measure results.

Reference 1: Harvey Ross, Retired General Manager, Dycon Systems, 617-555-1676 cell, 617-996-5345 home, harveyrl@hostway.com

---

Relationship: As Controller then, I was part of the Dycon Systems Business Management team and Sales Management team under Harvey, and we reached extraordinary goals as teams.

Reference 2: Steve Handel, Chairman and CEO, American Industrial Applications, 203-239-5651 cell, 203-995-4894 office, stevehandel1@aia.com

Reference 3: Brian Otis, COO, Acme Seals Corporation, 312-321-7294 cell, 312-666-0203 office, brianotis1@acmeseals.com

Relationship: I worked with Steve and earlier with Brian, especially on drastically reducing inventory costs by Pareto efficiency, improving our forecasting, centralizing our inventory, aligning our metrics and decreasing the amount of time needed to manufacture products.

14. Compensation Plan and Equity Purchase Plan parameters in the Investor CFO position description are acceptable (if you are seeking a higher salary than our client's range or a higher bonus plan than that offered, this is a zero rating, and "deal killer". Equity investment requirement can be lowered from $100K to $60K for the hired CFO candidate who is not in a position to invest). __8__

Candidate comments:

I believe I can creatively address this issue. One option is to use funds that would have gone toward relocation. Another option is a sign-on bonus to compensate for this year's lost bonus opportunities with Acme Seals.

Completed retained search: SITG Chief Operating Officer. All actual names and data have been edited for privacy.

SITG COO Candidate: David Ritter

Edited Client Company Summary

Well established National Association of Securities Dealers Automated Quotations (NASDAQ),$110MM multi-plant and multi-state producer of custom-engineered components, products, and specialty packaging primarily for the medical, automotive, aerospace and defense, electronics, consumer, and industrial markets. Based in the Northeast.

Checklist – Rate yourself on a scale of one to ten on these points related to these critical Chief Operating Officer specs.

Take your time (24 hours) and reflect about your responses before you make them your final answers. Thank you.

1. Technical Degree. __10__; MBA

Candidate Comments:

M.S., Manufacturing Systems Engineering, Cornell University

B.S., Physics, Rensselaer Polytechnic Institute (RPI)

2. Raw material converting, or medical device, or automotive parts manufacturing experience producing highly engineered products. __10__

Candidate comments:

Since 2007 in the Ferrocom Corporation High Performance Division (HPD), I've been directly involved in the development and commercialization of specialty high performance materials targeting applications in both the medical device and automotive markets. Examples of medical products include orthotics, prosthetic padding, and other biomechanical support products using PEREN Medical® urethane foams that meet ISO 10993/FDA G95 requirements for primary skin contact, and Transbak® advanced dermal materials used in wound dressing backings, transdermal patches, IV site dressings, and EKG electrodes. In the automotive market, PEREN® urethanes and CORACO® silicones were specified in dozens of applications from noise and vibration blocking to water sealing and high temperature under the hood applications.

During the twelve years from 1992 to 2004 at the Ferrocom Corporation Components Division, I held positions in Quality, Engineering, R&D, Manufacturing, and General Management in an automotive components business that produced Rynophyl® gas tank floats sold to tier one automotive OEMs such as Exide Systems, Valeo, Delphi Automotive Systems LLC, Cooper-Standard Automotive, Inc. and Bosch. The custom molded foam floats were highly engineered to withstand years of immersion in hydrocarbon fuels with negligible absorption. The entire business was conducted under the QS9000 Quality Management System (later upgraded to TS16949).

My first position following graduate school was at General Motors as a Manufacturing Development Engineer, where my job was to develop new manufacturing methods enabling improved automotive component designs.

Reference 1: Bob Wallace, Former CEO, previously President Ferrocom Corporation 860-799 3570 office, rwallace1@gmail.com

Relationship: Bob was my direct supervisor for nine years as GM Elastomer Components Division, VP Corporate Manufacturing and GM High Performance Foams.

Reference 2: Frank Gilbert, Retired VP Ferrocom Corporation, 480-415-3801 home, fgillern@aol.com

Relationship: We worked on and off for fifteen years or so until 2009. Sometimes I was a peer of David's and later his boss in both a direct and matrix reporting structure.

Reference 3: Mike Bissel, Vice President, Technology, CTO. Ferrocom ACCORN USA, 480-223-1575 office, mbissell@accornusa.com

Relationship: Mike was a former Ferrocom ACCORN USA BoD Member and former peer member of Joint Venture Executive Leadership Team. Ferrocom is a Japanese company with over $400B in worldwide sales you never heard of that produces all industrial products for consumer health care, medical, and surgical. ACCORN USA has a 50/50 joint venture with Ferrocom Corporation and Mike used to run it until I replaced him.

---

3. Has solid progressive manufacturing knowledge including Continuous Improvement, KPI measurements, Lean, 5S, Six Sigma, Kaizen, Value Stream, etc.__10__

Candidate comments:

Since early in my career, I have driven continuous improvement in operations utilizing all of the above named tools with proven results. For three years, my primary job function as VP of Manufacturing was to lead a team of Six Sigma Black Belts in the elimination of waste, and process variation through Lean and DMAIC (Define, Measure, Analyze, Improve, and Control) projects. As a General Manager, I have always championed the use of these tools to achieve business results.

Reference: Mike Sherman, Former VP, Ferrocom Corporation, 480-888-1044 cell, sherman@gmail.com

Relationship: Mike was a peer member of the Ferrocom Executive Leadership Team. I have worked with him in various roles that overlapped us together for twenty years.

4. Hires and retains good people, and has team building skills (motivation and coaching). __10__

Candidate comments:

I have a solid track record of building and leading high performance teams. Direct reports receive clear expectations, honest feedback, and coaching. I require direct reports to have active development plans that I routinely review. Employees describe me as a manager who motivates them to be their best.

Reference 1: Albert Carlson, Plant Manager, High Performance Silicones, Ferrocom Corporation, Springfield, IL, 708-535-5921 cell, albertcarlson1@yahoo.com

Relationship: Albert is a former subordinate I hired. He worked for me for two years before I left Ferrocom. He successfully closed a money losing Hamburg, Germany silicone plant and transferred production lines to Springfield, IL under budget. He now has it profitably running.

Reference 2: Katum Kimu, General Manager, High Performance Foams and Urethanes, Ferrocom Corporation, South Korea, +82-31-223-7970, office-katumkimu@gmail.com

Relationship: I helped Ferrocom Corporation acquire Katum's company that had been a direct competitor of ours. He reported to me for three years and consistently made good profits for Ferrocom Corporation. I visited his plant twice yearly and we kept in constant phone contact in between.

5. Supply chain, purchasing background helpful, pro-customer attitude; will interface well with customers. __10__

Candidate comments:

I am extremely customer-focused, and routinely interact directly with customers. Since 2007, I've held Customer Advisory Council meetings with key customers twice each year in the US, Europe, and Asia. In these meetings, direct interactive customer feedback is gathered, and that feedback is used to drive continuous improvement in customer satisfaction.

I led the Supply Chain organization for nine years as General Manager of the Elastomer Components Division, and later at the High Performance Foams Division. My direct interactions with key suppliers have been at a strategic level. A recent example is the strategic alliance I formed with a European manufacturing partner to supply silicone sponge products that are sold under a Ferrocom brand.

Reference 1: Carl Bond, President, Johnson & Thomas, Timmons, Ontario Canada, 249-776-8802 office, cbond@johnsonthomas.com

Relationship: Carl is a twelve year Ferrocom Corporation customer. His company is a vertically integrated specialty materials supplier and also a competitor. Carl provided good input when I ran the Advisory Council.

Reference 2: Bill Simmons, President and CEO, Simmons Die Cutters & Fabricators, Pittsburg, PA., (412) 335-3005 office, wsimmons@simmons.com

Relationship: Bill is a ten year Ferrocom Corporation customer. Simmons are die cutters and fabricators of Ferrocom components to OEMs. I have dealt with him through exchanging productive ideas in Advisory Council meetings with him that I formerly led for several years.

6. Manage eleven plants from the Northeast to the West Coast through Plant Managers, Regional Managers, and GMs. Willing to travel 25%-50% as needed. Consistent in communication with plants and fosters inter-plant communication. __10__

Candidate comments:

I've managed both union and non-union plants in the US, Germany, Korea, China, and Japan since 2007. Direct reports in each location have either been General Managers or Plant Managers. Travel has been consistent with the requirements of this position. Consistent employee communication has been a key component of my role in both business leadership and corporate staff positions. Monthly employee communications meetings via simultaneous video conferencing assured consistency of the message.

Reference 1: Konrad Monsen, General Manager, Ferrocom GmbH, Hamburg, Germany, +40-057-3322-7172 office, konrad.monsen@gmail.com

Relationship: I helped Konrad set up this plant. Konrad reported to me for six years and I would visit his plant twice yearly. They manufactured ceramic substrates for power electronics solutions.

Reference 2: Stephen Zhao, Plant Manager, Ferrocom Technology(Suzhou) Co., Ltd., Advanced Circuit Materials Division, Suzhou, Jiangsu, China, (86) 555 13844803210 office, fax-(86)10355066380.

Relationship: Stephen reported to me for four years. I would visit him twice annually. His plant had advanced PCB technology, the latest laminates, and produced structured sequential laminations along with multiple metal finishes.

Reference 3: Yuriko Tanabe, Ph.D., General Manager, Ferrocom Japan Ltd., Ogawa-Cho, Kawasaki-Ku, Kawasaki-city, Kanagawa 210-0023, Japan, +81-44-322-7761 office, fax +81-44-888-9990.

Relationship: Yuriko reported to me for four years. I worked closely with Yuriko to improve PCB and IC substrate manufacturing towards denser and more complex boards, constructed of higher layer counts and finer lines. I visited his plant twice annually and was always available to Yuriko by phone for issues.

7. Work closely with the VP Sales and Marketing as a business partner on a variety of ongoing issues from people and customers, pricing, quality, products, and delivery schedules. ___10___

Candidate comments:

I've had broad commercial experience since 2000, successfully navigating the many issues that had the potential to impact the business. In the capacity of VP and General Manager, my role has been to lead my commercial and operations team in the resolution of a variety of ongoing issues from people and customers, pricing, quality, products, and delivery schedules. As a member of the CEO's Executive Leadership Team, I have consistently demonstrated strong collaboration with my peers to resolve broader issues that affect the entire company.

Reference 1: Bob Wallace, Former CEO, previously President Ferrocom Corporation, 860-799 3570 office, rwallace1@gmail.com

---

Relationship: Bob was my direct supervisor for nine years as GM Elastomer Components Division, VP Corporate Manufacturing, and GM High Performance Foams at Ferrocom Corporation.

Reference 2: Jim Shaw, Vice President of Marketing, High Performance Materials, (860) 666-3115 cell, jimshaw1@.ferrocomcorporation.com

Relationship: Jim and I worked closely together as peer members of Ferrocom Corporation's Executive Leadership team. The company invited a cross section of customers to group discussions on a wide variety of customer sensitive topics such as pricing, on time delivery, quality, and the expense of new materials replacing the old.

Reference 3: Ben Lawrence, Director of Sales, High Performance Foams, (719) 242-6770 cell, benlawrence1@.ferrocomcorporation.com

Relationship: I hired Ben who brought a strong background in electronic materials sales. He reported to me for fifteen months until I was let go by Ferrocom Corporation in the summer of 2013. Ben developed a big piece of new business from Hewlett Packard Corp. I traveled with him as he targeted potential big customers for sales presentations as the technical resource.

8. Work with CFO on financial measurement, contracts and legal issues, financial forecasts, HR issues (example: benefits) and IT strategy. <u>10</u>

Candidate comments:

I'm skilled at connecting financial metrics with the underlying root cause issues that affect business results. I routinely worked very closely with my Finance Manager in the High Performance Materials Division on a wide range of topics, including financial reporting, variance analysis, forecasting, cash management, strategic planning, capital investment analysis, and M&A analysis. I've been directly involved in the creation and approval of contracts, including strategic supplier agreements, joint venture agreements, acquisitions, and joint development agreements. I led the corporate IT function at Ferrocom Corporation for two years, driving business standardization and ERP implementation.

Reference: John Emerson, Finance Manager, High Performance Materials Division, (860) 333-1114 office, (860) 412-5546 cell, johnemerson1@ferrocomcorporation.com

Relationship: John was the de-facto CFO of Ferrocom Corporation's High Performance Materials Division. He reported directly to the Corporate VP Finance and on a dotted line to me as CEO. John and I worked closely regarding financial reporting, variance analysis, sales and profit forecasting, cash management, strategic planning, and capital investment analysis.

9. Works with VP of Engineering on developing and approving capital investments, prioritizing improvement activities and prioritizing development. __10__

Candidate comments:

A key responsibility during my three year tenure as VP of Manufacturing was to plan, prioritize, and approve all major capital investments, with an annual budget of approximately $20M. As VP and General Manager of the High Performance Foams Division, I developed the strategic and annual plans for capital investment, operational improvements, and new product development.

Reference: Angelo Costa, Ferrocom Corporation's VP Engineering, High Performance Materials, (860) 221-323-7890 office, (860) 661-956- cell, angelocosta1@ferrocomcorporation.com

Relationship: When I was General Manager of Ferrocom Corporation's High Performance Foams, Angelo and I were peers and we worked closely developing strategic and annual plans for capital investment, operational improvements, and new product development in manufacturing locations in Hartford, CT (US), Suzhou, China and Seoul, Korea.

10. Work with IT on developing and measuring key indicators, automating business processes and improving decision making information. __10__

Candidate comments:

In my experience, the CEO of Ferrocom Corporation, Hartford, CT and his Executive Leadership Team (Operating Committee) first agree on the most critical, must-do business results that will drive every decision in the company. The Operating

Committee then agrees on how to measure results, and the execution is driven by a collaboration between IT and Operations. As VP of Manufacturing and IT, I drove the standardization of business processes in order to facilitate automating them in our ERP system. This was later enhanced through the addition of standard reporting tools that drove improved decision making.

Reference: Sam Lowenstein, Ferrocom Corporation's Global IT Director, (860) 222-5550, office, (860) 431-6890 cell, samlowenstein1@ferrocomcorporation.com

Relationship: As Vice President of Corporate Manufacturing and Information Technology, Ferrocom Corporation, I hired Sam to be Ferrocom Corporation's Global IT Director in September, 2007. He and I worked closely together for five years until I was promoted. We drove corporate wide business process standardization, reducing fixed IT costs by $500K, and simplified ERP implementation.

11. Manage by metrics including measuring KPI results. __10__

Candidate comments:

As Ferrocom Corporation's VP and General Manager of the High Performance Foams Division, I managed the business using a KPI dashboard that made the status of key results visible. This in turn set the agenda for a bi-weekly staff meeting of my direct reports, where any variances from plan were reviewed and action items assigned. The same basic process was cascaded down throughout the organization at the functional department level, using KPIs specific to each team.

Reference: Charles Bowen, current CEO, Ferrocom Corporation, 860 995-1112 office, charlesbowen1@ferrocomcorporation.com

Relationship: Charles Bowen became CEO of Ferrocom Corporation in 2011 and he promoted me to Vice President, High Performance Foams, in January, 2012. I inherited several manufacturing locations in Asia, and the US.

12. Improve labor productivity. __10__

Candidate comments:

As VP of Manufacturing, I championed and led many projects across Ferrocom that resulted in higher labor productivity. This was accomplished primarily through value stream mapping and other Lean tools, such as SMED (rapid changeover). In several other cases, mini Kaizen events were highly effective at removing waste and improving labor productivity.

Reference: Nick Alexander, Plant Manager, High Performance Materials, Ferrocom Corporation, St. Louis, MO (314) 248-3412, office, (314) 321-5590 cell, nickalwxander1@ferrocomcorporation.com.

Relationship: Nick reported to me and helped me fold in a losing Belgium Silicones operation into our St. Louis Ferrocom Corporation facility. I worked with Nick instituting Lean Manufacturing principles removing waste, and greatly improving labor productivity.

13. Spearhead strategic evaluation of optimizing the company's footprint, including how many facilities should Client Company have and where. Consider strategies for plant consolidation and identify what the risks and rewards are. __10__

Candidate comments:

During my tenure at Ferrocom, I moved the Elastomer Components Division to Suzhou, China and closed the US factory, acquired a Korean competitor and consolidated their operation with our China plant, closed an underperforming non-woven's business, consolidated two silicone manufacturing plants, closing a facility in Bremen, Germany, and formed a strategic alliance with a European silicone manufacturer to supply a product line that did not make sense to move in the consolidation.

Reference: Bob Wallace, Former CEO, previously President Ferrocom Corporation 860-799 3570 office, rwallace1@gmail.com

Relationship: Bob was my direct supervisor for nine years as GM Elastomer Components Division, VP Corporate Manufacturing, and GM High Performance Foams at Ferrocom Corporation.

14. The Chief Operating Officer ideally will grow with our client company and eventually prove herself/himself able to assume greater, longer-term responsibilities and duties should the opportunity arise. __10__

Candidate comments:

I am a continuous learner, and a strong believer in personal and professional development. During my entire career, I have maintained mentoring relationships and worked with executive coaches to assure that I continuously increase my value to my employer. Whether or not this position someday leads to a larger position in the future, I will always grow and strive to bring new value to the role.

Reference: Dennis Friedman, Retired former Corporate Vice President, Human Resources, Ferrocom Corporation 401-332-6693 home, dfriedman12@gmail.com

Relationship: Dennis Friedman was at Ferrocom Corporation during my entire career at Ferrocom Corporation. He worked with me closely on many of my positions at the company. He recommended me for my three last promotions with Ferrocom Corporation.

15. Base salary range and bonus plan are acceptable. __8__

Candidate comments:

In my previous role, base salary was $250K, plus a 45% bonus target with the potential to double that based on meeting financial targets. Long-term incentive compensation included a blend of time-based and performance-based restricted stock. With the opportunity for skin in the game, I will accept a lower base salary and bonus.

Completed retained search: SITG Vice President Sales and Marketing. All actual names and data have been edited for privacy.

SITG VP Sales and Marketing: Randall Swanson

Edited Client Company Summary

Growing profitable $65M in sales New England manufacturer and fabricator of engineered materials and components for industrial customers. The most significant end-use segments are heavy construction, rotor vanes, power generation, electronics, aerospace, and cryogenics.

Checklist – Rate yourself on a scale of one to ten on these points related to these critical VP Sales and Marketing specs.

Take your time (24 hours) and reflect about your responses before you make them your final answers. Thank you.

1. Technical degree__10__; BS Chemistry plus equivalent industry/functional experience (twenty years) __10__; MBA a plus. __10__

Candidate comments: BS Chemistry, Brown University; MBA Marketing and Finance, Northeastern University; Equivalent industry/functional experience (twenty+ years).

2. Several years of successful hands-on experience in combination of technical sales (sales engineer and/or applications engineer) and sales management experience, nationally, in broad specialty materials preferably thermoplastics materials, reinforced, elastomers, resins, boards and custom molded. ___10___

Candidate comments:

Multiple industry and product experience with materials, including composites, specialty elastomers (including reinforced), various resin types and casting systems, and especially custom molding business. Have held positions of Director of Sales, Marketing and Engineering, for industry leader in thermoformed material handling leader, and VP Sales, Marketing and Engineering, for market leader in custom thermoformed components. Aerospace experience fundamental to understanding composites. Good material science background.

Reference: Carl Zeller, Chairman, CEO and President of Clark Plastics Technologies Corporation, Peoria, IL, 309-444-7908, carlzeller1@clarkplastics technologies.com

Relationship: I reported directly to Carl Zeller as Business Unit Director during my final year at Clark Plastics Technologies. I worked extensively with him on our joint venture with Collins Packaging Company.

3. Relevant customer knowledge in either bearings or wear, vanes or cryogenics applications, heavy construction equipment manufacturing, power generation equipment manufacturing or electronics manufacturing. ___7___

Candidate comments:

Strongest in heavy construction (Caterpillar, etc.), electronics manufacturing, and building composites for items like antennas, vanes, etc. as VP Sales, Marketing and Engineering, for Eldorado Thermoformed Products, experienced in low and high temperature electronic applications.

Reference: Brad Bennett, President of Eldorado Thermoformed Products, LaCrosse, WI, 608-567-4331 office, bradbennett1@eldoradothermaformed products.com

Relationship: Brad Bennett was brought in as a turnaround guy when our market lost 50%of its business in the economic downturn. He eliminated almost a dozen C-Level executives and consolidated operations at Eldorado Thermoformed Products. I reported to Brad for eighteen months with a mandate to open up new large accounts, which I did. I replaced Brad as an interim President for three months until the board hired his replacement.

4. Experience in either technical sales/sales management, or sales engineering from any of the following industries: textile, paper, or related producers of cotton, linen, canvas, fiberglass or paper substrates. __7__

Candidate comments:

Experience in vinyl reinforced materials (fabric or paper) and substitution of canvas and other materials. Significant fiberglass replacement substitution thereof. Gasket experience includes paper, specialty materials, and composites.

Reference 1: Tom Salvin, Chief Financial Officer of Westerland Materials, Los Angeles, CA, 213-777-8695 office, tomsalvin1@westerland materials.com

Relationship: Tom Salvin and I collaborated together on different projects during the seven years I was with Westerland Materials. We worked on budgets and planning, and the sale of our cork and rubber aftermarket division.

Reference 2: Linda Ouelette, VP Industrial Relations of Eldorado Thermoformed Products, LaCrosse, WI, 608-221-6789, office, lindaouelette@eldoradothermaformed products.com

Relationship: Linda was involved with my hiring as VP Sales and Marketing at Thomson Plastics, which was soon after acquired by Eldorado Thermoformed Products. She checked my previous references at Westerland Materials and knows a lot about me professionally.

5. Experience calling on and overseeing national sales coverage calling on engineering as well as purchasing at OEM customers and prospects, and closing the sale. __10__

Candidate comments:

Comfortable in both an engineering "solution sell' or negotiating with purchasing. Significant company engineering management experience. Negotiated numbers agreements with Fortune 100/500 companies. Like to "ask for the order". Tactics in the sales process are to early on identify potential objections and begin to work towards overcoming them. Like to ask sales personnel why they will not get an order as a means of validating true potential. Also, my international experience should be valuable in helping build revenues.

Reference 1: John Shuler, CEO of Progressive Packaging, Columbus, OH, 614-777-1189 office, johnshuler1@progressive-packaging.com

Relationship: John Shuler, CEO of Progressive Packaging, put together a partnership involving intellectual property he owned for Clark Plastics to produce and market new products. John worked with me for three to four years while I was Director of Marketing, Sales and Engineering, with Eldorado Thermoformed Products, and Business Unit Director with Clark Plastics Technologies after they acquired Eldorado. Unfortunately John and my boss never got along well.

Reference 2: Chris Sullivan, Northern Region Sales Director of Clark Plastics Technologies, Peoria, IL, 309-444-0042 cell, chrissullivan1@clarkplasticstechnologies.com

Relationship: Chris has known me for over five years. He was brought in by Clark Plastic Technologies as VP Sales and Marketing on the vacuum forming side of the business in NA. My responsibility was Director of Sales and Marketing of the Eldorado Thermoformed Products Division of Clark Plastic and their business is automotive returnable packaging and drainage products. We were peers and we worked on the same deals together. At John Deere we'd sell them external plastic parts – colored hoods, etc. and my division made the packaging containers for the shipped parts. Chris would introduce my group to his existing customer base, consisting of heavy trucks and snowmobiles.

---

6. Proven national sales organization management experience encompassing hiring/firing/upgrading/training/motivating Independent Sales Reps, Direct Sales Rep employees and Customer Service personnel. __10__

Candidate comments:

The sales growth my employers have achieved is a function of hiring and developing the best people. I am a firm believer in the "Consultative Selling" process to the total organization. Used an MBO management style and a process called EMFA to develop employees (Expectation, Measurement, Follow-up, and Accountability–with the objective to move from a supervisor to a Partner and help sales related personnel make better decisions independently). Numerous sales incentive plans developed. Built successful national and international independent rep/master distribution programs.

Reference 1: Brad Bennett, President of Eldorado Thermoformed Products, LaCrosse, WI, 608-567-4331 office, bradbennett1@eldoradothermaformed products.com

Relationship: Brad Bennett was brought in as a turnaround guy when our market lost 50%of its business in the economic downturn. He eliminated almost a dozen C-Level executives and consolidated operations at Eldorado Thermoformed Products. I reported to Brad for eighteen months with a mandate to open up new large accounts, which I did. I replaced Brad as an interim President for three months until the board hired his replacement.

Reference 2: Harry Spencer, Plant Human Resources Manager of Eldorado Thermoformed Products, LaCrosse, WI,

608-212-4440 office, harryspencer1@eldoradothermaformed products.com

Relationship: Harry reported to me for five years. He can verify I managed six outside Sales Territory Managers and two Customer Service Reps. He can also verify 50% of our sales were engineered products versus commodity sales. He knows I trained the Eldorado Thermoformed Products' sales force in solution selling techniques versus price.

7. Experience analyzing and targeting US growth markets related to Spaulding Composites' products, applications, or customers, and designing and implementing aggressive sales strategies to capitalize on them. __7__

Candidate comments:

Knowledgeable of applications, but have excellent abilities to identify market opportunities and determine viability. Revenue results of my employers are a result of a very focused and aggressive marketing program, all components of the organization understand and support plan.

Reference: Bob Kellogg, formerly Head of Group Sales for Eldorado Thermoformed Products LaCrosse, WI., and then former Director of Marketing and New Business Development after Eldorado's acquisition by Clark Plastics Technologies Corporation, Peoria, IL, 262-888-3311 cell

Relationship: I hired Bob and he worked for me as Head of Group Thermoplastic sales for four years at Eldorado Thermoformed Products. That included some work on the

Eldorado joint venture with Clark Plastics Technologies which became Eldorado being acquired during our fifth year working together. Bob became Director of Marketing and New Business Development, and I became Business Unit Manager for Clark Plastics Technologies. He and I left Clark Plastics about the same time.

8. Knowledge of composite material and filament winding applications. __8__

Candidate comments:

Have a working knowledge of both composites and filament winding and the manufacturing process of each. My technical degree and engineering management experience provide a basis to quickly learn new technologies, as has been required upon entering new business management roles.

Reference: Dr. Tejal Mehta, Head of R&D, Supervisory Chemist of BASF, Florham Park, NJ, 973-245-000 office, tejalmehta1@basf.com

Relationship: Dr. Mehta was a peer of mine at BASF in NJ for seven years. He was Group Leader and Head of R&D. Our sales were based on being spec'd in after being qualified. He knows of my good relationship with our former VP boss in the US and his boss at BASF in Germany. Both have left the company. We made bonding panels for the automotive market and for Boeing aircraft. Our flame retardant chemistry expertise was used to make products for airlines that had experienced toxic fume inhalation deaths after their planes had non-lethal crashes. We generated $23M in new sales by my second year and 60% gross margin.

---

9. Has traveled 40%-50% nationally. __10__

Reference: Linda Ouelette, VP Industrial Relations of Eldorado Thermoformed Products, LaCrosse, WI, 608-221-6789 office, lindaouelette@eldoradothermaformed products.com

Relationship: Linda was involved with my hiring as VP Sales and Marketing at Thomson Plastics, which was soon after acquired by Eldorado Thermoformed Products. I had a heavy travel schedule part of the year. She checked my previous references at Westerland Materials including my heavy travel schedule there training new salesmen, and knows a lot about me professionally.

10. Experience spearheading new product development objectives based on customer input. __10__

Candidate comments:

Firm believer in documenting customer requirements. Use this process to ask customer, "If we make such a product – are you going to buy it?" Also try to verify customer pricing and volume expectations. Like to consider the impact of a new project upon obtaining additional business.

Reference 1: Brad Bennett, President of Eldorado Thermoformed Products, LaCrosse, WI, 608-567-4331 office, bradbennett1@eldoradothermaformed products.com

Relationship: Brad Bennett was brought in as a turnaround guy when our market lost 50%of its business in the economic downturn. He eliminated almost a dozen C-Level executives and consolidated operations at Eldorado Thermoformed Products. I reported to Brad for eighteen months with a mandate to open up new large accounts, which I did. I replaced Brad as an interim President for three months until the board hired his replacement.

Reference 2: Bob Kellogg, formerly Head of Group Sales for Eldorado Thermoformed Products LaCrosse, WI. and then former Director of Marketing and New Business Development after Eldorado's acquisition by Clark Plastics Technologies Corporation, Peoria, IL, 262-888-3311 cell

Relationship: I hired Bob and he worked for me as Head of Group Thermoplastic sales for four years at Eldorado Thermoformed Products. That included some work on the Eldorado joint venture with Clark Plastics Technologies which became Eldorado being acquired during our fifth year working together. Bob became Director of Marketing and New Business Development, and I became Business Unit Manager of Clark Plastics Technologies. He and I left Clark Plastics about the same time.

11. Experience developing budget for new sales tools, trade show material, and upgrading company's website. __10__

Candidate comments:

Samples of new sales tools are being sent, highlighting capabilities. Similarly, I have directed the development of user friendly web pages, including positioning for high priority slotting when someone Googles a specific product. Firm believer in using case histories and key customer comments on webpage. Need customer service personnel with ability to respond to initial customer questions.

Reference: Tom Salvin, Chief Financial Officer of Westerland Materials, Los Angeles, CA, 213-777-8695 office, tomsalvin1@westerland materials.com

Relationship: Tom Salvin and I collaborated together on different projects during the seven years I was with Westerland Materials. We worked on budgets for new sales tools, trade show materials, and upgrading company's website.

12. Experience in working closely with company's manufacturing function in championing customer issues including new product trials, prototypes and other priorities. __10__

Candidate comments:

Based on my experience running a manufacturing operation, I fully support a partnership with manufacturing. Manufacturing needs to sign off on large quotes and products requiring new processes. The objective is for the new business to run at projected costs and make money for the company.

Reference: John Shuler, CEO of Progressive Packaging , Columbus, OH, 614-777-1189 office, johnshuler1@progressive packaging.com

Relationship 1: John Shuler, CEO of Progressive Packaging, put together a partnership involving intellectual property he owned for Clark Plastics to produce and market new products. John worked with me for three to four years while I was Director of Marketing, Sales and Engineering with Eldorado Thermoformed Products, and Business Unit Director with Clark Plastics Technologies after they acquired Eldorado. I worked closely with manufacturing, especially on high volume new products production.

Reference 2: Tom Salvin, Chief Financial Officer of Westerland Materials, Los Angeles, CA, 213-777-8695 office, tomsalvin1@westerland materials.com

Relationship: Tom Salvin and I collaborated together on different projects during the seven years I was with Westerland Materials. Since our boss, Tony Evans, passed away last year, Tom can verify that as Vice President over two specialty elastomer manufacturing operations, I fully supported a partnership with manufacturing. Manufacturing had to sign off on large quotes and plastic products requiring new processes for the automotive aftermarket in successful product redesigns giving us a sole source position.

13. Experience establishing and tracking appropriate metrics and measuring progress related to sales, sales forecasts, shipments, pricing, DSO, margins, and taking corrective action where necessary to improve unsatisfactory situations. __10__

Candidate comments:

My MBO style fully supports using metrics to monitor and provide the "alerts" as to when an action is required. My performance rating systems have generally used metrics as part of the overall employee evaluation. Generally a corrective action consists of defining the issue and developing a game plan, including who takes control and dates for resolution.

Reference: Brad Bennett, President of Eldorado Thermoformed Products, LaCrosse, WI, 608-567-4331 office, bradbennett1@eldoradothermaformed products.com

Relationship: Brad Bennett was brought in as a turnaround guy when our market lost 50% of its business in the economic downturn at Eldorado Thermoformed Products. I reported to Brad for eighteen months with a mandate to open up new large accounts, which I did. He required that I report weekly on my Key Performance Indicators including actual sales calls, updated sales forecasts, closed sales and average sale size. Brad will verify I managed my twenty-two person sales team by MBO, measured their performances and took action to shore up any correctible sales weaknesses.

14. Interested in the equity investment opportunity and would like to learn more about it. __10__

Candidate comments:

Look forward to understanding more details. Like the concept that there is a real "pay for performance" opportunity.

15. Salary/Bonus range in package in the position specs is acceptable. $175K -190K base; annual bonus range - 10% to 100%. __10__

Candidate comments:

The total compensation range is acceptable. I am interested in the skin in the game opportunity.

---

16. Would eventually relocate with spouse/family to the New England locale within reasonable time period and distance. __10__

Candidate comments:

My wife and I are in agreement to relocate. I plan to rent a condo until we sell our home. My wife will then join me and we can look for a home in the general company area.

Exhibit Items to Bring to your PEG Interviews in your Multi-packet Portfolio

In chapter 8, I covered what "show and tell" exhibit items you might bring with you for PEG networking meetings. Now it's "show time" for interviewing with a PEG Partner about a C-Level job. For "show and tell exhibit" items I suggest using Esselte Oxford Blue Poly 8-Pocket Folders - Letter Size - 9.1 x 10.6 x 0.4. They open wide easily and fit into a larger valise or briefcase. Practice pulling out the item(s) before your interview.

Ask yourself what exhibit items, if any, might be relative to the C-Level job, industry, products or markets for which you are being considered? PEGs are metrics, data, and Excel spreadsheet results hungry. Non-classified quarterly financials showing tremendous gains. Annual labor cost reduction chart. Improved productivity gains, minimal turnover, no plant accidents in thirteen months. Anything come to mind, there? The fewer exhibits, the better. Its impact and effect you are seeking. Mull it over and decide.

Bring duplicates of your completed SRQ and Indiana Jones Bio and resume in case the PEG has a surprise additional interviewer at your job interview. That will keep the extra interviewer busy and help prevent the interviewers "ganging up on you". You already FedEx'ed your Indiana Jones Bio and completed self-rating quiz to the PEG Partner.

Face-to-Face Generic SITG C-Level Job 1st Interview with a PEG Partner

This generic interview example is the result of SITG C-Level candidates including CEO, CFO, COO, or VP S&M each networking to connect with a PEG Partner. Next comes a 1st interview with him about a SITG job that theoretically fits each function example. If this 1st interview goes well, there would be a 2nd interview with each function's potential direct boss.

The generic PEG SITG C-Level interview with a PEG Partner should focus on these core subjects:

1. Your Completed Self Rating Quiz including your high ratings and listed references in support of them. If you have actual written reference letters from any of them, it's "show and tell" time.

2. The Descriptive Memorandum will present opportunities to ask specific questions of the PEG Partner based on your C-Level job responsibilities.

3. Your Indiana Jones Bio; ask the PEG Partner if he had any specific questions about it. If you were an Eagle Scout, or from the PEG Partner's home county or worked for employers where there are mutual contacts or were a veteran as he was. These topics aren't typically written in a C -Level person's resume. Why did you write an IJ Bio? It's just a "due diligence" resume. The more

a hiring authority knows about the job contenders the better informed their hiring decision.

Make good eye contact with the PEG Partner without staring. Look at his face and features when he speaks to you and especially when you speak to him. Nod your head when in agreement with the PEG Partner's comments. Your body language should be relaxed, show attentiveness, and focus.

I often suggest that the SITG C-Level candidate have a note pad and make notes of important info given to him. It helps when you email the PEG Partner a follow-up thank you note and reinforce the positive mutual job fit with his key statements from your notes.

PEG Partners are masters of letting people with which they are dealing and negotiating feel as if they have made a deal with the PEG Partner. At least that's the candidate's impression. They let their guard down when, in fact, they have obtained nothing from the PEG. C-Level job interviewers should never let the PEG lull them into a false confidence before they can recover the situation.

What signals are you picking up from the PEG partner's line of questioning? If you submitted an IJ Bio and SRQ to him in advance, do you feel he's read that material? Bottom line, are you being treated like a serious candidate? If you've been with the PEG Partner for long enough to have asked most of the questions in the sector below and others I have suggested, it's time to do a trial close to try to secure a 2nd interview. Time is now of the essence. I have heard of PEG Partners arranging a phone call at the 30 minute mark. If the interview isn't going anywhere as far as the PEG Partner is concerned, it gives him the opportunity to excuse himself for an important call from an Ivy League school's head of investments and can't wait. Goodbye to you Mr. Candidate (for good).

So, you ask the PEG partner, at this point, does he feel you're still a bona fide SITG C-Level candidate of interest for this PEG job opportunity? If not, why not? Often the potential "deal killer" is weak explanations for your last 3 rather rapid job changes. Some clients and PEGs, and many of my headhunter friends, HATE frequent job changes. Middle market and lower middle market PEGs generally hire SITG C-Level qualified and interested job candidates for 4-5 years until the exit or liquidity event.

The other reason some the candidates' references are checked is because they are mutual contacts to both candidate and PEG, this being unknown to the potential hire. Maybe from one or two who may have served on a company board, removed from the candidate's day to day C-Level job duties. The end result is negative comments. Hearsay negative references have hurt many candidates for SITG searches I have handled. The candidates should have been hired, but I couldn't take a chance. Ask the PEG Partner if he would like to check your references? You'd like to give them a heads up, but don't let that halt moving the hiring process along.

One area job candidates must be prepared to answer crisply, sharply and honestly is their reasons for changing jobs. Don't practice your job changing answers during a PEG job interview. The skin in the game C-Level job seeker isn't just trying to get hired no matter what. You have to learn what you're getting into for your sake and the PEG's.

The SITG C-Level Job Candidate's Suggested 1st Interview Questions for the PEG Partner

- Would I be a replacement hire in this C-Level position? If so, why?
- Why were you interested in interviewing me for this C-Level job?
- Does the PEG Partner have any questions about your Indiana Jones Bio?
- Answer PEG Partner's questions regarding your submitted SRQ.
- What are the main reasons the PEG acquired this portfolio company?
- How long do they plan to keep this company?
- How do they envision implementing their growth plan?
- Are they acquisition minded regarding their fragmented competitors?
- Do they envision any new product introductions?
- How can you be a good fit within the company culture?
- What is the PEG Partner's management style?
- Do the key managers in the company have some skin in the game?

If the PEG Partner focuses on "Tell me about yourself," that is the equivalent of a welterweight being pinned on the ropes. If that happens give him your elevator pitch.

- Ask the PEG Partner if he can provide an explanation and illustration of how the management stock value was calculated by the PEG and an overview of the PEG client's Management Common Stock Ownership

Program. Again, these documents are routinely provided by the PEG client as part of the SITG C-Level hire's job offer package.

- Ask the PEG Partner to see a Management Equity Valuation Estimation Worksheet based on PEG's estimate of the company's low, medium and high growth performance based on Earnings, Taxes, Depreciation and Amortization) EBITDA after 5 years of ownership (illustration example below).

ASI Manufacturing- Management Equity Valuation Estimation Worksheet

This worksheet is purely for illustrative purposes. Equity figures are based on management estimates of performance. Actual results can vary from these figures due to many factors. Equity investments in smaller private companies are inherently riskier than investments in large public companies.

Growth Scenarios-Performance of Company in Year 5 of Ownership:

EBITDA	Sales
A) Low Growth (5%) - $2,817,118	$9,236,451
B) Medium Growth (10%) - $3,729,684	$11,655,262
C) High Growth (15%) - $4,657,982	$14,556,194

Hypothetical Sale Prices after Year 5 of Ownership

Sale Price as a Multiple of EBITDA

7X EBITDA	5X EBITDA	6X EBITDA
A) Low Growth (5%)		
Sale Price $19,719,823	$14,085,588	$16,902,705
Less-Outstanding Debt ($3,805,368)	($3,805,368)	($3,805,368)
Less-Repayment of Preferred Equity ($4,788.333)	($4,788.333)	($4,788.333)
Value of Common Stock $11,126,121	$5,491,886	$8,309,003
B) Medium Growth (10%)		
Sale Price $19,719,823	$18,648,420	$16,902,705
Less-Outstanding Debt ($2,704,270)	($2,704,270)	($2,704,270)
Less-Repayment of Preferred Equity ($4,788.333)	($4,788.333)	($4,788.333)
Value of Common Stock $18,615,185	$11,155,817	$14,885,501
C) High Growth (15%)		
Sale Price $19,719,823	$23,289,910	$16,902,705
Less-Outstanding Debt ($2,326,207)	($2,326,207)	($2,326,207)
Less-Repayment of Preferred Equity ($4,788.333)	($4,788.333)	($4,788.333)
Value of Common Stock $25,491,333	$16,175,369	$20,833,351

Management Equity Valuation at Year 5 of Ownership

Assumptions

Management invests $50,000 in the company. As a result of this investment, management receives $50,000 of Preferred Equity and 1.15% of the company's Common Stock.

Management also received stock options that will vest over five years. These options total 5% of the Common Stock.

Upon the sale of the company, after all debt obligations of the company are paid off, the Preferred Equity Investment is repaid along with an 8% compounded return. All remaining sale proceeds are distributed to the Common Stockholders.

Sale Price as a Multiple of EBITDA

7X EBITDA	5X EBITDA	6X EBITDA
Hypothetical Value of $50,000 Preferred Equity Investment & 1.15% of Common Stock		
A) Low Growth (5%) $163,531	$118,024	$140,778
B) Medium Growth (10%) $224,020	$163,771	$193,896
C) High Growth (15%) $279,558	$204,314	$241,936
Hypothetical Value of Stock Options for 5% of Common Stock		
A) Low Growth (5%) $556,306	$274,594	$415,450
B) Medium Growth (10%) $930,759	$557,791	$744,275
C) High Growth (15%) $1,274,567	$808,768	$1,041,668
Hypothetical Combined Value of $50,000 Preferred Equity Investment & 6.65% of Common Stock		
A) Low Growth (5%) $719,838	$392,618	$556,228
B) Medium Growth (10%) $1,154,779	$721,562	$938,171
C) High Growth (15%) $1,554,125	$1,013,082	$1,283,604

The above format is a real example, with the company name edited for confidentiality, of a lower middle market OEM manufacturing company with roughly $9.3M in sales and the opportunity it offered for sales and earnings growth. The CEO I placed in this company invested $50K in receipt of 1.15% of the common stock. He also received a stock option of 5% of the common stock fully vested in five years. These figures from my client PEG are hypothetical examples he was shown before he accepted his job offer of low, medium and high growth based on EBITDA multiples. I almost always furnish my SITG C-Level job candidates with a two or three example projection of earnings from my client PEG for their purchased equity and their options, plus their earned interest if they receive Preferred Stock versus Common Stock. My hired SITG CEO did very well at the exit sale. In the above example, a $50K skin in the game equity purchase could net the hire in a high growth result of $1,554,115. Grow sales, grow profits, sell the business equity for multiples of the EBITDA, and enjoy the shareholders' liquidity event.

There are a zillion books in the libraries, bookstores, and online outlets on interviewing. There is *Forbes* magazine's *"Ten Toughest Interview Questions Answered"*. If you Google "Knock their socks off", other similar book titles and articles on the subject of how to interview and answer tough questions will pop up. Collectively they do not apply to SITG Hiring. In my opinion, nobody can perfectly answer all those difficult questions. The funny thing is, many interviewers, especially from Human Resources, ask a lot of those tough questions and end up recommending the job candidate who answered them the most persuasively. That doesn't mean they hired the best candidate. Regular compensation C-Level job candidates go into their interview trying to memorize the right answers to difficult "sharpshooter" interview questions they may never be asked.

There used to be a weekly TV show when I was growing up called *What's My Line* with a panel of famous celebrities. Three guests would then appear and each would claim to be employed either as a doctor, chef, plumber, or whatever. The panelists would ask each one questions until they took a guess to try to select their correct job title. Often the panelists were completely wrong. That's how I used to be interviewing C-Level job search candidates. I mostly mistook a sharp candidate interview for the best candidate. For the past twenty-eight years my C-Level search candidates live or die by their reference checks. If you couple your completed self-rating quiz that contains specific references in support of your high ratings, and share the results with your interviewer, that is a strong start to a good interview experience for you and the PEG interviewer.

Gilreath Consultancy assembles a three ring binder on every one of our SITG C-Level search candidates. These binders contain resumes, Indiana Jones Bios, copies of degrees and certifications, honorable discharges, (confidential) exhibit items related to a candidate's jobs and at least a dozen written reference checks per candidate. My search agreement requests that the client interviewers must review this material before they interview each of our candidates. In roughly 70% of every interview, our PEG client will open the interview by asking the candidate, "Tell me about yourself." A WSJ article once said that next to public speaking, most executives were apprehensive about their interviewing skills. My proven approach is to have the interviewer focus on the SITG C-Level job to be filled and the SITG C-Level candidate's completed SRQ listing the specific references who would support the high ratings. Next would come the candidate's questions about the company's Confidential Descriptive Memorandum.

SITG C-Level job interviewers don't have to deal with some of the same toughest questions that non SITG job candidates face, if they're smart. You should have FedEx'ed your completed SRQ based on the C-Level job specs you were given rating yourself 1 to 10 on key aspects of the job. A PEG Partner might ask you, "Why should we hire you?" That opens the door for you to ask if he would go over the SRQ questions and your answers with you. Another unnecessary tough interview question is, "What are your goals five years from now?" Job tenure at typical middle market portfolio companies is four to five years until the exit.

If you are asked about your compensation expectations, your SRQ usually rates it against the offered compensation in the job specification. My advice on compensation is you are in agreement with the salary range and bonus plan in the SRQ. Your main interest is in the potential EBIDTA growth at the time of the company's liquidity event in four to five years or so.

Tough C-Level SITG Job Candidate Interview Questions:

- What have you learned from reading our Confidential Information Memorandum?
- Based on what you've learned, describe the type of candidate I need for this C-Level job?
- How have you gotten along with your last three bosses?
- What are your reasons for leaving your last two jobs?
- What is the best way to manage you?
- What do you do to keep your own and your team's focus on satisfying the customer?
- What have you used for Key Performance Indicators to monitor results of your team?
- What's, truthfully, the worst thing any of your references can say about you professionally speaking?
- What lesson (s) have you learned from your last performance appraisal?
- What goal and objective have you set for yourself and what is your target date for accomplishing them?
- How do you see yourself contributing to the success of this portfolio company?

- Why are you interested in investing some of your money in the equity of this company if you are hired for this job?

How The SITG C-Level Job Candidates Should Each End Their PEG Partner 1st Interviews

Keep in mind if you feel confident you can do this job well, mention that based on what you know about the company after reading the Confidential Information Memorandum, and the PEG Partner's comments about the functional job at hand, you can "land on your feet running" (if it's true, it isn't bragging).

Ask the PEG Partner if he has any concerns about whether you can do this job well? If so, what are they?

Tell the PEG Partner that you want the job that you can do the job, and you want to be successful once the scoreboard is tallied (at the company's exit).

Ask the PEG Partner what his time frame is for making a decision then ask what the next step is and when? Would there be an interview for you with others?

Does he want to set up a date and time now while you both have your calendars?

Does he want to contact any of your references listed on the SRQ? (You would like to give them a heads up first, but don't let that be a hold up.) He might want to email you the names of those references he wants to call. Or he might just go ahead and email them directly if time is of the essence.

If it's true, mention that this job opportunity is number one on your list of the SITG jobs in which you are a contender.

Be sure to follow up this interview with a thank you email to the PEG Partner.

In addition to the above, the CFO, Chief Sales &Marketing Officer, and COO should ask the PEG Partner whether each would be a good fit with the portfolio company CEO.

If there are any concerns, urge the PEG Partner to check with specific appropriate references of yours. Hand him the references contact info and specific reference letters from your show & tell info in your valise.

If the PEG Partner expresses no major concerns, press him about when he might set up your meeting with the CEO. If hired, the CEO is the dotted line report of the CFO and the direct boss of the COO and Chief Sales & Marketing Officer.

In their follow-up thank you email, the CFO, Chief Sales &Marketing Officer and COO should ask the PEG Partner if he could send their respective Indiana Jones Bio and completed SRQ form to the PEG portfolio CEO in advance of meeting with him. Thank him for doing so.

PEG job interviews tend to be "cut to the chase", not schmooze sessions. Newly hired C-Level non-performers, especially in lower middle market PEG's portfolio companies, can fairly quickly get fired working for PEGs. Middle market PEGs are more demanding of their C-Level hires but the increased equity growth payoffs at the exit confirm the PEG's general approach works. For example, a newly hired SITG CEO for a lower middle market OEM manufacturing company inherits a computer system that's outdated. Some of the machinery often breaks down. There's no lean manufacturing techniques implemented. There's too much outdated inventory. The labor costs are out of control. Too many plant accidents. These are just some examples of issues that need fixing. If the CEO isn't hands-on and neither he, nor his references, can convince the PEG he can "land on his feet running", he'll never get hired, or worse, he'll never last to the liquidity event.

I have interviewed many Fortune 500 C-Level applicants that did not make my screening cut for my PEG searches. In my skin in the game hiring world, PEGs seek hands-on results-oriented performers. They want doers willing to wear more than one functional "hat", if necessary, to achieve the company's goals and objectives. If an SITG job candidate withholds his strongest references from me and the PEG, unless he is a superstar interviewer, his candidacy could die in a weak interview. Team up with your references and parlay their support for you with my pre-interview preparation process into your becoming a potential skin in the game hire.

Psychological Testing Tips:

- If you have any past psych test results that were positive, you might mention it to the PEG Partner during your interview and offer to email him a copy.
- You may end up having to go to a recommended website and use a furnished password to access it and answer dozens and dozens of questions there for about one hour. If that goes well, you may end up visiting the psychologist if he's local for a meeting lasting another

hour or having a phone discussion with him for about an hour.

- Try to deal with the psych test in the morning if possible, when you are the freshest and have had breakfast and coffee. Either way, just relax and answer the questions honestly. Don't try to get "cute" and outthink the psychologist and what the test is probing by trying to outguess the test. If you answer the questions the way you think the psychologist wants to hear them, you are "cooked".
- Some PEGs require you make a round trip flight to meet with the psychologist in Florida the same day and return home that evening. I advise going the night before and getting a good night's sleep and a hearty breakfast. Some of the psychologists test a candidate for eight hours. No lunch or refreshment. Unbelievable!
- Personally, given a choice of doing twelve employment professional references on a C-Level executive versus taking psych tests, I am all over the former versus the latter from forty plus years of screening executives.

If you can learn what type of psych tests you will be given, there are books in the library on various psych tests to become familiar with the formats and types of questions and what the tests are supposed to reveal.

Face-to-Face SITG CEO Job 2nd Interview with a PEG Partner

Add to your own due diligence by obtaining answers to the following generic questions:

- Ask the PEG Partner if he would be your direct boss if you were hired for this PEG SITG CEO job. If so, what is his management style, typical meeting frequency, and general "modus Operandi"? In this example, the PEG Operating Partner turned out to be this CEO position's actual boss. The lesson here is for the PEG SITG C-Level job interviewer to ask the above questions for answers. The PEG Partner 1st job interviewer in this example was actually the PEG's General Partner and the direct boss of the PEG Operating Partner. This PEG SITG CEO job candidate had a successful interview with that PEG Partner interviewing him and referred him to the PEG Operating Partner with a strong recommendation that this candidate be interviewed. He also emailed this SITG CEO candidate's SRQ, Indiana Jones Bio and resume to the PEG Operating Partner.
- Does the PEG Operating Partner have any questions about the SITG CEO candidate's completed SRQ? Expect that he will.
- Does the PEG Operating Partner have any questions about the SITG CEO candidate's resume or IJ Bio?
- The PEG Operating Partner will want to verify this SITG CEO candidate has had full P&L experience and will ask if the companies this candidate ran as CEO were profitable. If not, why not? (Here is where having an Excel spread sheet of older profitable company financials as part of this candidate's show and tell will go over well.)

Do not leave sensitive show and tell documents with any PEG interviewers. Show for effect and put them away.

- Ask the PEG Partner about your direct reports by title. How strong a team is this group? Have they each put skin in the game? The CFO will be a dotted line to the new CEO but have a direct line to the PEG Partner. Inquire about the CFO's background and find out if he has skin in the game?
- If the PEG has owned this portfolio company more than a few months, ask PEG Partner if you would be replacing the former CEO if hired? What can you learn from that separation that might help you be a better CEO? (If a portfolio company hires SITG C-Level executives shortly after acquiring the company, these new SITG hires buy their equity at the "strike price", the same as the PEG's investors and the way the tax payments are handled, in my experience, was different than SITG hires a year or two after the company was acquired. That is because the equity has usually grown even though the PEG might still offer the stock at the strike price. A tax on the increase was due. I am not giving tax advice other than to alert the hired SITG C-Level hire that he must have a tax accountant advise him of any equity investment transaction. The PEG will probably alert him about this fact in the offer letter).
- Ask who the board of directors of the portfolio company are and what their backgrounds are. What role do they play, if any, with the CEO in the day-to-day business?
- You probably have already met one or more of the company board members. If not, suggest you ask to meet one or two if possible. If they reside out of the area, ask the PEG Partner if he will arrange for you to

have a brief phone conversation. Suggest they be emailed your Indiana Jones Bio as well as your resume. Often, in lower middle market PEG portfolio companies, the board tends to be more active with phone calls to the CEO, and unplanned or planned company visits and lots of suggestions for the CEO.

- If it's ongoing as opposed to tapering down after the new CEO's first month, then maybe it's OK. If the former company owner is invited on the company's board after the PEG has acquired the business that can be helpful to the PEG and the company's current CEO. However, there can be negatives unless the PEG has provided guidelines to this former CEO owner such as keep out of your former facility unless invited. The CEO has to trust his PEG boss that the board after the initial onboarding period will take its lead from the PEG Managing Partner. If not you have to clear the air on this if it could lead to your resigning from this job. It's happened to me once. I had to refill the CEO job.
- Ask if you can speak with a few of the PEG's CEOs from other portfolio companies who report to the same PEG Partner you will have as your new boss. Make a note of their backgrounds or ask the PEG Partner to email them to you before you speak with them. If they are within reasonable driving distance, try to meet with each of them. Otherwise request the PEG Partner if he can arrange for you to phone these CEOs as well as have your resume emailed to them. Positive responses by the PEG Partner to these few typical requests by skin in the game CEO finalist candidate indicate a promising mutual relationship job fit.

- Verify you will be allowed to invest $100K of your own funds or whatever the skin in the game amount the PEG portfolio company CEO job calls for. Confirm your zeal for doing so.
- Ask if there are any "sacred cows" among your direct reports. A sacred cow is untouchable in the eyes of the PEG and can't be fired without the PEG's approval, or possibly at all. Sacred cows are rare but have existed, especially the (subordinate) VP or Director of Information Technology, or the Head of Engineering or R&D. The latter two may be peers. Inheriting a sacred cow has been a deal-killer especially in a manufacturing company when the CEO has successfully managed Engineering and R&D in the past. Often the head of IT reports to the CFO. Many CEOs prefer that arrangement. I suggest the CEO be guided by the PEG Partner's explanation of why there is a sacred cow. Is it a permanent situation or temporary? The arrangement could be temporary until the CEO is on board and functioning for a few months. The SITG CEO candidate might ask to meet the sacred cow before accepting the offer but this could backfire on the CEO sabotaging his candidacy. If there are sacred cows, then try to make a case to change this arrangement before accepting any offer. I have never known a CEO or President or GM to survive permanent sacred cows in any company going back forty years. Better to do your due diligence on such "surprises" before you accept a job offer.
- Is the PEG SITG CEO job a board position or not?
- Ask the PEG Partner if he can provide an explanation and illustration of how the management stock value was calculated by the PEG client and an overview of the

PEG client's Management Common Stock Ownership Program. Again, these documents are routinely provided by the PEG client as part of the SITG C-Level hire's job offer package.
- Ask if the PEG Operating Partner has any other questions?

One question the PEG Operating Partner may ask is: if you were hired, how long would it take you to have a strategic plan to show the board? Normally it takes ninety days.

Most PEG Partner interviewers are usually almost overwhelmed by receiving a completed SRQ containing references and their contact info support for the interviewer to check with. Next they see the IJ Bio and select candidate confidential or sensitive exhibit items in support of SITG candidate's accomplishment claims. I often have a PEG client look over this material and call me asking, "What else am I supposed to ask this SITG candidate?

Ending PEG Partner 2nd Interviews

Keep in mind if you feel confident you can do this job well, mention that based on what you know about the company after reading the Confidential Information Memorandum, and both PEG Partners' comments about the functional job at hand, you feel you can "land on your feet running" (you would still like to speak with a couple of portfolio company CEO's sacred cows in my experience are far and few but if there is one, you'd like to meet with that person).

Ask the PEG Partner if he has any concerns about whether you can do this job well? If so, what are they?

Tell the PEG Partner that you want the job that you can do the job, and you want to be successful once the EDITDA scoreboard is tallied (at the company's exit).

Ask the PEG Partner what his time frame is for making a decision then ask what the next step is and when? Would there be an interview for you with others?

Does he want to contact any of your references listed on the SRQ? (You would like to give them a heads up first, but don't let that be a hold up). He might want to email you the names of those references he wants to call. Or he might just go ahead and email them directly if time is of the essence.

If it's true, mention that this job opportunity is number one on your list of the SITG jobs in which you are a contender.

Be sure to follow up this interview with a thank you email to the PEG Operating Partner and the PEG Partner that referred you to him.

A job offer usually occurs after the 2nd interview. The PEG Operating Partner will leave it that he will be in touch shortly by email and you will be able to speak with other portfolio company CEO's reporting to him if you are the finalist candidate (the same goes for your sacred cow chat).

Face-to-Face SITG CFO Job 2nd Interview with a PEG

Looking at the various steps in the hiring of a PEG SITG CFO, let me explain the variables. Gilreath Consultancy's main PEG client's CEO was the direct boss of any portfolio company

SITG CEO or CFO. Naturally the SITG CFO had a dotted line to our major PEG client's portfolio company CEO. However, no client PEG Operating Partner or client PEG CFO exists there. This major PEG client CEO would typically have their PEG President also interview portfolio company SITG CFO and SITG CEO candidates. That made the SITG CFO and SITG CEO interviews simple to explain to our candidates. In most of our PEG SITG CFO hires, the Operating Partner was our day-to-day PEG client, the CFO reported directly to another PEG Partner and dotted line to the portfolio company CEO, The latter reported to the PEG Operating Partner.

In our conducting a PEG SITG CFO search for a few other middle market PEG clients of Gilreath Consultancy, the CFO reported directly to the PEG CFO, who was a PEG staff officer, and indirectly to the PEG portfolio company CEO. However the PEG Operating Partner, (who was the direct boss of the portfolio company CEO) was my day-to-day client and the SITG CFO's 1st interviewer. Not every CFO can work effectively in that reporting structure. So the portfolio company SITG CFO might be answering financial questions from the PEG CFO, in this example, a very smart friendly guy, as well as the CFO's indirect boss, the portfolio company CEO and occasionally a board member. In this example, not as much from the PEG Operating Partner who has other day-to-day priorities.

If a PEG SITG CFO candidate prepares himself properly, he should know the title and background of the PEG Partner interviewing him and the PEG's reporting structure in the portfolio company where that PEG SITG CFO will work day to day if hired. In previous chapters, I have explained how to prepare yourself for a PEG interview, what items to request beforehand from the PEG (or headhunter) and what to bring with you. I have also mentioned how to conduct oneself in a PEG SITG C-Level job interview, generally speaking.

This PEG SITG CFO candidate's hiring challenge is compounded by the fact that the board probably contains former PEG CFOs. Even the hired CFO's direct boss may be a CPA or MBA in Finance. The CFO is subject to second-guessing and walks a delicate line in that the CFO, whose primary responsibility is to the board, must also gain the trust of the CEO. CFOs should conduct due diligence on this PEG SITG CFO job opportunity for mutual fit. The following 2nd SITG CFO interview is the result of a referral by the PEG CEO (CFO direct report) to the portfolio company CEO (CFO indirect report). Be sure you have a copy of the CFO job from the PEG Partner referring you. Check that this CEO has a copy of your resume, IJ Bio and completed SRQ. Below is the PEG CEO/SITG CFO become acquainted job interview as the CFO would report directly to this CEO's boss who recommended him for this CFO job.

(CEO) **Describes his background and how he was hired as a PEG SITG portfolio company CEO.**

(CEO) **Did you have any questions about the Confidential Descriptive Memorandum?**

(CFO) Discuss questions you have about this critical document.

(CFO) Do you have any questions about the completed Self Rating Quiz I emailed you?

(CFO) Discuss the SRQ and reinforce your qualifications.

(CEO) **Have you dealt with this type of CFO reporting structure before?**

(CFO) Provide CEO reference you dotted line to in the past.

(CEO) **Have you dealt with the PEG Partner and board's insatiable desire for financial information before?**

(CFO) Provide CEO references and their contact information from your past.

(CFO) What is your management style, preferred frequency of meetings and what types of reports do you routinely want?

(CFO) Review the titles and number of your direct reports. How strong are the direct reports and do any need upgrading or just training?

(CFO) Does the CFO have any responsibility for the HR or IT departments? If so, explain details. What are the backgrounds of these department heads?

(CFO) Ask about the portfolio company board's makeup and how active they are in the day-to-day company activities.

(CFO) Verify you will be allowed to invest $60K of your own funds or whatever the skin in the game amount the PEG portfolio company CFO job calls for up to $100K. Confirm your zeal for doing so.

(CEO) **How effectively have you typically interacted with Operations?**

(CFO) Discuss your dealings with Operations and how you've helped them. Provide a reference to verify your effectiveness there.

(CEO) **How effectively have you typically interacted with Sales & Marketing?**

(CFO) Discuss your dealings with Sales & Marketing and how you've helped them. Provide a reference to verify your effectiveness there.

(CEO) **What are your main priorities as CFO if you were hired?**

(CFO) Accurate and timely financial reports, risk management, monitoring cash flow, help promote growth and profitability analysis.

(CFO) What would be on your priority list for your next CFO?

(CEO) **Automating budgeting and forecasting and improving the access and assessment of enterprise data for use by myself and the company other key executives.**

(CFO) Do you have any concerns as to whether I could do this CFO job well? If so what are they?

(CEO) **How long would it take for you to come up with a strategic plan for the Finance Department for presentation to the board?**

(CFO) About three months.

(CEO) **Based on my PEG boss recommending you for this CFO position and from speaking with you and from your questions and completed self-rating quiz, I feel we could work well together, chemistry-wise.**

(CFO) Would you like to speak with any of my references listed in the SRQ?

(CEO) **Asks to speak to a few former bosses of the CFO listed.**

(CFO) Gives his OK.

(CFO) I feel I can do this job well and have wanted a CFO position where I could invest some of my own money in the stock of the company and risk it as the PEG investors have.

(CEO) **If you were hired as our SITG CFO, what's the first thing you would do?**

(CFO) Meet with my subordinates to evaluate how much training each one needs to elevate their technical skills. Then I would meet with each department head and discuss how I might help them and how they might help me be of more value to the company.

(CFO) What is the next step?

(CEO) **I'll be speaking with my boss and one of us will get back to you very soon. We are both interested in your CFO candidacy.**

Reminder: follow up with a thank you email to both the PEG CEO and the portfolio company CEO. Ask for the job in that email as well.

Face-to-Face 2nd Interview Regarding PEG Portfolio Company SITG COO (or VP Operations) Job

In this scenario, the SITG COO (or VP Operations) candidate originally networked through an M&A referral to meet the PEG Partner (actual title is PEG Operating Partner). In following up their mutual contact's emailed introduction, the candidate emailed his resume to the PEG Operating Partner and followed up with a call a few days later to arrange an exploratory meeting with this PEG Operating Partner. As luck would have it, he was told there was a PEG SITG VP Operations job within one of the PEG's portfolio companies. There were also other candidates under consideration by the portfolio company CEO, who reported to this Operating Partner. So time was of the essence and both individuals set up an interview date two days later.

The VP Operations candidate asked for a job description to be emailed to him and after reviewing it, felt he was a promising fit. He rated himself on the key points of this job in an SRQ as evidence and emailed it to the PEG Operating Partner together with his Indiana Jones Bio with both documents marked "Highly Confidential" at the top. The PEG Operating Partner read the candidate's completed SRQ (containing specific references in support of certain ratings) and his Indiana Jones Bio and interviewed the SITG candidate for the PEG SITG VP Operations vacancy (see Face-to-face SITG C-Level job 1st Interview with a PEG Partner above). The Operating Partner was impressed enough with this SITG VP Operations candidate, by referring the SITG candidate to the portfolio company CEO together with his resume, SRQ and Indiana Jones Bio.

This is an ideal situation for the SITG VP Operations candidate going into an interview recommended by the boss of the CEO who will be interviewing him. Most portfolio companies hiring CEOs would be "blown away" with this much information about a SITG VP Operations candidate. Having the CEO's boss refer you is gravy! This type of interview setting is typically called the mutual chemistry fit between the potential boss and this qualified and recommended VP Operations, who already was a chemistry fit with the PEG Partner who highly recommended him. But this candidate's not hired yet!

During my career I have conducted a number of PEG SITG searches where the PEG client has been referred someone they want considered as a C-Level candidate for the search. This candidate may have come from a PEG Partner colleague within the PEG from another PEG Limited Partner. Once the new candidate was the brother of the portfolio company CEO! These candidates were given the opportunity to be screened by my due diligence screening process. Those who refused to go through my screening thought my process was too time consuming, overwhelming, and unnecessary info and detail. None had 2nd interviews.

Now, getting back to this SITG VP Operations candidate interviewing with the PEG portfolio company CEO after being referred by the PEG Operating Partner as a good candidate. The VP Operations' research on the CEO showed that he was a former CFO in a different PEG portfolio company. He had successfully filled in as interim President there while his former boss recovered from colon cancer. That info gave the SITG VP Operations candidate insight into how to focus his interview comments and questions. Such as how he stuck to his Operations budget while achieving goals and objectives, how he watched the labor expense in costs of goods sold, how he reduced excess inventory costs and increased inventory turnover. Most importantly, by the VP Operations implementing lean manufacturing, wasteful practices will be eliminated and their corresponding costs.

Tough questions for COO/VP Operations to answer include, "We expect our C-Level executives to wear more than one hat." One of my SITG hires answered such a question by saying he could fill in for the Supply Chain Manager vacancy to handle products to customers logistics, to minimize raw material shortages and keep costs down. He would also fill that job with a top notch individual from his contacts file.

"What's the worst thing your references could truthfully say about you?"

The lesson I recap here is qualified and interested PEG SITG C-Level job candidates can help control their job interview success by going on the offensive taking the initiative. Stop defensively memorizing great responses to anticipated tricky questions and worrying about body posture. Prepare to have a solid interview and keep it focused on their mutual job fit. Below are 10 action item reminders for the C-Level candidate to execute. Then they relax and enjoy their productive interview:

1. Research the PEG's website and their current and former portfolio companies.
2. Research the PEG's team including the background of the PEG CEO you will interview with.
3. Research the PEG portfolio company needing the SITG COO or VP Operations job filled. Make notes on synergies with your background.
4. Get a copy of the PEG SITG C-Level job description and study it.
5. Prepare a SRQ of the key job requirements with how well your background and experience fits, 1 (lowest) to 10 (highest).
6. List appropriate career references that you know will support your high job qualifications ratings in your SRQ. After you've alerted them, list their contact info.
7. Be certain that you email the PEG portfolio company CEO interviewer your completed SRQ and confidential IJ Bio with your resume in advance of your interview. Mention you will be glad to go over the SRQ with the CEO and answer any questions regarding your IJ.
8. Bring an extra copy of the items listed in #7 in case a PEG Partner attends your interview session.
9. Confirm your desire to put some of your own money at risk as the CEO and other key C-Level executives have to help grow this company and achieve the PEG's goals and objectives.

10. Lastly, consider **selectively** any relevant item(s) to bring with you in your valise that might impress the CEO interviewer (see chapter 8-c Fine Tuning Your Presentation).

How the SITG C-Level Job Candidates Should Each End their PEG 2nd Interviews

Keep in mind if you feel confident you can do this job well, mention that based on what you know about the company after reading the Confidential Information Memorandum and the PEG Partner's comments about the functional job at hand, you can "land on your feet running".

Ask the PEG Partner if he has any concerns about whether you can do this job well. If so, what are they?

Tell the PEG Partner that you want the job that you can do the job, and you want to be successful once the scoreboard is tallied (at the company's exit).

Ask the PEG Partner what his time frame is for making a decision then ask what the next step is and when. Would there be an interview for you with others?

Does he want to set up a date and time now while you both have your calendars?

Does he want to contact any of your references listed on the SRQ? (You would like to give them a heads up first, but don't let that be a hold up.) He might want to email you the names of those references he wants to call. Or he might just go ahead and email them directly if time is of the essence.

If it's true, mention that this job opportunity is number one on your list of the SITG jobs in which you are a contender.

Be sure to follow up this interview with a thank you email to the PEG Partner.

Face-to-Face 2nd Interview Regarding PEG Portfolio Company SITG VP Sales & Marketing (VP S&M) Job

PEG SITG VP S&M has been the most challenging job I've had to fill. If I interview 5 VP S&M candidates, I usually end up liking them all for the job search I'm conducting. They are hard to interview. Instead of preparing they'll ad lib their way through. VP S&M, typically, are much more sales-oriented than marketing. They generally have big egos, are charismatic, brag often, have convenient memories for failure details and often will take credit for the success of every one of their employers. Next to the head of IT, the VP S&M can have more job changes than all other C-Level functions. It's difficult to get them to complete an IJ Bio or a SRQ. They are on the road 6 or 7 times a month traveling, in sales meetings, customer conference calls, and interviewing sales people to replace their turnover. VP S&M, outside sales people and inside sales force are vital to the success of the majority of companies. Without sales, there's no use coming to work. Checking references on a typical SITG VP S&M, is difficult. Why? They are very likeable and make a lot of friends. Their former subordinates will sometimes cover for the VP S&M's failures and shortcomings, many are terrific bringing in sales but carry baggage that negatively impacts their long term PEG client hireability. They furnish you with a dozen references to call about their job performance including past customers, independent manufacturers, representatives, former subordinates, and maybe one former boss. CFO references and VP Operations references are scarce or non-existent. Any hiring authority weak on interviewing skills will mostly enjoy an interview session with the VP S&M. It's typically afterwards when their references are checked or attempted to be checked that reality sets in. If you are an SITG VP S&M, note the points I'm making in this section's intro. Don't ad lib. Prepare for the PEG interviews. If you have a slew of bad references, forget the SITG PEG market sector. Try the Fortune/Forbes 1000 job market where all they are allowed to provide for references is your length of employment and your former title, if that. Employees aren't allowed to provide references,

Setting the scenario of this PEG SITG VP S&M job interview. This candidate was part of the Face-to-Face Generic SITG C-Level job 1st interview with a PEG Partner example above. The SITG VP S&M networked to meet a PEG Partner referred through a mutual M&A contact. It turned out that the PEG Partner liked this VP S&M and told him there was a SITG VP S&M position open in one of the PEG's portfolio companies. The PEG Partner recommended this VP S&M job candidate to the PEG portfolio company CEO (the PEG Partner's direct report) and suggested he interview this SITG candidate. The VP S & M's resume, IJ Bio and completed SRQ were emailed to the CEO in advance. Their interview (the 2nd with the PEG about this SITG job) follows:

(CEO) **Asks the VP S&M candidate how he knows his boss, the PEG Partner that recommended him for this.**

(CEO) **Describes his background and how he was hired as a PEG SITG portfolio company CEO.**

(CEO) **Has the VP S&M seen the Confidential Descriptive Memorandum? Does he have any questions after reviewing it?**

(VP S&M) It seems the company needs a change agent since the sales top line has been stagnant for the past 2 years. Does the company envision acquiring new product lines from fragmented competitors? They discuss this and the candidate pulls out an Excel spread sheet of his past performance in a stagnant company showing metrics and data in support of improvements in sales & marketing under this VP S&M.

(VP S&M) Have you any questions related to my completed SRQ? They discuss the ratings which were 10s (highest).

(CEO) **Is it OK if I call a few of those references listed in your SRQ?**

(VP S&M) Sure. I'd like to give them notice and then I'll email you tomorrow afterwards.

(CEO) **What questions did you have about the Descriptive Memorandum?**

(VPS&M) Discuss specific concerns related to VP S&M 's role.

(VP S&M) I am curious if the company bonus increases for exceeding the annual sales goals?

(CEO) **Yes. If you are hired that will be explained in your job offer. I note my boss said you wanted to put skin in the game if hired? Why is that?**

(VP S&M) True. I think the possibility of a huge sales increase for this company is doable. I know the markets, the product lines, new customer base potential due to other uses and applications of this company's specialty chemicals product line. There are a few top notch sales people I plan to recruit here if possible. I feel I can land on my feet running. I want to own a piece of the company and help drive up the company EBITDA so at the exit all of the equity owners will hopefully gain wealth.

(CEO) **How have you worked with the VP Operations in your prior VP S&M positions? That combination can involve friction as you know.**

(VP S&M) I work well with Operations. I'm bringing in a customer for a plant tour I always schedule that with the VP Operations. If I need product shipped earlier than the date Operations has it scheduled to go out, again I try to get Operations to rob Peter to pay Paul, but don't do it purposely. VP S& M pulls out a reference letter from his former VP Operations from his show and tell items. It goes over very well.

(CEO) **How have you worked in past jobs with the CFO?**

(VP S&M) I have generally worked well with the CFO. I have collaborated with the CFO on improving sales forecasts and turning in my monthly expense reports in a timely fashion. Working closely with the CFO, I developed, recommended, and implemented pricing strategies and profitability (based on market trends and internal costs), for product offerings and alternatives. Here is a copy of a reference letter from the CFO of Arnish Specialty Chemicals which was acquired by Dow a few months ago.

(CEO) **I notice you rated yourself a 10 (highest) on Maintains an awareness of competitor's activities and its effect on: customer interest, impact on market share and capital investment commitments.**

(VPS&M) Yes, as my reference, the former CEO of Spaulding Chemicals will tell you I am constantly researching and analyzing our main competitors through solid industry contacts.

(CEO) **I am very interested in checking with some of those references in your SRQ.**

(VP S&M) Ask the PEG Partner if he has any concerns about whether you can do this job well. If so, what are they?

(VP S&M) Tell the PEG Partner that you want the job, that you can do the job, and you want to be successful once the EDITDA scoreboard is tallied (at the company's exit).

(VP S&M) Ask the PEG Partner what his time frame is for making a decision then ask what the next step is and when. Would there be an interview for you with others?

(VP S&M) The big Specialty Chemicals Trade Show is in Las Vegas next month and it would be good for the VP S&M to plan for it and make appointments ahead of attending it.

Be sure to follow up this interview with a thank you email to the PEG Operating Partner and the PEG Partner that referred you to him.

I have participated in hundreds of PEG SITG C-Level job interviews. The first hour is critical and sets the tone for the rest of the session. I believe the PEG SITG job candidate must be more prepared than their interviewer. How, by producing an IJ Bio, a solid elevator pitch, make the effort to get some reference letters from a group that encompasses bosses, subordinates, peers, board members, PEG Partners and customers. Get a copy of the job for which you will be interviewing. Then complete an SRQ containing references in support of your ratings. Ask for the Confidential Descriptive Memorandum and prepare questions for the PEG Partner from it. If any SITG C-Level executive trying to be hired by a PEG keeps striking out, if I did an audit of his approach, it's weak and strives for short cuts, OR he can't really perform the PEG's job requirements, know thyself! Good luck.

Chapter 11

From the Job Offer to Being Hired

As you get closer to getting an SITG job offer, reflect on the following: the M&A industry is not for the faint hearted. There are risks. I am not placing altar boys in skin in the game jobs, and PEGs aren't hiring "Big hat, no cattle" types. There is always mutual risk for the candidate and for the PEG hiring authority. Besides the mutual due diligence being right, the chemistry between you, the skin in the game candidate, and the Managing Partner/Partner/PEG must be very positive. If not, do not pursue this SITG job opportunity. If things are heating up on the employer's side, be courteous, listen, thank them, and say you'll think it over. Send your "Dear John" the next day. Why? Because once you are on the job, odds are that working relationship between you and the boss in question will only get worse. Job security for SITG C-Level hires in the middle market PEG sector can be tenuous. Time to pursue the next skin in the game job opportunity. It's out there if you're prepared properly, especially references-wise, and do your own due diligence thoroughly.

If you are about to receive a SITG PEG job offer and invest up to $100K of your own funds in portfolio company equity, hopefully you have researched this PEG the best you can through the website and the web in general as well as through contacts you have made confidentially. You like the C-Level job and the portfolio company and the PEG Partners you've met. Some of the answers to your questions weren't that illuminating. Their CDM showed some rough financials the last 2 years. Do they really want to grow this acquisition or put the company in play getting out from under this problem portfolio company? You have been seeking such an SITG job for a long time, but you still feel uncertain beyond the typical anxiety about such a move.

With so much at stake, you might want to speak with my friend, Kenneth S. Springer, a Certified Fraud Investigator I've known over 20 years. His clientele is mostly PEGs. Ken is the founder and President of Corporate Resolutions, Inc. Check out their website: *www.corporateresolutions.com.* Ken's email is: KenSpringer@corporateresolutions.com. Mention I referred you. Ask what he might learn about the PEG making you a job offer and what his charges might be? He may already have information on your PEG that will help you make a better decision. A great read is Ken's book, *Digging for Disclosure* for insight into his practice.

Negotiating Your SITG C-Level Job Offer

As I completed SITG C-Level search assignments for middle market PEGs over twenty-five years, the majority of my SITG hires received fair, competitive offers. Some were lateral salaries, most were performance based bonus plans. The best offers involved performance based stock option plans in addition to purchased equity at the start. You have to look at the big picture, not just the salary, not just the risk of not earning a bonus.

During my commercial search experience representing Fortune 500 companies, the total compensation was more generous on average. Often, the stock options were under water. The clients wanted employed candidates not out looking for their next move. In a number of cases, such candidates will take their job offer into their boss's office and solicit a counter offer. So our client might lose such a candidate but the candidate typically loses in the end too by accepting a counter offer.

My advice is not to risk what you perceive as a bona fide job opportunity by going into an SITG C-Level job offer with a PEG trying to greatly increase your starting salary and bonus plan. I know there are books by "experts" about tricks to negotiating a big total compensation increase in your next job offer. PEGs interpret a qualified and interested C-Level job candidate willing to put skin in the game as a positive. Ninety-five percent of my PEG C-Suite searches require skin in the game from our candidates. Occasionally the skin in the game amount required by our PEG client is flexible. There are even times when our client PEG C-Suite candidate wants to invest more than the amount required. Often that request is approved by our PEG client. The same goes for negotiating a job offer with emphasis on modest salary increase and merit bonus plan being acceptable. That's received as a positive. After all, it's the opportunity to increase the value of your total equity both purchased and earned that is the focus of this opportunity. I have never charged a PEG client or skin in the game hired C-Suite candidate anything for their mutual skin in the game agreement. Gilreath Consultancy charges our traditional retained search flat fee based on a percentage of the projected annual total compensation amount,

I am not exaggerating when I tell you that many of my hires took less total compensation for my SITG job offer than they were earning in their previous non skin in the game job. I have witnessed over and over a number of my hires investing their hundred thousand, and even hundreds of thousands, in equity after they were hired and then receiving millions back for their increased equity value at the company's exit. The former owner and CEO of the business acquired expressed skin in the game hiring nicely as, "Specifically, the compensation approach in skin in the game hiring has a significant wealth accumulation creation orientation, balancing that aspect with current income."

Secure your job offer in writing before you resign or give notice from you're current job. Ask if all the reference checking is done. Do they require a company physical and that you successfully complete a substance abuse test before you can accept this job offer?

Should you meet your SITG direct reports and the CFO before accepting the job offer? In my experience the SITG CEO has 24 hours to accept or reject his emailed written offer. Rarely do my SITG candidates want to meet their fellow SITG PEG portfolio company team before accepting a job offer, unless the PEG Partner suggests it or makes it part of the hiring routine. Most of the time the new CEO will be asked to fill an SITG C-Level vacancy or evaluate the COO/VP Operations and the VP Sales & Marketing after he is aboard. If your subordinates do not have skin in the game, it may signal that the PEG wants a change agent, especially if they are from the old ownership before the PEG acquired their company. I try to avoid putting one of my CEO candidates into a situation where the direct reports think they have a major say in whether their new CEO boss is hired or not. The CFO is almost always replaced by the PEG after their former employer is acquired by the PEG. The CFO always reports in a matrix, direct to the PEG Partner or the PEG CFO and dotted line to the portfolio company CEO. In the case of the SITG CFO, SITG COO, and SITG VP Sales and Marketing, I do not think it's necessary to request meeting them in a one-on-one situation. Meeting the PEG Partner and CEO are the most critical for the COO and VP Sales & Marketing.

Let's Review an Actual SITG CEO Job Offer

President and Chief Executive Officer (CEO) Skin in the Game Job Offer

Nomanus Hydraulics Company – Frank Brooks, President and CEO Summary Terms

Anticipated Start Date: July 14, 2013

Reporting Structure: as President and CEO, you will report to the PEG Managing Partner.

Base Salary: $325,000 per year

Bonus Potential: up to 50% of Base Salary, for total annual cash compensation potential of $487,500. Existing Nomanus bonus plan is based on management objectives and financial performance.

Benefits: health, disability, life insurance, 401(k) and vacation consistent with existing Nomanus plans.

Vacation: vacation will be four weeks per year.

Auto: auto allowance will be provided based on the current Nomanus program for a mid-sized branded automobile.

Relocation: Nomanus would pay for moving household goods expenses to Chicago and temporary living expenses of $5,000/month for up to six months for a total of $30,000.

Stock Options: 5,150 options representing 2.0% of company on fully diluted basis. Vesting is time-based over five years (i.e. 1,030 options at each anniversary of start date). Upon a change of control, existing Nomanus stock option plan provides that if you are employed for more than twelve months, all options will vest (5,150 options). If you are employed for less than twelve months, you will receive one year of accelerated vesting (1,030 options).

Exercise Price: $190 per share

Equity Investment: ability to invest up to $500,000 at a price of $190 per share if it is in the form of a cash or Wells Fargo IRA investment. Should the Wells Fargo IRA investment not be possible, we would provide a line of credit to enable you to invest up to $250,000 at a price of $190 per share.

Severance: if employee is terminated not for cause or resigns for good reason, twelve months of current salary. If employee is terminated for cause or resigns for no reason, no severance.

Unbelievable, but it's true. In reviewing a number of Gilreath Consultancy SITG C-Level hires, I remember in the handful of instances when one of my hires was let go (not for cause), that my candidate's initial investment money was always returned to him.

Here Are My Thoughts on this CEO SITG Job Offer:

Regarding Base Salary

Speaking about your total compensation negotiation, in my experience, middle market and lower middle market PEGs do not typically offer big salary increases. They don't like to guarantee bonuses either, if it's a merit bonus. Middle and lower market PEGs start with a fair compensation range in mind. They want to hire qualified, interested, and motivated risk takers. I have always found that PEGs project a portfolio company employer's future equity valuations realistically, if not conservatively. If one of my search candidates is earning a bit more salary and bonus compensation than the PEG client is offering, I try to determine if the significant skin in the game opportunity based on the three equity valuation future projections will account for a lesser salary and non-guaranteed bonus if they get a job offer. My candidate job search philosophy is, "When in doubt, knock them out." With PEGs, the SITG job candidate shouldn't go into their PEG interview with unrealized expectations. As I already mentioned, I have experienced a number of CEO hires of SITG candidates accepting a surprisingly lower amount in salary to accept a PEG's job offer. They wanted skin in the game job opportunities. Overall the majority did well on the job. Determine if you are a good fit for the SITG job, with your future PEG Partner boss and how he manages other PEG company CEOs. Research the PEG's overall track record for solid acquisitions and lucrative exits. Those items should be higher up on your focus ladder than salary. Don't forget the PEG's Management Equity Valuation Estimates. You will either consider the compensation range or you won't, or look at the big picture. Just don't expect to go into a job offer discussion persuading the PEG Partner that you are worth abandoning his total compensation budget for the opportunity for you to invest thousands of your own money to make perhaps a million or so at this portfolio company's exit. That's why I wrote this book, to share with C-Level executives in the current job market.

Regarding Bonus Potential

Expect a merit bonus plan based on both personal objectives and financial targets (usually EBITDA growth during the year). Occasionally bonus plans can be exceeded and surpass the plan. Ask about the latter.

Regarding Auto

For a CEO only, in my experience, but I don't take it for granted, usually a full-size mid-luxury car. Once in a while for a VP Sales in a regional business. I have had top caliber SITG CEOs kill a job offer wearing one of those $10K watches and bragging to the PEG Partner how many he has! The client was not impressed. A few have self-destructed, having their offers withdrawn after pushing for a Mercedes Benz or BMW auto as part of their offer!

Regarding Relocation

I admire my branded brother headhunters handling searches for the Fortune 500 clients. They work with Human Resources on a full blown relocation package for their C-Level hires, especially CEOs. Lower and middle market PEGs typically ask the hired candidate to total his estimated relocation expenses, minus realtor fees, and will pay a lump sum total for the relocation as they occur. Most lower middle market PEGs prefer the wife to be with the husband, especially if they are empty nesters, especially if the CEO is hired soon after the PEG acquired this business. Figure four or five years before this company is sold, normally. They offer three to six months paid temporary housing near the job site and a few house hunting trips for the CEO's spouse. If the CEO has teenagers, a family relocation becomes difficult or impossible and may figure into the CEO candidates' hiring prospects if relocation is required. On the other hand, typically paid home visits bi-weekly are not unusual. Bottom line, if you come from an employer with a generous relocation package, lower your expectations in dealing with a PEG job offer. A SITG CEO "pro", especially in PEG-owned middle market manufacturing portfolio companies will try to rent a decent place for him and his wife within commuting distance to the job and perhaps rent out their main residence. I try to avoid presenting SITG C-Level candidates who plan to permanently commute home twice monthly due to their teenage kids wanting to remain in their local home area high schools. Invariably, there occurs a "crisis at home involving a child requiring the CEO to fly home for an extended unanticipated event". Bring up your latter relo status early in the 1st interview versus beating a dead horse and hoping your wife will help work things out.

Regarding Stock Options

Ask the PEG Partner how the management stock value was calculated. My best PEG client offered their SITG C-Level hires a merit annual bonus plan and merit stock options vested in five years or at the sale of the company, whichever occurred first. In the case of any annual goals and objectives not being met, no stock options were awarded that year. Others offered automatic annual stock options vested in five years or at the sale of the company, whichever occurred first.

Regarding Equity Investment

For a CEO, the purchased equity, required the first day (or week) he reports to work, is usually their check for $100K. Also, in my experience, a number of my SITG CEO hires have been allowed to purchase more than $100K (typical maximum SITG C-Level hire investment allowed) in company equity. Those occurrences were motivated by the PEG client being very satisfied with my CEO hires. My top CEO hire invested $100K in equity upon being hired then invested another $400K in equity in his portfolio company. When he cashed out at the exit he had earned in excess of $11 million.

Regarding Exercise Price

Most of my SITG C-Level hires purchased their equity at the "strike price" at the same price as the PEG investors and Limited Partners did. The taxes in such cases weren't payable immediately. If an SITG C-Level hire purchases equity after the company has been owned by their PEG employer for a few years, when the stock typically has increased, then the hires have to take into consideration their incurred equity tax obligations and its timing. In any case, consult your tax advisor before reporting on the job, or sooner if possible. In my experience the PEG clients have loaned the new C-Level hires the money to pay these taxes for non-strike price equity purchases.

Regarding Severance

Hired SITG CEOs are usually offered six months' severance if they are terminated without cause or resign for good reason. In some cases the severance, if a long distance relocation is involved can be nine months, or rarely, one year. If a CEO is terminated for cause such as repeated willful misconduct or resigns for no good reason, there is no severance paid. I am fortunate in that I have only had one CEO fired for cause. He invested $100K in our client's private label candy business, but continued spending time on his former consulting business. The PEG Partner concluded that this CEO was neglecting his duties at their portfolio company and fired him and returned his $100K.

The SITG hired CEO has a place to sign the offer letter under agreed & accepted and then date and return it to the PEG Managing Partner. Offer letters are typically void after three business days.

Prepare your employment lawyer ahead of time to review your offer letter in a "time is of the essence manner". The same goes for your tax accountant. There are typically 3 days for you to sign the offer letter or mutually agree with the PEG Partner on changes or an extension for good reason. My advice would be, don't jeopardize being hired over your "petty wants, would like to haves, and preferreds". If you have a possible "deal-breaker concern" that needs clarity, then bring it up cordially. If you don't like the offer and are willing to turn it down over an unresolved issue, then do it cordially. That's why the 2nd interview with the PEG is so important to get answers to those key questions you have. Remember President Reagan's mantra, "Trust, but verify."

Chief Financial Officer (CFO) Skin in the Game Job Offer

Jupiter Machinery Corporation – Marty Clark, CFO Summary Terms

Anticipated Start Date: May 03, 2013

Reporting Structure: as Chief Financial Officer, you will report directly to the PEG Managing Partner and dotted line to the President and CEO of Jupiter Machinery Corporation.

Base Salary: your annual base salary will be $200,000, less applicable taxes and other withholdings as required by law or the policies of the company, payable in weekly installments.

Annual Bonus: you will participate in an executive incentive compensation plan based on achieving annual corporate EBITDA and debt reduction targets. Within this context you are eligible for an annual bonus of up to 25% of base pay less applicable taxes and other withholdings.

Employee Benefits: the company provides a variety of employee benefits as summarized in Exhibit 1, including health, disability, life insurance, 401(k), vacation and auto allowance consistent with existing Jupiter Machinery Corporation plans. There is a thirty-day waiting period for participation in the company's health benefit program.

Vacation: vacation will be four weeks per year.

Equity Investment: it is understood that you are prepared to invest approximately $50,000 in the common stock of Jupiter

Machinery Corporation at approximately $177 per share through a self-directed IRA. The common stock purchased by you will be subject to three year vesting. (The PEG loaned this CFO the money to pay the due taxes on the EBITDA gain of the shares since the original strike price five years earlier. It will be repaid from future bonus money earned).

Stock Options: you will be entitled to participate in a stock option plan with a grant of 1,000 shares of the common stock in Jupiter Machinery Corporation based on achieving certain earnings targets (to be established by you and the company's Board of Directors) over a three year period. In the event that the annual earnings target is not met, grants for that particular year will not be made.

Confidentiality: during your employment with the company and afterward, you agree to keep confidential all business-related information about the company including, without limitation, information about business contacts, transactions, contracts, intellectual property, finances, personnel, products and pricing, borrower, customer or corporate affairs of which you may become aware, whether or not relating to or arising out of your specific job duties. ("confidential information") and you shall not disclose or make known any such confidential information to any person except (i) to officers, directors, employees, agents and advisors of the company and such other persons as may be authorized by them in writing or (ii) to the extent such confidential information (a) is or becomes publicly known through no wrongdoing of yours, (b) was available to you on a non-confidential basis prior to its disclosure by the company, (c) is independently developed or becomes available to you on a non-confidential basis from a source other than the company, or (d) is required to be disclosed pursuant to the order of a governmental agency or a court of law.

Non-Competition: the company's standard non-compete agreement must be signed prior to employment.

Life and Accidental Death: the company provides life and accidental death and dismemberment insurance of $95,000.

401(k) Plan: after one year of employment you will be eligible to participate in the 401k Plan with Jupiter Machinery Corporation, that currently provides for matching the first 3%, and 50% of the next 2%. There are Federal Tax Regulations that impose a limit on individual tax deferred contributions, and you should discuss this with your accountant.

Physical Exam: this job offer is contingent upon evidence of your having a satisfactory, comprehensive physical examination by a licensed physician. Written results of such a physical examination should be furnished to me as soon as possible. You must also successfully complete a substance abuse test before you can accept this job offer. Our company will make arrangements for the latter as soon as possible coordinated with you by our VPHR, Stella Harris.

Involuntary Termination Without Cause: in the unlikely event that you are terminated for any reason other than for illegal conduct or repeated willful misconduct, or the sale of Jupiter Machinery Corporation, you will be paid six months' severance pay upon such termination.

Voluntary Termination: in the unlikely event that you resign from Jupiter Machinery Corporation, no severance payments would be due to you.

Terms of Employment: while we anticipate an ongoing employment relationship, we would like you to understand that no guarantee of continued employment for any specific length of time is intended or implied by this job offer and that your employment may be terminated at will

If Jupiter Manufacturing Corp. is Sold: when Jupiter Machinery Corporation is sold while you are an employee, all of your shares become vested.

Before the CFO writes his check for $50,000 for his equity share of skin in the game, he will be given a detailed document covering all aspects of his investment and the terms and conditions associated with it to review with his attorney. I have found these documents disclose fairly standard industry terms and operating procedures. Some have wording that is more legalese than plain. Offer letters are typically void after three business days.

Some of our PEG clients will accept a lesser preferred dollar amount the C-Level candidate has to invest. This should be discussed at the 1st interview. A number of C-Level SITG candidates ask me if the PEG client will lend them their required equity invested amount and have it taken out of their future bonuses. That should be discussed at the 1st interview once you feel the job is a good fit with your background, My advice is not to plan on the latter happening after an offer has been made.

The vacation issue comes up once in a while when an SITG C-Level job candidate has 4 weeks of vacation in his current employment. The PEG client occasionally offers 3 weeks of vacation. The PEG client typically expects the SITG C-Level job candidate to take their vacation at a time when the portfolio company can afford the SITG C-Level hire's absence. If the SITG C-Level candidate presses for 4 weeks rather than 3 weeks some PEG clients take that as a red flag in the candidate's priorities. Normally, though, it's not a deal-breaker.

Another sensitive issue with the PEG client is inserting 12 months severance (instead of 6 months) in the unlikely event the SITG C-Level hire is let go not for cause. This will sometimes happen if the SITG C-Level candidate has another job offer or is considering joining a startup or (God forbid) contemplating a counter-offer from his employer. The PEG typically expects their offer letter to be no surprises and agreed upon in short order. If the PEG C-Level candidate's, offer letter back and forth discussions involve issues that could have been discussed or questioned during the 1st or 2nd interview stage. It can send a signal to the PEG that diminishes their confidence in you. Take notice that during your SITG C-Level job interviews, you have to ask plenty of questions, reading documents such as the Confidential Descriptive Memorandum and getting answers as if you will be receiving the SITG C-Level job offer. If you wait until you have the offer letter to bring up surprise issues you are questioning, PEGs don't like surprises. Send them the right signal they expect at the job offer letter time.

Chief Operating Officer (COO) Skin in the Game Job Offer

Winslow Precision Corporation – Harold Goldman, Chief Operating Officer Summary Terms

Anticipated Start Date: Jan 02, 2012

Reporting Structure: as Chief Operating Officer, you will report directly to the President and CEO of the Company.

Terms of Agreement: subject to earlier termination as hereafter provided, this Agreement shall have an original term of five (5) years commencing on the start date, and shall be automatically extended thereafter for successive terms of one (1) year each, unless either you or the company provide notice to the other at least two (2) months prior to the expiration of the original or any extension term that the agreement is not to be extended.

Base Salary: the company will pay you a base salary at the rate of two hundred and fifty thousand dollars ($250,000) per year, payable in accordance with the regular payroll practices of the company and subject to yearly increases (but not decreases) commencing on January, 2013 which are, at a minimum, equal to the percentage increase in the Consumer Price Index for the immediately preceding calendar year.

Annual Bonus: for each fiscal year completed during your employment under this agreement, you will be eligible to earn an annual bonus. Your target bonus will be 30% of your base salary, with the actual amount of any such bonus being determined by the board, based on its assessment, in its discretion, of your performance and that of the company against financial goals established by the board after consultation with the President, CEO and you.

Enhanced Bonus: in addition to the annual bonus set forth above, for each fiscal year completed during your employment under this agreement, you will also be considered by the board for an enhanced bonus if the financial goals established for that given year are exceeded. If the board elects to provide you such a bonus, the amount of the enhanced bonus, if any, shall be determined by the board, in its sole discretion.

Bonuses Payable: any annual or enhanced bonus due to you hereunder shall be payable not later than two and one-half months following the close of the fiscal year in which the bonus was earned or as soon as administratively practicable within the meaning of Section 409A of the Internal Revenue Code, as amended.

Employee Benefits: you will be entitled to participate in all employee benefit plans from time to time in effect for employees of the company generally, except to the extent such plans are duplicative of benefits otherwise provided to you under this agreement (e.g., a severance pay plan). Your participation will be subject to the terms of the applicable plan documents and generally applicable company policies.

Vacation: you will be entitled to earn up to four weeks of vacation per year, in addition to holidays observed by the company. Vacation may be taken at such times and intervals as you shall determine, subject to the business needs of the company.

Business Expenses: the company will pay or reimburse you for all reasonable business expenses incurred or paid by you in the performance of your duties and responsibilities for the company, subject to any maximum annual limit and other restrictions on such expenses set by the company and to such reasonable substantiation and documentation as may be specified from time to time.

Relocation Expenses: you will relocate from Chicago, Illinois to the Indianapolis, Indiana area. The company shall reimburse you for all reasonable and customary out-of-pocket expenses incurred by you in connection with such relocation including but not limited to costs for visits, moving expenses, and temporary housing, up to a maximum of thirty-five thousand dollars ($35,000) in the aggregate for all such relocation expenses and subject to reasonable substantiation and documentation as may be specified by the company.

Purchased Equity: you will be purchasing a minimum of $100,000 of the PEGs equity position at fair market value. Its equivalent value is .015% of Winslow Precision Corporation common equity. We are flexible on additional purchased amounts of common equity up to $300,000 at fair market value.

Stock Options: the PEG is proposing a value of 3.0% of the common equity as stock options, which equates to a value of $1.45 million on a five year fully vested time horizon, assuming a start date in Q1, 2012.

Liquidity Event Bonus: in the event of a company sale, you shall be entitled to the vested portion of the Liquidity Event Bonus. The Liquidity Event Bonus shall vest on a level basis each quarter over a three year period commencing on the first day of the quarter following the start date. Payment of such Liquidity Event Bonus is subject to the following conditions:

a. In the event of a company sale while you are employed under this agreement, all unvested portions of the Liquidity Event Bonus will, upon the closing of such transaction, immediately vest such that you will be entitled to receive 100% of the Liquidity Event Bonus, payable within thirty (30) business days of the company sale

b. In the event that your employment hereunder is terminated pursuant to sections 13(a) or 13(c) below, you will forfeit all of the vested and unvested portions of the Liquidity Event Bonus;
c. In the event that your employment hereunder is terminated pursuant to sections 13(b) below, you will be entitled to receive 100% of the vested portion of the Liquidity Event Bonus, payable within thirty (30) business days of the company sale; and
d. In the event that your employment hereunder is terminated pursuant to section 13(d) below, you or, if applicable, your designated beneficiary or, if no beneficiary has been designated by you, your estate will be entitled to receive 100% of the vested portion of the Liquidity Event Bonus, payable within thirty (30) business days of the company sale

Termination of Employment: notwithstanding the provisions of section 2 hereof, your employment under this Agreement shall terminate prior to the expiration of the term hereof under the following circumstances:

a. The company may terminate your employment for cause upon notice to you setting forth in reasonable detail the nature of the cause. The following, as determined by the board in its reasonable judgment, shall constitute cause for termination: (i) your failure to perform, or material negligence in the performance of, your duties and responsibilities to the company or any of its affiliates;

(ii) your material breach of this agreement or any other agreement between you and the company or any of its affiliates; or (iii) other conduct by you that is or could reasonably be expected to be harmful to the business interests or reputation of the company or any of its affiliates.

b. The company may terminate your employment at any time other than for cause upon sixty (60) days' notice to you.
c. You may terminate your employment at any time upon sixty (60) days' notice to the company. The board may elect to waive your notice or any portion thereof, but in that event the company shall pay you your base salary for that portion of the first sixty days of your notice waived.
d. This agreement shall automatically terminate in the event of your death during employment. In the event you become disabled during employment and, as a result, are unable to continue to perform substantially all of your duties and responsibilities under this agreement, the company will continue to pay you your base salary and to provide you benefits in accordance with section 2 above, to the extent permitted by plan terms, for up to twelve (12) weeks of disability during any period of three hundred and sixty-five (365) consecutive calendar days. If you are unable to return to work after twelve (12) weeks of disability, the company may terminate your employment, upon notice to you. If any question shall arise as to whether you are disabled to the extent that you are unable to perform substantially all of your duties and responsibilities for the company and its affiliates, you shall, at the company's request, submit to a medical examination by a physician selected by the

company to whom you or your guardian, if any, has no reasonable objection to determine whether you are so disabled and such determination shall for the purposes of this agreement be conclusive of the issue. If such a question arises and you fail to submit to the requested medical examination, the company's determination of the issue shall be binding on you.

Confidential Information: during the course of your employment with the company, you will learn of confidential information, as defined below, and you may develop confidential information on behalf of the company and its affiliates. You agree that you will not use or disclose to any person (except as required by applicable law or for the proper performance of your regular duties and responsibilities for the company) any confidential information obtained by you incident to your employment or any other association with the company or any of its affiliates. You agree that this restriction shall continue to apply after your employment terminates, regardless of the reason for such termination.

Protection of Documents: all documents, records and files, in any media of whatever kind and description, relating to the business, present or otherwise, of the company or any of its affiliates, and any copies, in whole or in part, thereof (the "documents"), whether or not prepared by you shall be the sole and exclusive property of the company. You agree to safeguard all documents and to surrender to the company, at the time your employment terminates or at such earlier time or times as the board or its designee may specify, all documents then in your possession or control.

Assignment of Rights to Intellectual Property: you shall promptly and fully disclose all Intellectual Property to the company. You hereby assign and agree to assign to the company (or as otherwise directed by the company) your full right, title and interest in and to all Intellectual Property. You agree to execute any and all applications for domestic and foreign patents, copyrights or other proprietary rights and to do such other acts (including without limitation the execution and delivery of instruments of further assurance or confirmation) requested by the company to assign the Intellectual Property to the company and to permit the company to enforce any patents, copyrights or other proprietary rights to the Intellectual Property. You will not charge the company for time spent in complying with these obligations. All copyrightable works that you create shall be considered "work made for hire" and shall, upon creation, be owned exclusively by the company.

Non-Competition: you acknowledge that in your employment with the company you will have access to confidential information which, if disclosed, would assist in competition against the company and its affiliates and that you will also generate goodwill for the company and its affiliates in the course of your employment. Therefore, you agree that the following restrictions on your activities during and after your employment are necessary to protect the goodwill, confidential information and other legitimate interests of the company and its affiliates:

i. While you are employed by the company and during the twelve (12) months immediately following termination of your employment pursuant to section 4(a) and (c) below (in the aggregate, the "Non-Competition Period"), you agree not to work or provide services, in any capacity, whether as an employee, independent contractor or otherwise, whether with or without compensation, to any person that is engaged in the design and custom production of specialty rotary valves, micro valves and micro precision feeders

ii. You agree that during the Non-Competition Period, you will not, directly or through any other person, (i) hire any employee of the company or any of its affiliates or seek to persuade any employee of the company or any of its affiliates to discontinue employment, (ii) solicit or encourage any customer of the company or any of its affiliates or independent contractor providing services to the company or any of its affiliates to terminate or diminish its relationship with them or (iii) seek to persuade any customer of the company or any of its affiliates to conduct with anyone else any business or activity that such customer conducts with the company or any of its affiliates. For purpose of your obligations hereunder after your employment terminates, an employee, independent contractor, or customer includes only those who are such on the date your employment terminates or at any time during the preceding six months.

Severance Payments and Other Matters Related to Termination:

a. In the event of termination of your employment with the company, howsoever occurring, the company shall pay you (i) your base salary for the final payroll period of your employment, through the date your employment terminates; (ii) at the rate of your base salary for any vacation earned but not used as of the date your employment terminates; and (iii) for business expenses incurred by you but not yet reimbursed on the date your employment terminates; provided you submit all expenses and supporting documentation required within sixty (60) days of the date your employment terminates and provided further that such expenses are reimbursable under company policies, as then in effect; and make all required contributions to any retirement or other deferred compensation plan in which you are enrolled as of the date of your termination (all of the foregoing, "Final Compensation")

b. In the event of termination of your employment by the company other than for cause, the company, in addition to Final Compensation, will pay your base salary for the period of twelve (12) months from the date of termination ("Severance Pay"). Any obligation of the company to provide you Severance Pay under this section is conditioned, however, on your signing a timely and effective release of claims in the form attached to this agreement as exhibit A. Any Severance Pay to which you are entitled will be provided in the form of salary continuation, payable in accordance with the normal payroll practices of the company, with the first payment, which shall be retroactive to the day immediately following your termination, being due and payable on the company's next regular payday for executives that follows the expiration of thirty (30) calendar days from the date your employment terminates. Notwithstanding anything to the contrary contained in this agreement, however:

Terms of Employment: while we anticipate an ongoing employment relationship, we would like you to understand that no guarantee of continued employment for any specific length of time is intended or implied by this job offer and that your employment may be terminated at will.

Physical Exam: this job offer is contingent upon evidence of your having a satisfactory, comprehensive physical examination by a licensed physician. Written results of such a physical examination should be furnished to me as soon as possible. You must also successfully complete a substance abuse test before you can accept this job offer. Our company will make arrangements for the latter as soon as possible coordinated with you by our VPHR, Mary Ellis.

Accepted and Agreed: ______________________________

Date: ____________________________

Be sure to return this offer letter signed and dated to the PEG Managing Partner. Offer letters are typically void after three business days.

The above SITG COO offer letter is more reflective of a middle market manufacturer's offer letter to a C-Level executive job candidate. This company has a VP Human Resources. Especially in the non-compete clause. Their involved NDA document also reflects their desire to protect their unique patented capability in designing and manufactured products processing. This PEG portfolio company was a great acquisition by our PEG client and their exit in about 5 years brought a generous equity payout for the COO and all other stockholders. This company employed several engineers who set the tone for the company's conservative culture. Reminder that all SITG C-Level job candidates must show their offer letter to their employment lawyer (ideally) and their CPA tax professional.

VP of Sales and Marketing Skin in the Game Job Offer

Kronan Advanced Materials, Inc. – Bill Flavin, VP Sales and Marketing Summary Terms

Anticipated Start Date: September 7, 2011

Reporting Structure: as VP Sales and Marketing, you will report to the President and CEO.

Base Salary: $180,000 per year

Performance Bonus: you will be eligible for a performance bonus that will range from 0% to 25% of your base salary upon achievement of a combination of personal goals and financial targets. After you join Kronan Advanced Materials, Inc. as Vice President, Sales and Marketing, you and I will meet to mutually agree upon your personal goals and objectives for FYE 2011.

Benefits: you will be eligible for benefits as provided to other salaried employees of Kronan Advanced Materials, Inc. Benefits include, but are not limited to, a Group Medical Plan, Life and Disability Insurance.

Vacation: you will be entitled to three (3) weeks' vacation during your first year of employment and four (4) weeks upon your first employment anniversary date.

Relocation: Kronan Advanced Materials, Inc. shall reimburse you for all reasonable and customary out-of-pocket expenses incurred by you in connection with your relocation from CT to VA, including but not limited to costs for visits, moving expenses, and temporary housing, up to a maximum of fifty thousand dollars ($50,000) in the aggregate for all such relocation expenses and subject to reasonable substantiation and documentation as may be specified by the company.

Stock Options: you will be entitled to participate with other key managers in a stock option plan providing for the grant of options totaling 3,000 shares of the common stock in Kronan Advanced Materials, Inc. based on achieving certain annual earnings targets established by the company's Board of Directors. In the event that the annual earnings target is not met, grants for that particular year will not be made. Your stock option allocation will be 600 of the 3000 shares.

Equity Investment: at your option, Kronan Advanced Materials, Inc. hereby extends to you the opportunity to invest a minimum of $30,000 and up to $60,000 in return for approximately 0.92% up to 1.83% of the common stock at the same price per share paid by the PEG. Should you exercise your option to purchase common stock, the purchase must be executed within ninety (90) days of your employment date. The common stock is subject to five-year vesting.

401(k) Plan: after one (1) year of employment, you will be eligible to participate in the 401k Plan with Kronan Advanced Materials, Inc. matching the first 3%, and fifty percent of the next 2% subject to vesting. You should be aware that there are Federal

Tax Regulations that impose a limit on individual tax deferred contributions, and you should discuss this with your accountant.

Severance: if employee is terminated not for cause or resigns for good reason, twelve (12) months of current salary. If employee is terminated for cause or resigns for no reason, no severance.

Drug Screen/Physical: our offer is contingent upon evidence of your having passed a pre-employment drug screen. You will receive information necessary to take the drug screen under separate cover from our Human Resources Director. You must also undergo a satisfactory, comprehensive physical examination by a licensed physician, within the next ten (10) days; written results of such examination should be furnished directly to me as soon as possible.

Non-Compete Agreement: you agree that, while you are employed by Kronan Advanced Materials, Inc. (the company) and for one (1) year following your employment, you will not, directly or through any other person: i) compete with the company, ii) hire any employee of the company or seek to persuade any employee of the company to discontinue employment; or iii) solicit or encourage any customer of the company to terminate or diminish its relationship with the company. During the course of your employment with the company, you will learn of confidential information, as defined below, and you may develop confidential information on behalf of the company and its affiliates. You agree that while you are employed by the company and at all times thereafter you will not use or disclose to any person (except as required by applicable law or for the proper performance of your regular duties and responsibilities for the company) any confidential or proprietary information obtained by you incident to your employment or any other association with the company or any of its affiliates. You agree to disclose to the company any and all intellectual property and other proprietary rights relating to the business of the company developed by you during your employment and agree to assign to the company all such rights.

Terms of Employment: while we anticipate an ongoing employment relationship, we would like you to understand that no guarantee of continued employment for any specific length of time is implied by this offer, and that your employment may terminated at will.

If Kronan Advanced Materials, Inc. is Sold: when Kronan Advanced Materials, Inc. is sold while you are an employee, and should you purchase shares in the company, all purchased shares in the company shall become vested.

Accepted and Agreed:______________________________

Date: _____________________________

Be sure to return this offer letter signed and dated to the PEG Managing Partner. Offer letters are typically void after three business days.

Before You Accept a Written Job Offer, You Should Have Completed the Following Action Items:

- Be sure to have already read a copy of the job description you will be performing for any questions you may have to clear up.
- Learn the management style of the PEG Partner or the CEO for whom you will be working. Do it before you have to sign an offer sheet acceptance. If you are an SITG CEO candidate, request the PEG Partner to at least have a phone chat with one or two other portfolio company CEOs to learn about the PEG's culture and their management style as soon as possible.
- Be sure to get an explanation and copy of how the company's common stock valuation was accomplished.
- Request at least two or three different Equity Valuation Estimation Worksheets for the company you are joining projecting examples of lower EBITDA performance, targeted EBITDA performance, and above targeted EBITDA performance (see earlier examples in this chapter). Typically these EBITDA projections are understated.
- Some PEGs make job offers subject to credit and criminal background checks. Some credit checks are not current and may show inaccuracies. Be prepared to demonstrate how you are working on correcting this misinformation. If you have been incarcerated or convicted of a crime with probation, you should be prepared to deal with a report indicating this information. Again, if you have the right references who can vouch for your character and current lifestyle, you should be prepared. Normally I would advise my candidates to put this info in their

bio, especially if things are improved for the better and can be substantiated.

- The other issue you might have to deal with is the PEG checking unauthorized references on you through their own network, or you may have separated from a former employer after a mutual settlement and signed an agreement not to divulge specifics of your separation. The PEG could extend a written job offer subject to checking "other references" on you. I tend to honor such off limits reference checking at the request of my SITG job offer candidates if their overall references are above average to superior. You can never have enough knowledgeable positive references on yourself to cover as much of your career as possible. That's the crux of the Gilreath skin in the game hiring philosophy. Forearmed is forewarned. An ounce of prevention is worth a pound of cure.

Keep in mind you are trying to land an SITG job offer with a PEG whereby you will be a peer with all the other equity investors/owners of the portfolio company you will be helping grow. Hiring due diligence is a two way street. The PEG is doing theirs on your candidacy and you are doing yours on the PEG's reputation and track record, as well as their modus operandi. Keep in communication with your lawyer and CPA. Hopefully they have expertise in doing business in the M&A sector and have dealt with PEGs before.

CHAPTER 12

CONCLUSION

So now we're at the end of the skin in the game job hunting trail in the middle market and lower middle market M&A sector. By this time you should know yourself, your skills, qualifications and accomplishments, and how to go about substantiating them. You know the work culture you fit and you've assembled the strategy, documentation, references support and hit the SITG C-Level job search trail. You learned one last thing on this subject from me. There are no short cuts in implementing my strategy. Start executing the "due diligence" way. Once you have decided that you really want the SITG C-Level job opportunity, strive to associate yourself with a trainload of networkers, successful M&A contacts, and winning PEGs. Find one that makes sense for you and them, because you are a SITG C-Level executive match with their portfolio company's industries, markets, related products, acquisitions integrations, processes, growth potential, and entrepreneurial risk-taking team. It's rewarding for you, it's good for them. If you have the skin in the game (equity investment money), goals, drive and ambition, now you have the formula for eventual success. All you need is the opportunity In the interim of landing a skin in the game opportunity. Consider handling a project for a PEG.

Your two favorite phrases describe your SITG job hunting effort: *slow but*, *steady*, and solid, day by day. You're on your way.

Avoid going off half-cocked! Prepare yourself thoroughly for the SITG job hunting campaign. Complete your Indiana Jones Bio, then produce an honest, influential, metrics driven resume. Call in a resume/cover letter expert if you must. It's money well spent. Then tackle your references until you have the one or two paragraph testimonials for your "show and tell" material. Assemble your impressive, select "show and tell" items. You will need these to fortify your networking presentations and PEG job interviews. LinkedIn has made that easy for you to achieve written references with their recommendations and skills endorsement capability in your profile page.

But don't believe everything you read. For example, I have received recommendations from connections I've never met or spoken with, and don't know me well enough (if at all) to be writing recommendations about me. Notice on my Jim Gilreath LinkedIn page, I don't post such well-meaning recommendations.

Meanwhile work on your elevator pitch until it's polished and effortless to communicate it impactfully. Practice, practice, practice says Profile Research LLC's President, Bob Bronstein. Start identifying and compiling your networking contacts. Email them your M&A master target list from chapter 9. Become a LinkedIn member and produce your career profile site. Upgrade to a Premium membership listing for its increased volume capability for research and networking contacts. Start having coffee or lunch or cocktails with important networking contacts, their referrals, and hopefully PEGs. Make sure you have a good activity follow-up tracking system like Outlook or whatever you're comfortable with.

Get involved with the Association for Corporate Growth. Attend an ACG C-Series breakfast hosted by a local chapter for potential mega networking. Make ACG member contacts and follow up.

Research Dealmaker Portal to identify appropriate PEGs to cold network with by email or cold calling by telephone. Explore targeted "blast" mailings to PEGs. Talk it over with Bob Bronstein (see chapter 9).

Cold call networking, at first, like standing at the edge of the ocean surf at Hampton Beach, New Hampshire. It's always bone chilling. Yet there are hundreds of shivering swimmers slowly creeping into the ocean with the surf crashing against their lower torsos. At some future point (which could be hours later) the plodding, shivering swimmer wants to dive below the chilly ocean surface. They jump up and dive again. Wow, somehow it's getting warmer. Approach networking the same way. Prepare to engage contacts and referrals and PEGs. Get momentum going! Jump in, the water's fine!

The bottom line is to thoroughly read this book, and to make up your mind to go for it. You follow my chapters, produce your documentation, and practice your communication techniques on your spouse, close friends, colleagues, and your inner circle. You're getting better. You're gaining confidence. You're making your networking plans and implementing them. You're experiencing rejection, disappointment, elation, and success sometimes all in the same morning. Solid M&A referrals at times can be far and few between. Keep at it! Time for an ACG networking event. Look at all these M&A sector business cards to follow up. Keep up your slow, steady, and solid routine and make things happen through email, phone, LinkedIn, coffees, lunches, cocktails, meetings, and interviews. Finally the right SITG job offer will arrive. You could end up making a million dollars or more at the company's liquidity event. I have seen it happen, over and over again using my system. I am rooting for you!

In July I asked Mary Kathleen Flynn, Editor-in-Chief, Mergers & Acquisitions, a SourceMedia publication, what the latest trends are in middle market and lower middle market M&A deal value and volume, to which she replied "On the surface, the news seems good. The first half of 2015 delivered around the same level of middle-market M&A deal value and volume as the same period in the previous year, according to preliminary data from Thomson Reuters. Considering that 2014 was the best year for M&A since 2007, the fact that 2015 is holding steady is a reason to cheer. But, while the early flurry of activity sounds encouraging, it's also possible that 2015 is front-loaded. Dealmakers say they are more optimistic about M&A growth over the next three months than they are about the next 12, according to Mergers & Acquisitions' monthly surveys. There's a nagging sense that the current wave of middle-market M&A may have already peaked. Nevertheless, many transaction pros argue that niches of the middle market will continue to be very active, even if the economy shifts. Some of the most promising sectors are technology, especially software, mobile, security and e-commerce; and health care, especially medical devices, physician groups and services aimed at the aging population. The lower middle market, in which small companies have a lot of room to grow, also provides fertile ground for investments".

Mergers & Acquisitions, a SourceMedia publication, covers all aspects of middle-market dealmaking, including identifying acquisition targets, negotiating transactions, performing due diligence, and closing deals. With more than 42,000 unique monthly visitors, the brand's website at www.TheMiddleMarket.com is continuously updated, providing real-time information and analysis of news and trends in M&A. The monthly magazine, which serves nearly 20,000 subscribers, is published in partnership with the Association for Corporate Growth (ACG), a global organization comprised of thousands of private equity firms, corporate officials and intermediaries. Mergers & Acquisitions' online video series features interviews with high-profile dealmakers, including private equity Partners, strategic buyers, investment bankers and other advisers.

CPSIA information can be obtained at www.ICGtesting.com
Printed in the USA
BVOW08*1727270316

441524BV00001B/2/P